A MORAL THEORY OF SPORTS

A MORAL THEORY OF SPORTS

Richard J. Severson

ROWMAN & LITTLEFIELD
Lanham • Boulder • New York • London

Published by Rowman & Littlefield
An imprint of The Rowman & Littlefield Publishing Group, Inc.
4501 Forbes Boulevard, Suite 200, Lanham, Maryland 20706
www.rowman.com

6 Tinworth Street, London SE11 5AL

Copyright © 2019 by The Rowman & Littlefield Publishing Group, Inc.

All rights reserved. No part of this book may be reproduced in any form or by any electronic or mechanical means, including information storage and retrieval systems, without written permission from the publisher, except by a reviewer who may quote passages in a review.

British Library Cataloguing in Publication Information Available

Library of Congress Cataloging-in-Publication Data

Names: Severson, Richard James, 1955– author.
Title: A moral theory of sports / Richard J. Severson.
Description: Lanham, MD : Rowman & Littlefield Publishing Group, Inc., 2019. | Includes bibliographical references and index.
Identifiers: LCCN 2019003219 (print) | LCCN 2019008197 (ebook) | ISBN 9781538128879 (Electronic) | ISBN 9781538128862 (cloth) | ISBN 9781538158364 (pbk) Subjects:
LCSH: Sports—Moral and ethical aspects. | Sports—Philosophy.
Classification: LCC GV706.3 (ebook) | LCC GV706.3 .S49 2019 (print) | DDC 175—dc23
LC record available at https://lccn.loc.gov/2019003219

To Cody Rufer, Kent Knutson, and John McDermott,
and to Uncle Red, who lived and breathed it.

All that I know most surely about morality and obligations I owe to football.—Albert Camus

CONTENTS

Introduction: The Joy of Running — ix

1. Bullying, Teasing, and the Birth of Conscience — 1
2. The Land of Pretend — 19
3. Coaches and Referees — 37
4. Imitation, Ritual, and Transcendence — 53
5. Excellence without End — 71
6. Neuroscience, Mirroring, and Complementarity — 89
7. Fandom: Why We Watch and Care So Much — 103
8. Cockfighting, Gambling, and Villages — 119
9. Situationism and the Dynamics of Misbehavior — 133
10. Whither the Future? — 147

Appendix: On Moral Psychology and Ethics — 157
Notes — 167
Bibliography — 177
Index — 183
About the Author — 191

INTRODUCTION
The Joy of Running

Growing up, I participated in a wide range of sports, mostly at the neighborhood backyard level. We played everything—football, baseball, basketball, hockey, volleyball, tennis, golf, badminton, horseshoes, racquetball, ping-pong, foosball, marbles, even square ball. We wrestled, boxed, raced our bikes and electric cars, swam, dived, bowled, chased one another in foot races, skied on the modest prairie hills of eastern South Dakota, and organized neighborhood-wide snowball fights. "I'm going to kill you!" was a common (empty) threat when you couldn't quite catch the person or persons who had swiped your long-tailed stocking cap and wouldn't give it back.

The competition wasn't cutthroat, but we got to know who was good at what, who the alpha kids on the block were. Growing up is about learning your place, and sports was an important proving ground for my tribe of friends.

None of us was groomed to be a professional athlete like the lucky Canadian kids who happened to be born in January, who Malcolm Gladwell wrote about in *Outliers*.[1] According to Gladwell, they were the ones most likely to end up in the National Hockey League because the eligibility cutoff date for youth hockey made them the oldest kids in their cohort. So they got most of the playing time and attention from coaches, which meant they were afforded the best opportunities to further succeed as they got older. Eventually, there came a point when the rest of the kids would never be able to catch up.

The rich get richer, accumulating their advantages.

We weren't treated like young prodigies in my neighborhood, and many of us bear the minor scars of being passed over in the sports selection processes that determined our fates. I wanted to be a pitcher on my little league team, for example. The coach had me throw a few balls, then shook his head and sent me to the outfield. *C'est la vie.*

In high school, the only organized sport I participated in was wrestling. It wasn't because I had no interest in football, basketball, or other sports. I wasn't good enough to make the teams. Even though I grew up in a rural state, with a population of far less than a million souls (and far more cows and pigs than that), my high school in Sioux Falls had 2,400 students. The competition was stiff.

I'd have had better opportunities if I'd gone to the smaller Catholic high school, like my parents wanted. (It went against the grain of being a rock and roll bewitched teenager in 1969 to follow the sensible advice of one's parents.)

As a sophomore I wrestled in the 105-pound weight class, and I made the varsity team simply because the upperclassmen had grown too big. As it was, I had to lose 10 pounds from my already-rawboned frame. I remember chewing gum in the evening (after skipping supper) so that I could get the juices flowing and spit about 10 ounces worth of saliva into a glass while watching television with the family. It was as gross then as it sounds now.

Another trick we had for making weight was rolling ourselves up into the wrestling mats after practice until we could slide in a pool of our own sweat.

As a junior I wrestled at 132 pounds, meaning I finally had the big growth spurt I had been praying about for half my life. I was in the 145-pound class as a senior, and by the time I graduated, I weighed 155.

I was a good wrestler in the practice room but not in the actual matches. I got too nervous and froze up. I lost a lot of matches with low scores of 2 to 1, or 3 to 2. I did just enough not to be humiliated, but I didn't have the "killer" instinct to try to win. I have often wondered how many people resort to that kind of play-to-survive-but-not-to-win strategy. Is surviving itself a kind of success? Is hanging with the best without actually beating them a kind of winning?

INTRODUCTION

When I got to college, I quit playing sports. My only aerobic exercise came from strutting through bars with a bottle of beer in my hand. I was smoking about a pack of Marlboros a day. If you smoke, I reasoned, then you shouldn't be a hypocrite and try to exercise for your health as well. We all have our standards. That's got to be about the dumbest bit of higher reasoning ever confabulated to justify bad habits and a wayward life.

Then something terrible happened. My mom and dad were on their way home from a weekend trip to Las Vegas with friends. They had flown out of the Twin Cities and were driving back to South Dakota. The car drifted over the highway line on a foggy Halloween morning, crashing head-on into a farm truck full of grain from the fall harvest. Only the woman in the front passenger seat survived. My parents were sitting in the back seat.

At the time of their deaths, 50,000 Americans died every year in automobile accidents. Of small comfort to families affected by such a routine modern tragedy, that number has now dropped to less than 35,000. The byways of America are getting safer. There's another noteworthy numbers comparison from that era: Approximately 58,000 Americans (mostly young men) lost their lives in the Vietnam war.

I turned 18 in 1973, and registered for the selective service, as required by law. Fortunately, my friends and I were never drafted because the Nixon administration ended that practice the year before.

Those of us of college age in the 1970s (before adult learning came along) were mostly too young to be hippies. Sure, we wore our hair long and dressed like shabby hobos. We smoked some pot and grooved to the music at Minneapolis rock concerts when we could afford tickets and gas money. One of my friends even drove a VW bus. But we weren't real hippies. They wouldn't have wanted to hang out in South Dakota in any case. The winters are too harsh.

With encouragement from friends who cared about me when I didn't care enough about myself, I rediscovered my love of sports and got caught up in the jogging craze. At first, I could barely run a mile without heart palpitations and fear of a collapsed lung. If cell phones had been around, I probably would have called for an ambulance at least once. I kept at it, however, and eventually started to run in road races. The first one was a 10-miler at the Howard Wood Relays in Sioux Falls. It surprised me that I was able to finish.

Running made me feel good and helped wean me off cigarettes. Buying my first Nike Waffle Trainers was a memorable experience. There were no specialty stores for athletic shoes in South Dakota at that time. But two elderly brothers who were fiercely passionate runners set up a little Nike shop in the basement of their furniture store. They didn't advertise the running shoe business. You just had to hear about it through word of mouth. They also organized a running club called Prairie Striders.

A friend introduced me to the Bartling brothers, and the younger of the two took me downstairs to purchase my Nikes. They were baby blue with a yellow swoosh and a black waffled rubber tread on a white foam cushion. They also sold me a tube of liquid goop and a little plastic mold for building up the waffle bumps as they wore down so that the shoes would last longer. I believe I paid $40, a sizeable sum for sneakers, or plain old "tennis shoes," as we called any athletic footwear at the time.

Bill Bowerman was the track coach at the University of Oregon who cofounded Nike with one of his former athletes, Phil Knight. In Bowerman's 24 years at the helm, Oregon won four NCAA track team championships and had 16 top-10 finishes.

Blue Ribbon Sports, which eventually became Nike, was originally an athletic footwear distribution company founded on nothing more than a handshake. At first it was a 50–50 proposition, with Bowerman staying put at the University of Oregon in Eugene and Knight managing the business from Portland. Bowerman experimented with different athletic shoe designs, famously ruining his wife's waffle iron while concocting a lightweight rubber sole. A few years later, the Waffle Trainer was born, fueling the meteoric growth of their legendary company.

Before inventing the Waffle Trainer, Bowerman learned about recreational jogging for health and fitness from Arthur Lydiard in New Zealand. He brought the concept back to the United States. *Jogging*, the book he authored, sold more than a million copies and is credited with igniting the jogging craze that helped me recover from my grief and self-neglect.

There is something about running outdoors that seems to satisfy an aboriginal need deep inside of us. That's what I began to ponder as I scampered hither and yon in my Waffle Trainers—through snowstorms and rain showers, bucking headwinds that could tear the hair from my scalp; on blistering hot days with humidity so high that my lungs felt more like gills; and on frigid mornings when even my bundled-up penis—not to mention toes, fingers, and nose—was in danger of frostbite. I ran on gravel roads, paved streets, and neglected highways; golf courses, park trails, and campus green spaces; and even farm fields and cemeteries. I loved my baby blue Nikes.

Of course, I read about the "runner's high" and no doubt experienced some of its euphoric effects. For decades, it was believed that strenuous exercise releases endorphins, feel-good natural opioid peptides that seduce the brain like an illicit drug. Recently, however, German researchers have found evidence in mouse studies that the endocannabinoid reward system is responsible for the runner's high.[2] It turns out endorphin molecules are too big to quickly cross the blood–brain barrier (a protective membrane).

The endocannabinoid hormone responsible for the runner's high is similar to marijuana or cannabis. According to Peter Kramer, author of *Listening to Prozac*, most psychotropic drug research follows a homologous arc.[3] That means researchers design new synthetic drugs by imitating the natural ones found in our bodies. Recreational street drugs follow the same arc—they make us high because they are able to imitate natural feel-good hormones like the endocannabinoids. Anabolic steroids, the most demonized of the performance-enhancing drugs (PEDs) in all of sports, are homologous with testosterone, the body's most potent natural performance enhancer.

In my senior biology seminar, a capstone class for biology majors, I was required to make a presentation about new research opportunities in a biological discipline. I chose to talk about ethology, the study of animal behavior through observation of living animals in their natural setting. Squeamish about killing animals and dissecting them in the lab, ethology appealed to my soul.

Jane Goodall was famous by that time for her observational studies of wild chimpanzees at Gombe National Park in Tanzania. Louis Leakey, the renowned paleontologist, raised the funds to sponsor Goodall's Gombe research and sent her back to England to finish her education as an ethologist.

At that time, ethologists were vigilant about the dangers of anthropomorphizing their animal subjects. They meticulously described what they saw in value-free language, never imputing human feelings, cognitions, or motivations. Apparently Goodall didn't get the memo.

She named the chimpanzees that she studied, instead of numbering them, as protocol required. Nor did she shy away from using human categories to describe their personalities and loving relationships (violent ones as well). The first chimp to accept her presence and allow her to approach him in the forest was called David Greybeard. "My own relationship with David was unique," Goodall wrote, "and will never be repeated. He allowed me to groom him, and on one never-to-be-forgotten occasion, gave me a gesture of reassurance when I held out my hand to him, offering a palm nut."[4]

The scientific understanding of primate behavior has exploded since the 1970s. It is now beyond dispute that chimpanzees and bonobos (formerly, pigmy chimpanzees) share many of our feelings and cognitive capabilities. They can recognize themselves in a mirror, which could indicate that they are one of the few species capable of human-like self-awareness. As primatologist Frans de Waal has argued, they practice their own brand of coalition-building *politics* and have proto-moral instincts regarding fairness and sympathy.[5]

By the early 1990s, genetic comparisons disclosed just how closely related to chimpanzees and bonobos we actually are. They share 98 percent of our genome, far more than imagined. And gorillas are not far behind. Because gene mutations accumulate at a predictable rate, it is now possible to pinpoint when archaic *Homo* species (hominids) split from the *Pan* species (chimps and bonobos). We shared a common ancestor as recently as 6 million years ago.[6]

In my seminar presentation, I also mentioned Lucy, the australopithecine hominid skeleton that had just been discovered in Ethiopia by Donald Johanson, an American paleoanthropologist. Lucy lived 3.2 million years ago. She was small—at 3-foot-7 and 64 pounds—and probably looked like a chimpanzee, except for one thing. Her pelvis and leg bones were similar to modern humans. That meant she walked upright with the bipedal gait of a hominid.

Fruit-eating chimpanzees walk only one to two miles per day. According to Daniel Lieberman, early hominids ate tubers and other hard-to-chew raw plant materials.[7] They were forced to trek as many as nine miles per day in search of food as open savannas replaced forests due to dramatic climate changes. A rhythmic bipedal gait is four times more efficient than the crouched arm and leg ambling locomotion of the other great apes.

INTRODUCTION

The need to travel so far to find food in the dry, hot African savannah led to evolutionary adaptations that made us different from our primate relatives: Our legs grew longer, making it harder to climb and live in trees; the foot's arch became more pronounced and stiff; and leg joints got bigger and bones grew thicker to absorb the impact of long-distance running. The fur on our bodies also disappeared as sweating, not panting, became a more efficient method for cooling down the body, and the nose began to protrude, creating air turbulence in the breath, adding another cooling and humidifying effect.

In addition to being foragers for plant-based foods and carrion, hominids experimented with hunting after they began making stone tools approximately 2.6 million years ago. To hunt faster, bigger animals than themselves, they used persistence tactics. They ran long distances at moderate speed, tracking an animal that could easily sprint away from them, then stop, then sprint away again when the hunters caught up with it. Eventually, the hunted creature would suffer heat stroke, unable to keep cool by panting as the blazing sun beat down on its fur-covered body. The vertical body orientation of the bipedal hunter is less exposed to the sun than the horizontal body orientation of the quadruped quarry, another advantage for the long-distance runner.

So it is true, what I suspected when I began jogging in the mid-1970s—evolution adapted us to be runners. It's why we have big gluteus maximus muscles, short toes, narrow waists, slow-twitch leg muscles, and brains responsive to neurochemicals that minimize pain while rewarding the metronomic monotony of putting one foot in front of another for hours on end if need be. For those first athletes in Africa, the runner's high was a foretaste of the feast hopefully to come.

Louis Leakey foresaw the convergence of primate ethology and paleoanthropology as a strategy for better understanding human evolution. That's why he sent Goodall to Gombe. The kind of history I was taught in college, on the other hand, began with the invention of agriculture at the end of the Stone Age. It also heavily favored the great books of Western civilization. It was as if nothing that occurred prior to that ("prehistory," it was called) actually mattered.

But it did matter, more than any other period in human history. Almost everything significant about us—our bipedal gate, large brains, use of language, music, art, culture, self-awareness, moral conscience, spirituality, caring for the sick, tool making, curiosity about the world, superstition, cooking, storytelling, collaborative hunting, playing games, competing, warfare, pair bonding, and on and on—evolved and took shape in the late Pleistocene epoch.

Thanks to the efforts of innumerable scientists and scholars from a wide range of disciplines, we now know a great deal about "prehistory," or the ancestral environment, as it is often called: the roughly 200 millennia between the time when *Homo sapiens* first emerged in southern Africa and the agricultural revolution that marked the beginning of civilization as we understand it today.

When I graduated from college, I never again stopped running or participating in sports at some level. How could I surrender what is bred in my bones to do? After a few years of working in less-than-satisfying jobs, I went back to graduate school, eventually becoming an academic librarian. I also studied religion and ethics, completing my PhD at the University of Iowa.

I have been curious about the archaic origins of morality for almost as long as I have been wondering why it felt so instinctively natural—so *joyful*—when I took up jogging. In *The Descent of Man*, Darwin suggested that morality is a group-fitness adaptation, meaning that moral societies, on average, will outcompete nonmoral ones because they are more cooperative.[8] That view was strongly rejected in the 1960s and 1970s by evolutionary biologists who fell under the spell of the "selfish gene."[9] They viewed evolution as strictly a matter of replicating genes. In that milieu, morality came to seem more like what de Waal called a "thin veneer" of false niceties covering up a nasty creature beneath the surface.[10]

In recent decades, Darwin's point of view has come back in favor as evidence has mounted for natural selection occurring on multiple levels, not just at the level of gene mutations. Even individual organisms can be viewed as social groups in the sense that their bodies represent collaborative communities of specialized cells. Multilevel selection theory is more attuned to the importance of groups in the evolution of social animals, particularly their natural tendencies toward altruistic behavior.

The idea that morality and the joy of running are closely linked in our ancestral past has been kicking around in the back of my mind for years. There is no question that running, jumping, throwing, climbing, hitting, grappling, and other skills of archaic humans are the basis for many modern sports. The link with archaic morality is less obvious. The moral life as it evolved in the ancestral environment has been transformed into something less relevant and effective—at times almost unrecognizable—in complex modern societies, which are forced to rely on legal systems and other bureaucratic mechanisms to monitor and control bad behavior. There is, however, at least one exception: A remnant of what moral life was like when all humans lived in small bands as egalitarian hunter-gatherers survives in modern sports. To interpret modern sports from the perspective of our ancestral morality is the purpose of this book.

This interpretive lens works the other way around, too: The moral life in modern times, I suspect, can be better understood, perhaps even reinvigorated, by analyzing it from the point of view of sports. In my rendition of them, morality and sports function as reciprocating metaphors, entangled narratives of aboriginal origin that are especially capable of illuminating the shadowy depths and passions of the human condition.

The play of sports is a competition (a play fight), a reenactment on artificial terms of the blood-and-tooth survival games of real life. In their ability to help us both forget and imitate harsh realities, sports grant us safe passage through dangerous terrain. They enable us to find leisure in practices that spill joy upon us like the lost fountain of youth that Ponce de León was never able to find in his circumnavigations of the New World.

Likewise, I am going to argue that morality is a sporting contest in essential ways. We compete with one another in our moral practices, just as we do in our sports. At this point, that probably sounds oddly mistaken. That is because the competitive side of our morality has been largely whittled away by civilization. That was not the case in the ancestral environment, however, as we shall see.

This is an adventure story, and it began millions of years ago when our species had yet to emerge on the African savannahs of the late Pleistocene epoch. So far, we are the only creature with a fully formed moral life. Yet, primatologists have discerned the building blocks of morality, the predispositions for it, in the empathy, sharing, play, intelligence, political alliances, trickster behavior, peace-making gestures, and so forth, of our nearest animal relatives.

In its existential purpose, the verve of sports is moral drama. That is my moral theory of sports in a nutshell. In the next chapter, I will investigate how bullying behavior led to the development of conscience in the ancestral environment. Teasing also played a seminal role in the evolution of morality. The line between the two—bullying and teasing—can be hard to appreciate sometimes. That is especially the case in modern sports. It's time to get into the thick of things.

I

BULLYING, TEASING, AND THE BIRTH OF CONSCIENCE

For thousands of years, ethicists have attempted to educate, civilize, groom, strengthen, codify, and extend the moral feelings, instincts, and dispositions ingrained in our nature. It is a commonplace of ethical judgment to decry the moral bankruptcy and illiteracy of our times (no matter what century it happens to be). It always seems to be the case, from an ethicist's point of view, that we are far too lax and inattentive about what the proper order of our concerns ought to be. There is a utopian urgency about ethics (and politics) that is not part of our instinctive morality.

Usually we think of the moral life as a life honestly and authentically lived, with integrity, virtue, good will, sacrifices of ego, friendship, sympathy, and the like. And if, on occasion, we happen to do something that is wrong, the inner voice of conscience prods us to clean up our act. That is the "goody two-shoes" version of personal morality that has been polished up throughout the years by philosophers and theologians. The morality of early humans was a bit rougher around the edges. It's that raw, precivilized version of morality that I am comparing to sports. The practice of morality was probably the very first sporting contest of our experience. To this day, we are all adept at playing the morality game.

According to biologist Richard Alexander, consciousness, foresight, and the other distinctive components of the human psyche evolved as part of a moral arms race.[1] While it is true that morality enabled early humans to cooperate effectively in small bands, it also unleashed the clandestine practice of reading the minds of others so that we might get the upper hand with them. "Consciousness," Alexander said, "is a game of life in which the participants are trying to comprehend what is in one another's minds before, and more effectively than, it can be done in reverse."[2] We are astoundingly clever at deception and manipulation, which is one important reason why we have such large brains and complex social (moral) interactions.

Sharing goals among individuals in small groups was the beginning of morality. But it has never reached the ideal state that ethicists dream about because moral deception is fitness-enhancing if you can get away with it. That is the other side of the story about morality that the goody two-shoes version ignores. Unconsciously, we all want other people to be slightly more moral than we are because then they will be slightly more generous toward us than required. That is to our advantage. Likewise, we want to appear to be more moral than others because then we will gain a reputation for being more generous than we actually are. I am reminded of Benjamin Franklin's efforts to deceive his neighbors—or "impress" them, as he put it in his autobiography—regarding his devotion to virtue and hard work by needlessly pushing a wheelbarrow up and down the street.[3] This is what I mean by the "morality game"—ploys and counterploys of advantage-seeking behavior nestled alongside our more generous, cooperative undertakings. In general, the greater the threat to its own survival that a group faces, the more cooperatively and honestly its members will behave. It's when times are less dire that the subversive aspects of morality come to life. Or, as I was taught in catechism, idle hands are the devil's workshop.

Alexander defined conscience as the small, still voice that tells us how far we can go without incurring intolerable risks.[4] If true, that makes conscience a cunning cost–benefit calculator, a cautionary voice rather than a purely inspirational one. The message is more along the lines of "be careful," instead of "be good for goodness's sake." What can I get away with without harming my good reputation? That is probably the original moral conundrum. The temptation to cheat or lie is a moral universal; strategic posturing vis-à-vis the interests of others is as well. That means everyone does it. (Maybe there are rare saints who actually rise above gaming the system.)

As the moral arms race progressed, we became almost supernatural in our abilities to discern deception in others. We are very good at sniffing out liars. We can read it in their faces and body language: averted eyes, sweaty brow, guilty blushing, hand wringing, and so forth. We prize honesty above almost everything in the moral universe because we hate being taken advantage of by free riders who only pretend to be cooperative and generous. Alexander hypothesized that the unconscious evolved as a way to counter the improved ability to uncover deception.[5] By pushing our own deceptive practices into the unconscious, we are no longer aware of them; therefore, we will no longer display the telltale signs of deception that others can easily read.

Think about that for a second. If you yourself aren't aware of your own deception because it has been relegated to the unconscious, then others won't be able to catch you in the act either. Unconscious self-deception is not a pathological behavior, as one versed in modern psychology might suspect. It is a way to deceive others by being more *believable* in oaths and declarations regarding one's own innocence when accused of bad behavior. Being in denial, to invoke a more familiar concept from everyday experience, is a state of mind that we often encounter in others but never in ourselves (because then it wouldn't be denial, right?). *League of Denial* is an aptly titled book that tells the story of how the NFL refused to acknowledge (relegated to the unconscious) the role of repeated concussions in the demise of Mike Webster, a gridiron hero of the fabled Pittsburg Steelers.[6]

It isn't only in our psyches that we play paradoxical moral games of innocent (unconscious) deception. For a long time, biologists have speculated about why humans are the only primate without an estrous cycle that clearly signals (like the swollen red bottom of a baboon) when a female is most receptive for getting pregnant. Human females conceal ovulation, even from themselves. Why such secrecy about when pregnancy is most likely to occur? One theory is that ovulation is like the unconscious, a place to hide secrets from both ourselves and others. Concealed ovulation frees the woman from having to lie to her mate about her own fertility or receptivity to sexual advances. "Honey, I have a headache," evokes a different level of significance in this case.

The incessant, mostly unconscious probing for advantage that occurs when humans interact is not a form of brutality. It is, after all, part of our *moral* constitution. I don't want to go so far in acknowledging the Machiavellian side of morality that I forget it has a gold standard, which is generosity of spirit. Greco-Roman wrestlers push and tug at one another, making head fakes and other movements designed to trick the opponent into thinking he knows what the other wrestler is planning. Then, when it is least expected, when the opponent's defenses have been lulled almost to sleep, the devious wrestler executes a perfect takedown maneuver. It's a contest of wits as much as physical strength or quickness. Yet, both wrestlers follow rules that forbid them from intentionally hurting one another. And, like all good sportsmen and women, they shake hands when the match has ended.

There is an etiquette to playing games, like the mannered tradition of smiling and saying, "Hello, how are you today?" to people we encounter on the street. It doesn't matter how any of us is actually feeling inside: suspicious of this overly friendly stranger, perhaps, or resentful of the prune who won't reciprocate a pleasant greeting. What matters is the pretense of being civil. Even a pretense—pretending—is a tiny step in the right direction of getting better at playing the game of being good. Morality is exactly like that. The deceptions involved are partly benign because they can only go so far. There are checks and balances—even for the all-important *games within the game*.

The tension between the interests of the group versus the varied and conflicting interests of individuals constitutes one of the playing fields of morality (the other being group-versus-group competitions). The group demands cooperation and generosity from its members; individuals scheme for advantage against both other individuals and the group itself. The reason why Machiavellian tendencies can only go so far is because group members watch one another. At least that was the case in the small bands of hunter-gatherers who lived together in the ancestral environment. If you got out of line, you heard about it from other members of the band. People behaved because the threat of being punished by the group was ever present. It is fascinating that gossip is seen as immoral in our day, yet it was vital for the proper functioning of moral society in the late Pleistocene. People talked about one another. Most of it had to do with reputations. To be called stingy was a serious matter to be avoided. It was probably comparable to being a convicted criminal today.

Bart Giamatti was the former Yale president who briefly served as commissioner of Major League Baseball before his untimely passing. His ruminations about baseball and the American character celebrate the tensions and contradictions inherent to both sports and moral society. "Baseball fits America so well," he said, "because it embodies the interplay of individual and group that we so love, and because it expresses our longing for the rule of law while licensing our resentment of law givers."[7] He also said that baseball is an opportunist's game, and that ultimately the virtuoso player is subsumed into the team ensemble. Regarding the peril of a batter's circumstance, he had this to say: "Part of what a batter must overcome, part of the secretive, ruthless dimension of baseball, is the knowledge that an opposing player, crouching right behind him, signals wordlessly in order to exploit his weaknesses."[8] This is the stuff of morality indeed; its cunning ploys, dramatic tensions, and saving grace—the knack for enabling social groups to prevail as something greater than their competitive individual parts.

The fact that modern humans voluntarily join and leave any number of organizations, clubs, teams, and so forth, probably gets to the heart of why we have come to view morality as a personal matter more than a social one. We believe the ebb and flow of our alliances is no one's business but our own. It's the manifest destiny of our freedom to be agents of our own social calendars. The basic sociality of human nature was more palpable to our ancestors. Get banished from a Stone Age band for misbehaving and you probably ended up dead from starvation or predation. Morality evolved as a means for people to thrive in groups despite their natural tendencies toward egoism and nepotism.

Put a number of young children together in a room, as social psychologists have in their studies, and the children will instinctively cluster into groups.[9] It was group or peer pressure that led to the development of a calculating conscience. Christopher Boehm argued that bullying was the most serious internal threat to the moral harmony of archaic humans, followed by stealing and cheating.[10] Boehm studied the hunter-gatherer societies that survived into modern times to speculate about what life must have been like prior to the agricultural revolution.

Humans resent being dominated, and other great apes share the same predisposition. Our ancestors ganged up on bullies and suppressed any kind of big-shot behavior. It was vital for the group to do so. The typical behavior of a bully would have been to take more than his fair share of meat, which was distributed equally among band members when large game could be successfully hunted.

The importance of ganging-up behavior as both a hunting strategy and a form of moral sanction cannot be overestimated. Successful mammalian social hunters use ganging-up techniques, whether it is lions, wolves, orcas, or humans. In fact, these mammals became so successful at ganging up that no other predator could seriously threaten them—except for us. We alone gang up on every other animal species as potential food or extermination target, and that includes ourselves. We hunt one another, group against group, and continue to do so in modern warfare.

Boehm surmised that in more than half of the cases where capital punishment was used by hunter-gatherers, it was for the purpose of putting down bullies.[11] In fact, he thinks conscience evolved so that bullies could learn where the boundaries lie regarding their unwelcome tendencies. Bullies use their conscience to determine how far they can go without incurring the risk of severe consequences from the group. In modern times, it is often the psychopathic bullies—those without a conscience—who get caught going too far and wind up in prison. Conscience is a remediation tool in this sense. It helps rehabilitate those of us who need extra incentive to control the impulse to dominate, steal, or cheat. As it turns out, most of us could use such assistance.

If conscience evolved to help bullies self-monitor their own desire to dominate—to interrupt themselves, as it were, before they got into real trouble—then it doesn't actually eliminate bullying so much as mask it. It pushes the bullying tendency underground, into the secretive regions of the psyche, like the relegation of deception to the unconscious. The bully's ability to hide his desire to dominate is what conscience enables him to achieve. There is an ironic twist to this story: Conscience evolved to suppress bullying, yet in the process it enabled bullying to persist in the human genome as a secret desire. It shouldn't come as a total surprise, then, that bullying has become an epidemic of our times, especially given the anonymity with which we coexist even with our nearest neighbors. When humans lived in small bands, they usually knew who was misbehaving and who wasn't, and what to do about it.

The moral instinct to gang up on bullies is endemic to modern sports. How do opponents respond to LeBron James or any other dominant alpha on the court? They double- and triple-team him, bump him, trap him: They do whatever it takes within the rules of the game to neutralize his dominance. On the other hand, how do basketball players respond when someone attempts to be too much of a big shot on their own team? They get after him/her, using such names as "gunner" or "ball hog," hoping that their admonishments will put an end to the selfish showboating. Scolding is typically the first line of moral sanction against recalcitrant group members among hunter-gatherers, followed by ostracism.

Sports teams and their leagues are like mini-societies, or cultures, in the sense that they develop unique codes and sensibilities (consciences) regarding how to get along. They also create governing bodies and write rule books. As anthropologists have been telling us for a long time, many of the nuances of a culture can never be completely captured in a set of rules or laws. That's why every sport includes traditions that are not covered by the official rules. Where in the rules of baseball does it say anything about the seventh-inning stretch? I will look at the issue of culture and rules in more detail in a later chapter.

When a baseball pitcher hits a batter, intentionally or not, there is a moment of suspenseful expectation. Will the batter rush the mound or let the transgression go unpunished? If he does rush the mound, it invariably triggers a team response—from both sides—as the dugouts empty. Not to participate in such a ritualized defense of a teammate would be a serious faux pas. We have not only a moral instinct to gang up on bullies, but also a natural tendency to dislike members of other groups. This xenophobic instinct probably evolved as a consequence of the often-violent interactions between rival Stone Age bands, particularly in times of drought and scarcity. It is the basis for team loyalties in modern sports. We can't help but look askance at the other team when we care deeply for our own. Loyalty is a moral virtue that, by definition, only extends to a selected group. If everyone was included, loyalty would be beside the point.

Social psychologist Muzafer Sherif and his colleagues explored the issue of intergroup conflict in the famous Robber's Cave experiments.[12] Researchers randomly assigned 22 boys to one of two groups, then transported them separately to a Boy Scout camp at Robber's Cave State Park in Oklahoma. Initially, neither group was aware of the other group's existence. This allowed them to bond within their own group as they engaged in team-building activities. One group called itself the Rattlers, while the other group chose Eagles for its name. They made flags and printed their group names on their shirts. In the second stage of the experiment, the groups were brought together for a series of activities designed to create friction between them. They had a picnic, but one team's food didn't arrive in time so they had to wait while watching the other team eat. They played a baseball game and only the winning team received awards. As expected, tension quickly rose between the groups. The Rattlers planted their flag on the playing field and threatened to harm the Eagles if they touched it. Things escalated until the researchers, posing as camp counselors, had to intervene to prevent fighting. The researchers concluded that intergroup conflict will occur whenever two groups compete for prizes or resources that only one group can have. It sounds like the perfect formula for creating a sports league.

The Lance Armstrong saga is perhaps the best example of how bullying in sports recapitulates the moral circumstances of ancestral humans. Armstrong, who grew up in Texas, won multiple professional triathlon championships while still a teenager. In 1992, at the age of 21, he became a professional bicycle racer when he joined the Motorola Cycling Team. His first major victory came at the World Road Race Championship in Norway. In 1996, he was diagnosed with advanced testicular cancer, which he managed to survive after intensive treatment. Less than three years later, he won the first of seven consecutive Tour de France races, an unprecedented achievement. He rode for the U.S. Postal Service team in six of those wins.

The Tour de France is the greatest cycling competition in the world. It is one of the most grueling events in all of sports, a three-week long war of attrition against machine, body, and spirit. For most of his racing career, Armstrong was dogged by doping allegations. That wasn't an unusual circumstance for many elite cyclists; the sport was often embroiled in doping controversies. Since 1967, when Tom Simpson died while competing in the Tour de France, 86 percent of the race's winners have been either sanctioned or incriminated for doping.[13] Simpson's autopsy revealed that he had mixed alcohol with amphetamines, a deadly diuretic combination when racing up a mountain in extreme heat conditions.

When accused of cheating, Armstrong always responded in the same intimidating manner: He attacked his accusers, smearing their character and threatening legal action. When his team's masseuse, Emma O'Reilly, claimed that she saw drugs in his bathroom, he sued her and called her a prostitute. To cross Lance Armstrong, as fellow cycling legend Greg LeMond and many others learned, was like descending into a hellish cage fight. Most accusers didn't have the stomach for Armstrong's no-holds-barred tactics. Despite rumors about cheating and mounting suspicions, he was able to amass a fortune exceeding $100 million by some accounts.

Lance Armstrong flatly denied ever having taken performance-enhancing drugs (PEDs) right up until his televised confession to Oprah Winfrey in January 2013. He was cornered into making that admission of guilt by a damning report from USADA (United States Anti-Doping Agency), published a few months earlier. The report charged him with running a massive doping ring when he rode for the U.S. Postal Service team. Nike and his other sponsors dropped him almost immediately, costing him dearly in terms of future earnings. Armstrong was banned for life from participating in any sports overseen by WADA (World Anti-Doping Agency).

After his disgrace, it's hard to appreciate the mythic stature Armstrong attained during the period when he was winning Tour de France races. It's probably what enabled him to forestall the ruin that finally caught up to him in 2012. Rayvon Fouche called him a "cancer Jesus" because his survival story was so heartwarming that millions of people practically worshipped him.[14] To be a cancer survivor is like being untouchable. People were willing to give Lance a pass on the nasty accusations, to believe that haters were trying to tear down (crucify) a good man. LiveStrong, his foundation dedicated to helping cancer survivors, raised more than $500 million. A major portion of it came from the sale of those formerly ubiquitous yellow wrist bands.

Armstrong is a classic case of an alpha male who saw the opportunity to dominate others and enrich himself. He couldn't resist. He used his double-heroic stature—gifted athlete plus cancer surviving philanthropist—to shame and silence critics who told the truth. He became a bully of epic proportions because, in his secret calculations, the risk of being punished for it was worth taking. He made his bet, and it sealed his fate.

In the end, it wasn't doping that brought Lance Armstrong down so severely. He never actually failed a drug test in his career. Compelling blood-doping evidence wasn't presented in USADA's 200-page decision until page 140.[15] Floyd Landis, his former teammate and chief critic, was suspended for only two years after being caught cheating en route to his 2006 Tour de France victory. Armstrong is banned for life—from participating in *any* organized sport. It could have gone differently, had he not become such a mean-spirited individual.

What brought Armstrong down was the testimony of Landis and 10 other teammates. Sports teams are moral communities, like hunter-gatherer bands, more egalitarian than hierarchical in the final analysis. Dominant stars carry teams to victory, but it's the team that is most important. Every coaching cliché revolves around the truism that there is no "I" in team. Teams desire humble leaders; they resent bullies. Sharing and generosity are more important than self-aggrandizement. The cancer Jesus behaved like a big shot, and his teammates brought him down. Finally, belatedly, they ganged up on him.

Armstrong never learned to suppress his own dominance sufficiently to survive (assuage) the resentment and vengeance of those he dominated. In that regard, his conscience failed him.

In their natural habitat, female bonobos will stand up to an alpha male and force him to back down if he tries to steal their food.[16] Female chimpanzees have never been observed standing up to alpha males in that way, at least not in the wild. They have been observed standing up for themselves in a zoo setting, however. Primatologists assume that the reason for the difference in how these closely related primates behave is due to their feeding patterns. Bonobos eat as a group, whereas chimpanzees tend to wander off to feed by themselves. What an alpha can get away with in seclusion is not tolerated when the entire troop witnesses it. When zoo chimpanzees are confined in a pen, they can't wander off to feed. So the entire troop can witness the bad behavior of an alpha male and respond accordingly.

The point I want to make is that Lance Armstrong was able to intimidate and bully his accusers when he could respond to them individually. In a one-on-one scrum, the bully wins. When 11 people finally came together and stood against him as a group, the bully didn't stand a chance. Predators cull their prey from the herd, using isolation and secrecy to their advantage. That is why a sexual predator like Harvey Weinstein could abuse so many women without suffering the consequences—until the #MeToo movement empowered women to respond as a group.

Another high-profile case of bullying in sports involved Richie Incognito and Jonathan Martin, professional football players on the Miami Dolphins.[17] Incognito and Martin were both offensive linemen, which meant they spent a great deal of time working together on drills, blocking schemes, game preparation, and so on. In the fraternity of NFL players, offensive linemen have the reputation of being an especially tight-knit group. That's why reports about Martin suddenly leaving the team in the middle of the 2013 season were so puzzling at first. He accused his own offensive line teammate of verbally bullying him. It seemed incredulous. How can you bully a 300-pound testosterone-stoked professional football player? Why didn't Martin just coldcock him and be done with it?

The evidence from text and phone messages made it clear that Incognito's behavior was reprehensible. Among other things, he called Martin racially charged names (Martin is black, Incognito white) and made derogatory sexual comments about his mother and sister. Incognito was suspended from the team and later released. The NFL hired attorney Ted Wells to investigate the matter. His report accused Incognito of spearheading a pattern of harassment on the Miami team.[18] The USADA accusation against Armstrong—ringleader of a vast doping scheme—shares a family resemblance. Incognito didn't get a contract with another team until a year after his eligibility to play was reinstated. No one wanted to take a chance on a man who became a public pariah regarding the latest social scourge of America. Every day, it seemed, there was another national news story about a school kid getting bullied on social media.

"I know it when I see it." That's what Supreme Court justice Potter Stewart said regarding obscenity and pornography.[19] The same thing could be said about bullying, mental illness, and many other complex social categories that manifest themselves in shades of gray rather than black and white. Unlike being afflicted with the measles, there is no definitive infectious agent or biomarker that enables us to point at it and say, "This is bullying, and that is not." Circumstances and personalities have a bearing on how we interpret interpersonal conflicts, as do cultural differences and social conventions. Jonathan Martin had a reputation for being a bit sensitive by NFL standards, and apparently Incognito had been encouraged to try to toughen him up. The week before he left the team, Martin's position had been switched from left tackle back to right tackle because of performance issues. Such added information doesn't excuse Incognito's behavior, but it gives us a fuller picture from which to judge.

The difference between bullying and horseplay is not always clear in the freewheeling give-and-take of social interactions. When dealing with a tone-deaf bully who (by definition) isn't good at picking up on the discomfort of others, normally we need to speak up for ourselves using forceful language, for example, "Stop that!" Some (most?) of us are more apt to try to laugh it off and avoid the bully at all costs afterward. Unfortunately, Martin was stuck with the guy.

When does teasing cross the line and become bullying? It's an interesting question because teasing is such an integral part of sports. Teammates play practical jokes on one another. They argue, laugh, boast, and make every little thing into a contest. Who can eat the most hot peppers without throwing up? Silly things like that. The camaraderie that is so necessary for athletic success is built upon the capacity to have fun together. Work without fun would be unbearable. That's true in all walks of life, not just sports. To laugh and joke about someone's clumsiness or minor misfortune—the outfielder who stumbled, lost the ball in the sun, then covered his head so the ball wouldn't strike him—is part of the game. To be able to take a ribbing gracefully is one criterion by which teammates are judged. It's a desirable trait.

Friendship is one of the blessings of a life well lived. To describe its full measure would require an entire book, or more. It's no accident that the *Epic of Gilgamesh*, one of the oldest literary texts ever uncovered by archaeologists, is a story about friendship.[20] The unlikely friendship of Gilgamesh (a king) and Enkidu (a wild man of the forest) began as a contest of strength. Fighting and competition is often the prelude to friendship.

Friends do things together. They hang out. They enjoy one another's company and prize a good laugh above almost anything else. They cover for one another and care about the other's well-being. They mourn the loss of a friend as if the world has somehow stopped turning. They also tolerate teasing that would be offensive if administered by a nonfriend. Perhaps that was part of the problem for Incognito. He didn't seem to know that Martin didn't want to be his friend. In his mind, they were teasing and horsing around. He was wrong about that, and he was equally wrong in how far he took the teasing. He crossed the line.

When I look back on my high school wrestling career, I mostly remember the fun things we did together. I can't recall much about my matches, but I'll never forget the swimming pool we discovered behind the showers after a dual meet in Sioux City, Iowa. My teammates and I decided to take a late-night swim, and the coaches couldn't figure out where we went. We laughed about that for the rest of the season.

Teasing and hazing are the perquisites of seniority. Rookies are "forced" to do laundry, eat strange foods, and do all kinds of silly (stupid) things as part of their informal orientation to the club. Sometimes things go too far. Martin complained that Incognito bullied him into paying $15,000 for a trip that members of the offensive line took to Las Vegas.

When I was in college, I worked the same job every summer for the street department of Sioux Falls. I was part of the same small road repair crew every year. Our job was to replace the bad patches in the asphalt after the northern prairie winter had wreaked its annual havoc. When I think about it, we functioned a lot like a sports team. Bob and Monty, the full-time heavy equipment operators in charge of our crew, were the veterans. They showed us the ropes and laughed at our mistakes. We worked hard and played hard. Basketball was a favorite game during breaks. Actually, it was more like a shoving contest. No one ever got around to scoring a basket. But we loved playing. Bob never participated, but Monty was always in the middle of it.

Monty—we called him Monty Montana, or Montana for short—was one of those bigger-than-life kind of guys who walked with a swagger and acted real tough. He always told us to get in the first punch because that was how 90 percent of all fights were won. He was the blade operator and principal mischief maker on our crew. In the world of heavy equipment workers, blade operators are the alphas. It is an incredibly difficult skill to be able to push a windrow of dirt, asphalt, or snow running a 15-ton steel machine at full bore. Above the steering wheel there were a dozen hydraulic pressure handles that had to be constantly adjusted so that the blade stayed level, with just the right amount of pitch, at just the right angle, to prevent the machine from gouging itself into the earth or skimming too high. Many times I sat next to Monty in the cab watching him perform like a maestro conducting his orchestra. While steering and keeping his eyes on the road ahead, he reached out to tap a different handle in a blur of constant no-look motion, the hydraulic system barking and hissing in response to his every move.

I asked him where he learned to run the blade like that. He said he got a job working on the Oahe dam near Pierre, his hometown. The foreman asked him if he'd ever run a blade before, and he said sure. He got the job, and he learned pretty quick how to run the thing.

Monty was always reciting what I took to be Wild West folklore ditties. "I'm wild and wooly and full of fleas," he'd shout, "never been curried below the knees; I've got a barbed wire tail, and I don't care which way I twitch it." He was kind of crazy, or colorful, like the Worm (Dennis Rodman) on the Chicago Bulls during some of their glory years. Or maybe like Richie Incognito on the Miami Dolphins if he could have learned to rein in some of his outrageous tendencies.

Once Bob asked me to unload the roller, a machine we used to compress the new asphalt. It had two giant drums for wheels that could be filled with water to make them heavier. We hauled the roller on the back of the truck. It had real wheels that you could lower and raise so that the drums would ride above the road when it was being towed. We were working in a fancy neighborhood called Tuthill Park. I climbed up on the roller and released the bar that held it to the truck. But I had forgotten to lower the towing wheels first. The roller started rolling and I tried to steer it and stop it, but nothing worked because the drums weren't touching the ground. It picked up speed, jumped the curb, and headed straight for the front door of a fancy home. Someone yelled "jump!" but I just sat there in a stupor of disbelief. The roller ran out of steam just before it got to the porch. Bob came over and quickly lowered the towing wheels and drove the machine back to the street. I never saw grown men laugh so hard that they cried before that happened. My dumb mistake was the highlight of their summer, and they never let me forget it. I laughed too, thanking my lucky stars that no one got hurt.

Teasing played a vital role in the moral systems of Stone Age hunter-gatherer societies. It was the first line of defense against dominant behavior. If one hunter was acting too much like a big shot, the other hunters would tease and ridicule him. Usually that was enough of a reminder for the offender to stop trying to dominate and be humble. On the rare occasions when that wasn't enough, things got more forceful. Teasing and ridicule were gentler forms of bullying that served the purpose of suppressing more aggressive forms of bullying.

Over time, the social pressure to be humble and careful with regard to bullying became internalized in a moral conscience. With the advent of that self-monitoring capacity, the social role of teasing became less urgent as a group strategy for disciplining moral deviants. It began to take on more of the friendly banter character that we see in sports today. More than likely, there is a parallel evolutionary trajectory between that shift—the internalization of discipline followed by the fraternization of teasing—and the invention of games and contests as the ritualized reenactment of practices essential to survival, for instance, hunting and fighting. In that sense, teasing as friendly banter and playing games (proto-sports) coevolved as recreational pursuits.

Teasing has always been an egalitarian pastime. No one was above being put in his place by teasing in the ancestral environment. Can you imagine a 16th-century commoner teasing oversized Henry VIII and living to tell about it? In the culture wars of our time, to make a joke about the president could result in a background check by the Secret Service. Intentions and motives are always subjects of suspicion. The Incognito–Martin case is of that ilk to some extent. There are limits to what a white man can say to a black man, even within the context of locker room camaraderie as a throwback to simpler times.

Teasing has always had a rehabilitative purpose as well. In general, hierarchical societies are more bent on punishing deviants (criminals) than egalitarian societies. Hunter-gatherers teased to get the misbehaving deviant to straighten up his act. Unless the survival of the group was threatened, second chances were usually forthcoming. Locker rooms operate in a similar manner. Pete Rose was banished from baseball because he gambled about games where he had a potential hand in the outcome. That threatened the integrity of baseball, akin to a recalcitrant bully threatening the survival of a hunter-gatherer band. Perverse and misguided as his behavior was, Incognito thought that he was helping Martin to succeed by toughening him up.

Teasing was also vitally important to the moral training of hunter-gatherer children. Children were treated differently than they are in modern societies. The group didn't try to protect their innocence or shield them from the harsher realities of life. They were treated like small adults. Based on her study of an Inuit three-year-old, anthropologist Jean Briggs showed how hunter-gatherer children learned to be moral agents through dramatic play, or teasing.[21] An adult might say to a child, "Why don't you die so that I can have your shirt?" To a modern person's ear, that sounds like cruelty. But in Inuit society, it is meant to help the child figure out how to resolve internal conflicts. Packed into that question sits the moral dilemma between wanting something for ourselves (a shirt, personal immortality) and the sacrifice it takes to achieve the generosity of spirit that Inuit culture admires (giving away a shirt, dying so that others might flourish). The question encapsulates a morality play for the child to wrestle with, not only in that moment, but also in the coming months and years as she grows up.

Coaches often chide their charges with similarly stark moral options. "Are you going to make the sacrifices it takes to become a champion, or are you just throwing away this opportunity?" "Do you want to be a party girl, or do you want to be a basketball player?"

There are degrees of bullying and teasing, some severe and more than obvious (punching someone's lights out), some less so (teasing that isn't malicious). The gentle teasing that is typical of friends is not bullying, although it can be construed as such if the friendship sours. Most teasing in sports probably falls into that gentler category. That's just a guess on my part, of course. I am not aware of any studies that would suggest otherwise. Rudeness is another gentler form of interpersonal conflict, not on the same scale as bullying, except in extreme cases.

In the ancestral environment, a rude person would have been scolded and ridiculed just like a bully but with less intensity because the threat to group harmony and survival would have been less. I think it is the same in modern sports. People resent rudeness—being spoken to in a harsh or condescending tone, typically—and often attribute it to arrogance, which is borderline big-shot behavior. It almost seems like there is a vicious circle between bullying, teasing, and rudeness: a not-so-merry merry-go-round.

Tennis player Maria Sharapova got a rude reception from many of her competitors when she returned to the WTA tour after serving a 15-month doping suspension. That isn't altogether surprising given the competitive nature of women's tennis. Sharapova is one of the wealthiest athletes in the world thanks to her endorsement earning power, which dwarfs her earnings on the court. That kind of success no doubt generates plenty of admiration—as well as envy. But the rudeness Sharapova met with upon her return to competitive tennis was particularly virulent. One top-10 player went so far as to say, "Nobody likes her or wants to see her back."[22]

Maybe I could agree that the rude reception went too far if it was just a matter of envy, as Sharapova's supporters liked to claim. But envy wasn't the most important factor. Some of her harshest critics referred to her as a doper and cheater who shouldn't be allowed to play ever again, evoking comparisons to Lance Armstrong. That is a real stretch. EPO is to meldonium as a PED what a lion is to a house cat. They aren't in the same league. Sharapova failed a drug test for meldonium at the 2016 Australian Open, just weeks after it had been added to the banned list by WADA. To suggest that she is a serious doper hardly seems fair. Doping wasn't the most important factor for the virulent reception she received either.

The animosity that greeted Sharapova's return was personal. I think that's why it was so virulent. In individual sports like tennis and golf, the league itself functions like a close-knit society, or a sorority. There aren't many tennis players good enough to earn a living by playing on tour. Maybe about 200 actually succeed in doing so. These elite athletes develop a sense of camaraderie, not as close as one would expect on a football or basketball team, but a sense that they all belong to the same group nevertheless. Not everyone is friendly with everyone else, but a certain level of friendliness is expected.

To appear unfriendly, or cold and indifferent—which is the reputation that Sharapova has earned among some of her colleagues—provokes resentment. It is the perceived rudeness of Sharapova herself that is the foundation for the rude reception she received upon returning to the fold. What goes around comes around; we resent rudeness like we resent bullying. That portion of the sorority of professional tennis players who perceived her as arrogant responded by ganging up on Sharapova when she returned.

Watching Sharapova compete throughout the years, I doubt that she is truly haughty, although she sometimes comes off that way even on the television screen. Her intensity is a two-edged sword. It gives her the tunnel vision to focus only on her own side of the net (her training and desire to win). But it opens her up to misinterpretation and resentment from others because, like Armstrong and Incognito, she hasn't learned to attenuate her intensity as a necessary step for getting along with one's peers. Sharapova's own conscience could better serve her understanding of how to be part of the group. There are no purely individual sports. There is always a group that is more significant than the sum of its individual members.

Morality, like sports, is a group-based endeavor. Conscience is a cautionary voice, not a saintly one. Its purpose is to help the individual understand her group.

In the next chapter, I will continue to flesh out my moral theory of sports by focusing on the often-contradictory roles of pretending and imitation in both morality and sports.

2

THE LAND OF PRETEND

The breadth of our moral experience is more extensive than ethicists have led us to believe in the past several millennia. The growing body of research literature in moral psychology bears witness to that circumstance. I don't blame ethicists for their efforts to civilize our moral instincts. It is a noble cause; however, it has also helped to deceive us about the true purposes of morality. There is more to morality than being honest and good, or aspiring to universal principles. One of the arguments I make in this book is that we must get out from under the spell of ethical idealism if we want to see morality for what it was intended to be. We know so much more now about the ancestral environment of our distant past, where morality and the other distinctive features of our nature took their current form. Guided by anthropologists, evolutionary theorists, primatologists, and others, I have been discussing what the moral life actually looked like for hunter-gatherer bands in the late Pleistocene epoch. My thesis is that the morality of our distant ancestors bears a remarkable resemblance to the moral experience of modern athletes. Championing group success is the epitome of hunter-gatherer morality; it is the epitome of modern sports as well.

In chapter 1, I focus on the birth of conscience as a response to the threat of bullying. The suppression of bullies who seized more than their fair share of resources was an important function of Stone Age morality. Bullying has become an epidemic in our time, and we see it in sports, as well as everyday life. Assaults on referees and other sports officials are becoming so common that many states—Alabama, for instance—now have laws that specifically address such conduct in an effort to protect officials. A recurrent sports page headline runs something like this: Parent goes ballistic because kid got raw deal in youth league game.

Bullying wasn't the only behavior that conscience evolved to suppress. Stealing, cheating, and lying were also moral problems that threatened the harmony of hunter-gatherer bands. They were tolerated more than bullying for two reasons. First, bullying was a more serious threat to group survival. If an alpha male were to intimidate everyone in the band without consequence, the cooperation necessary to hunt big game and share the meat equitably would have evaporated. Eventually, so too would the band. Second, cheating and lying—and sometimes stealing—are much harder to monitor and ferret out than bullying. It's impossible to hide the intimidation and violence that signify bullying. It's also fairly easy to catch a thief by finding the stolen goods in his possession. Cheating and lying, on the other hand, are subterfuges.

The subject of this chapter is the practice of deceptive arts—cunning, trickery, faking, subversion, cheating, lying, etc.—in morality and sports. Conscience is not above taking advantage of a situation when the benefit outweighs the risk of detection and punishment. Deception, in its many guises, is a pretender's game. Pretending is part and parcel of our very nature. Recall that I mention in the previous chapter what biologist Richard Alexander said about the evolution of the unconscious: It evolved as a place where we could push our lies so that others would not be able to catch us by reading our faces and body language.[1] Since we are better at detecting lies than covering them up, evolution hit on a strategy for self-deception. If I am not aware that I lied, then you can't be aware of it either. Check, and checkmate.

It's a hard timer's cliché that you'll never meet anyone in prison who doesn't proclaim his own innocence. The scary part of that is many of them actually believe it. Most Americans seem to think that disgraced football legend O. J. Simpson really did murder his ex-wife. We wonder how he could lie about that. Wouldn't his conscience eat him up inside? The truth is oftentimes more like a pretzel than a straight road. Even one's conscience can be fooled by the unconscious.

What about consciousness, our signature psychological capacity? According to Alexander, it evolved to make us *unpredictable* to competitors and prey.[2] Our big brains enable us to devise elaborate strategies for surprising those against whom we match wits. We trick others into thinking we are going to do one thing, and then we do something unexpected. We not only have great facility at detecting lies, but also are just as masterful at reading the intentions of others. The unconscious renders us inscrutable to lie detectors, and consciousness enables us to foil mind readers. Our capacity for cunning and craft evolved in lockstep with our moral evolution.

In Super Bowl LII, in 2018, the overmatched Philadelphia Eagles prevailed against the favored New England Patriots because they had the better trick plays, most notably the "Philly Special." The first half was coming to a close, and the Eagles had stalled on the two-yard line of New England. The down was fourth and goal. Backup quarterback and Super Bowl MVP Nick Foles lined up in shotgun formation. He drifted to his right, and the ball was snapped directly to the running back. He pitched it to Trey Burton, the tight end, who was wheeling around from the left side of the line. Burton threw the ball to a wide open Foles in the end zone. The Patriots had been thoroughly outfoxed by the Philly Special.

Foresight is another psychological capacity associated with moral evolution. It enabled us to postpone the need for immediate gratification when we did something generous—I scratch your back, you scratch mine—by predicting future benefits for favors rendered now. If I give a struggling family extra food that they will never be able to repay, others will notice my generosity, which will enhance my reputation as a good guy. Down the road, when I might need a favor, the good reputation I built up by being generous to those who couldn't reciprocate increases the likelihood that someone will help me. Morality is a reputation-based reward system. It pays to be generous, but not always right away. It takes time and foresight to build a reputation.

We evolved to be wily moral creatures—unpredictable, inscrutable, cautious, calculating. I don't think that means we are selfish at heart with only a thin veneer of niceness on the surface, as Frans de Waal described the position of those who base their cynical view of morality on the selfish gene theory.[3] There is ample evidence that social pressures favoring humility and generosity played a significant role in moral evolution. Generosity begets generosity, so long as free riders (those who take unfair advantage of generous individuals) are sufficiently shamed and suppressed. The worst free riders are bullies, followed by thieves, cheaters, and liars.

There are only a few strategies in nature that enabled large groups of animals to become a social organism in their own right. The bee hive is a perfect example of this unique evolutionary achievement. The life of the hive is more important than the survival of individual bees. Bees and other social insects achieved this group level of existence by restricting their own sexual reproduction to only a few specialized individuals: the queen and her drone mates. The rest of the bees are sterile siblings. The key to being able to exist as a super-organism or hive is the reduction of conflict between individuals within the group. Since bees are all siblings, competition between individuals is sufficiently reduced to support the hive due to the nepotism instinct that all animals possess. Like us, bees are naturally inclined to take care of their own family members.

The human strategy for achieving group level "hive" status—we usually call our hives cultures and civilizations—was very different. We reduced the conflict and competition between members of the group via a moral strategy. Morality is far from perfect, but it does a good enough job to ensure that human super-organisms will thrive. As large civilizations emerged after the invention of agriculture, morality had to be assisted by religious preachers, hierarchical governments, militaries, ethical manuals, and other means to help reduce the increasing potential for conflicts. The more that growing populations of people were forced to live in close proximity to one another, the more likely that conflicts would occur.

Monogamous pair bonding—we call it marriage—played a big part in our moral solution to the hive problem of reducing conflict. Rather than restricting sexual reproduction to specialized individuals, as social insects did, human morality took the opposite tack.[4] Every male had the opportunity to mate with one female, thereby reducing the likelihood that males would aggressively compete for sex. With marriage, everyone got a reasonable chance to mate.

The most common form of cheating, of course, is extramarital affairs. This is a story as old as conscience itself. Morality might not be as efficient and regimented as the sexual specialization of social insects, but no species on earth has proved to be more flexible and adaptive than our own. Ironic as it may seem, we have morality to thank for that.

Its *inefficiencies* in stamping out competition and conflict—and the deceptive practices that inevitably follow—also encouraged the risk-taking behavior that enabled us to settle every continent and major island on earth except Antarctica. We are risk takers at heart, and conscience is adept at evaluating the potential benefits and risks of our behavior.

In some instances, selfishness and nepotism become necessary for survival. In times of famine, the generosity toward nonfamily members that sustained the hunter-gatherer moral hive broke down.[5] Bands would split up because it was easier for a family to survive by scavenging on its own. If the group had stayed together—if nepotism and egoism had been thoroughly wiped out by moral generosity—everyone would have starved to death. There wasn't enough food to share equitably anymore, so the smart and flexible thing to do was break up. After the famine, when times got better, bands would naturally form again because they are more efficient when opportunities to hunt large game are available.

The imperfections of moral systems are their saving grace. Flexibility is more adaptive than moral perfection. It is okay to have some misbehavior going on so long as it doesn't prevent the group from thriving. Morality balances conflicts of interest, it doesn't obliterate them. Our strongest moral instincts are egoism and nepotism. While moral generosity may be less powerful as an instinct, it is aided by the watchful eyes of individuals who are naturally suspicious of the selfish intentions of others. Like consumer economies and modern democracies, moral systems function best when each individual is looking out for his or her own best interests. That is the gist of Adam Smith's "invisible hand" concept: Without intending it, as if every action had been guided by an invisible hand, the pursuit of self-interest leads to the most efficient moral/political/consumer societies. Smith's first mention of this idea came in *The Theory of Moral Sentiments* (1759), long before his more famous book, *The Wealth of Nations* (1776).[6] Looking out for our own best interests doesn't mean that we can't also be generous to others. Rather, it means that we have to be cautious about falling prey to deception.

The reason why our moral lives are leavened with cunning and other forms of deception, including self-deception, is because we have competing interests and desires. We compete against others in our group but not with outward abandon. We are sly about it because we don't want to be shamed for not being generous enough. There are rules to follow when playing the morality game. Go too far in taking advantage of others and you risk punishment from the group. On the other hand, a little bit of self-serving misbehavior is to be expected.

Intergroup conflicts constitute the most serious threats to survival. Moral cooperation increases to its most efficient levels in this circumstance. Groups that suppress the normal infighting between members and collaborate like a smooth functioning hive will outcompete groups that don't function so well together. Nothing sharpens moral resolve like an existential threat. Sports teams face similar threats, not all of them merely symbolic. Coaches are fired when they don't win. Professional players are released. Tragic injuries occur. Dreams are shattered, reputations sullied. The glory of achievement is all too quickly forgotten. On occasion, a life, not just a livelihood, is lost.

There is nothing quite like March Madness for its existential purity. Lose, and you go home. Win, and you survive to play another basketball game. Everything is reduced to that binary reality. We are strongly attracted to binary interpretations. Seeing things as black and white gives us a survival advantage. Gray is confusing, and leads to hesitation, which in a battle of wits could be costly, even deadly. It's why we tend to make instantaneous moral judgments about people: friend/foe; trustworthy/shifty; good guy/bad guy; truthful/untruthful; nice/mean.

If your team reaches the latter stages of the NCAA tournament bracket, each game becomes special in itself. The moral suspense builds, like the fervent anticipation for what is to come at the end of Ramadan, or Holy Week. Make it to the Sweet Sixteen and you've earned a coming-out party. Enjoy the moment, because there's a 50–50 chance you will be crushed before the candles get blown out. Make the Elite Eight, and you are only one step away from basketball heaven: a trip to the Final Four.

Winning is not some selfish triviality, as it is sometimes portrayed. It is the sign of a team's virtue, its achievement of the highest excellence. A championship team is greater than the sum of its parts. It is a hive, a super-organism, and to become such a thing is the true purpose of sports—and morality too. Bill Belichick, the mumbling, disheveled Patriots coach, is universally admired for his ability to cobble together winning teams by getting the most from castoff players not named Tom

Brady. "Do your job" is the Belichick mantra. That is hive speak. If you are a queen, be the queen. If you are a worker, be a worker. Don't try to be more than what you are. Trust the team to take care of itself.

The true purpose of winning is to achieve something seemingly impossible. It is to rise above the self-centeredness that preoccupies our lives far too much. Teams require sacrifice from their members. The transmigration from a group of individuals to a proficient hive is a birthing process. Midwifery is a coaching credential. When it works, well . . . honey never tasted so sweet.

There is no such thing as an "individual" sport. I've said that before, and it bears repeating. It's a convention for how we talk about sports when the competition is between two individuals. Great as they are, even Roger Federer and Rafael Nadal have teams behind them, as does every other tennis player, tournament director, league president, and so on. Nadal, the King of Clay, was taught the game by his Uncle Toni. A former professional table tennis player, Toni Nadal forced his nephew to do two things from an early age: play left-handed (he's a natural righty) and hold the racket like a ping-pong paddle to generate the most spin on the ball.[7] Lefties have a natural advantage because most players are right-handed. That means they don't often see the kinds of spin and ball movement that a lefty generates. No one spins the ball with the looping vengeance of Rafa. There has never been another player with a game like his. Couple that uniqueness with his burly physique—he looks like a middle linebacker among a league of bony punters—plus his love for the exhaustive suffering of battle, and witness perhaps the toughest out in sports. Would Nadal be so indomitable without Uncle Toni's shrewd coaching?

In the land of pretend, morality and sports are subterfuge royalty. The moral struggles that made us so deceptively clever are unmatched by any other creature. When our species left Africa to settle all parts of the globe, most of the large fauna that we encountered went extinct soon after our arrival. These outsized animals that were hunted to extinction—mastodons and mammoths, among many others—had lived by a different evolutionary standard. Being bigger had been the key to survival in the animal kingdom, until we came along and suddenly demonstrated that being clever was better. The largest animals didn't understand how dangerous we truly were because for millions of years their size alone had scared away potential predators. Most successful predators find a sustainable equilibrium with their prey. Otherwise, they would be putting at risk the long-term survival of their own species as well. The human ascendancy to dominance happened so quickly (tens of thousands of years instead of millions) that most of the largest mammals didn't have time to adapt.[8] Other species, like coyotes, known for their wily ways, have thrived alongside us. It can't be accidental that Native American cultures throughout the continent cherished trickster tales that usually featured Coyote, a mythical mischief-making creature.

In many ways, the human psyche is a set of subversive practices. Odysseus, the legendary Greek hero, was best known for his *metis*, or cunning intelligence. It was Odysseus' idea to build the fateful "Trojan Horse," which enabled the Greeks to finally overcome Troy. The horse was a hollow structure left on the beach as a tribute to Troy. The Trojans were so overjoyed to see the enemy ships leaving that they dragged the giant horse into their fortified city to celebrate. But the Greeks had only pretended to sail home. Some of their warriors were hidden inside the horse. After dark, while the Trojans slept, the Greeks slipped out of the horse and proceeded to sack the fabled city. It is a bitter lesson of history and poetry. The greatest strength of Troy—its impenetrable walls—was overcome by guile, not force. It was the Trojans themselves who authored their own demise by falling for Odysseus' ruse.

It is our nature and destiny to live and die not by the sword, but by the *metis* that wields it. We play games and invent sports because it is a practical necessity for us to do so. Just as our bodies require physical challenges to thrive and exist, our wits require opponents with whom to joust. Mental sparring is an itch that we cannot help scratching, as is the joy of being an embodied soul that must work to stay fit and ready. Such are the elements of athletic prowess. We wage pretend battles in sports, just as we conjure pretended experiences in dreams. Dreaming is to our sleep and restoration what sport is to our play and recreation. We cannot live without either one. Isn't it strange that imaginary things are as important to our self-identities as cells and organs?

The ancient Greeks adored Odysseus. The same can't be said for the Romans, who weren't normally averse to emulating Greek culture. One reason for their distaste regarding Odysseus traces back to the Trojan War. According to a legend beautifully rendered in Virgil's epic poem, Rome was founded by a vanquished Trojan. A more likely reason for

Roman coldness had to do with their law-abiding pragmatism. Compared to the stoic and sensible Romans, Greeks were passionate dreamers. On his wayward journey home after the war, the subject of Homer's other epic poem, Odysseus lashed himself to the mast of his ship to hear the mythical Sirens sing. He had been warned that it was certain death to hear their song because no one who listened could resist the temptation to steer his ship onto the treacherous rocks where they lived. Odysseus's clever solution—to hear the enchanting song without falling prey to the enchantment—was something any Greek would wish to do. But not a levelheaded Roman.

The most intriguing interpretation of Homer's *Iliad* that I have encountered was offered by Julian Jaynes, a psychologist who anticipated many of the recent discoveries in neuroscience.[9] Based on the changing meaning of some of Homer's language, Jaynes concocted a theory about how we acquired moral agency and self-consciousness. He noticed that Homer's portrayal of Achilles' decision to join the Greeks in their siege of Troy was not really a decision as we understand it. There was no agency involved—no Achilles taking responsibility for his own actions. Instead, Achilles swore an oath in which the gods commanded him to go to war. He didn't decide anything; it was the gods who made the "decision." But the decision was delivered by Achilles' own mouth, as if he were an oracle (vessel) reciting what the gods wished him to say.

What Jaynes noticed was that in the oldest versions of the poem that have been preserved, there was more oath-making talk than in the more recent versions. Remember that this poem was part of an oral tradition that reached back in time to the era before writing became widespread. The written versions of it that have survived to modern times are not all identical. Scholars have been able to date the different versions accordingly. So Jaynes formulated an interesting hypothesis: What if in these different versions of this ancient poem, what we are actually witnessing is the birth of human consciousness?

Jaynes argued that Achilles and other characters in the most ancient versions of the poem were without self-awareness. They lived as schizophrenic people live in our time. They heard voices that appeared to come from the gods. Jaynes believes that what we call schizophrenia is actually a vestige—not a disease—of how humans used to make decisions. Ancient people had bicameral minds, with hallucinatory voices. The birth of self-awareness happened in the process of breaking down the bicameral mind so that only one voice—the emerging self's voice—remained. Unlike Achilles, we don't rely on hallucinations to tell us what to do. We decide for ourselves.

What is prescient about Jaynes's theory is that he linked it to brain research. The brain is actually bicameral; it has two hemispheres that do operate independently in many ways. Most speech functions are controlled by three areas in the left hemisphere, most notably Wernicke's area.[10] The right hemisphere is largely silent. Why? Because, according to Jaynes, the area in the right hemisphere that corresponds to Wernicke's area is where hallucinatory voices come from. As we achieved self-consciousness and moral agency, the hallucinatory voices that used to tell us what to do were silenced.

The bicameral theory is interesting because it supports the premise that morality is a group phenomenon, not an individual one. John Geiger referred to Jaynes's work in his book about the prevalence of "third man" experiences in situations of extreme isolation and stress.[11] Mountain climbers, solo sailors, polar explorers, and others who find themselves in extremely traumatic circumstances are prone to experiencing the presence of a "third man" (or a guardian angel, as some have called it) who comforts them. Sir Ernest Shackleton described such an experience in his memoir about exploring the South Pole. In moments of exhaustion and desperation, many find comfort in an imaginary friend. It is the gesture of a mind adapted to acts of moral kindness. It is a bicameral experience of the close-knit group comforting a lost soul. I think athletes, in particular, have a sense for the greater-than-self (moral) quality of any effort that pushes us to the red line of the almost impossible.

Eight people died when they were caught in a blizzard as they were descending from the summit of Mt. Everest in May 1996. In his book about that disaster—the worst in climbing history—Jon Krakauer referenced a climber who said that people can't afford morality in the death zone above 8,000 meters (26,246 feet).[12] He meant that every person must look out for himself/herself when they reach that height because rescue from misfortune would be impossible. If something were to go wrong, your fate would be permanently sealed, along with the other 200 bodies currently frozen into the stony ice on Everest.

Just because rescue is impossible doesn't mean morality is irrelevant, however. The mind itself is a moral agency, and the will to survive in such dire circumstances is a moral feat. It is fitting that some mountain climbers—extreme athletes—are capable of finding comfort and encouragement in the silent presence of a "third man." There are no moral-free zones on earth because morality is part of our nature. Wherever we go, morality goes with us. Here, too, in the harshest circumstances, we find another form of self-deception that serves a moral purpose. We endure hardship in acts of will that are animated by mental cunning. Is it any wonder that the placebo effect (another form of self-deception) can play such an important role in our recovery from illness and injury?

There are degrees of deception and cleverness in sports, as in morality. When things go too far, we find it unacceptable. Cheating is a step too far. It is amazing how angry and upset we become when we think someone has cheated. We don't mind a little creative bending of the rules, however. The difference between the two can be hard to discern.

Was the NBA hack-a-Shaq strategy cheating? When Shaquille O'Neal was at his dominant best, no one could stop him if he got the ball in the paint. A power dunk was virtually automatic. But O'Neal was a poor free throw shooter, averaging only a little better than 50 percent for his career; therefore, many teams adopted the strategy of intentionally grabbing him when he got the ball deep instead of letting him dunk. That way he would need to earn his points at the line, which was an advantage for the other team.

Intentional fouling does not square with the spirit of the rules of basketball. Normally, a foul is supposed to be an unintended consequence of playing good, aggressive basketball. Despite that purist ideal, intentional fouling has become part of the game, and most commentators didn't view the hack-a-Shaq strategy as cheating. It is in a team's best interests to exploit the weaknesses of opponents. Shaq could have worked harder to improve his foul shooting, so he had some control of the vulnerability that he and his team faced when the game was on the line. Perhaps that is why public opinion didn't support the cheating label: He could have done something about it but didn't.

Muhammad Ali's rope-a-dope strategy against George Foreman when they fought for the heavyweight championship in 1974 similarly skirted the line between acceptable cunning and cheating. Foreman was a ferocious slugger. His uppercuts had lifted Joe Frazier right off the canvas, and that's not hyperbole. Some people expressed concern about Ali's safety before their Rumble in the Jungle. Round after round, Ali leaned far back over the ropes and invited Big George to flail away at his torso while keeping his gloves high to protect his head. He also did a lot of clinching and holding, which is against the rules. He only stood toe to toe with Foreman in brief flurries at the beginning and end of rounds. Eventually, Foreman tired from the ineffective heavy punches he had thrown, and Ali knocked him out. It was a fable-like ending: The opponent least expected to win somehow overcame the odds through courage and guile—like the tortoise and the hare.

Not all forms of deception come close to the red line of cheating. Toward the gentler end of things we find what I would call the mannered traditions. Kalahari Bushmen are so wary of being labeled big shots that they will never speak about their hunting success unless someone asks them first. The village could be on the brink of starvation, and a Bushman could be returning with a large antelope that would save the day. It's a cause for celebration, right? But the Bushman will sit as if he had nothing better to do all day, patiently waiting for someone to bring up the subject of the hunt. On the inside, he is eager to tell his story and share the meat. How could he not be? On the outside, however, he pretends not to care so much. That's what having good manners means: the ability to mask one's true feelings to be pleasant and get along with others.

Good manners are a hallmark of sports. When a sporting contest ends, invariably the protocol is to shake hands and wish the other competitor(s) well. At the end of a college basketball game, for instance, the teams form lines that move in opposite directions so that each person on one team can shake hands with each person on the other team. It is a typical scene in modern sports, where the expectations of good sportsmanship—behaving yourself and treating others with respect—are firmly upheld.

In sports where fighting frequently breaks out, for example hockey, we like to see gestures of reconciliation (a pat on the back, a handshake) afterward. "No hard feelings." That's what we expect to hear: not exactly a *mea culpa*, but close enough to satisfy our sense of good form. Even when fighting is the sole purpose of a sport, as in a MMA match, we look for and appreciate signs of basic decency. We warm to generous competitors, as we warmed to generous members of the hunter-gatherer band in ancestral times.

To be sincere in your congratulations to the winner, when you have just lost, is a social grace hard to come by. It takes practice, and goodwill. It shows a level of maturity and manners that most aspire to for their children. We tolerate temper tantrums in kids who are young and inexperienced. If it's our own kid making a scene, we probably can't wait to get home so we can scold him/her for being such an embarrassment. Tantrums from competitors old enough to have achieved self-control are subject to scorn and booing.

Not everyone wants their kids to be good losers. Even to mention the "l" word is avoided by some, as if mentioning it might cause it to occur. Superstitions run as deep in sports as good manners. The hard-nosed approach to playing a game—never give an inch to anyone—usually doesn't wear well in the long run with teammates and opponents. Pete Rose's "Charlie Hustle" antics—racing to first base when the pitcher had just walked him—were a little too gung-ho (borderline disrespectful) for many of us.

To be a gracious winner is almost as hard as being a gracious loser. Both are important. I'll never forget the picture of Rafael Nadal putting his arm around Roger Federer to comfort him after they played the final at the 2009 Australian Open. Federer had lost the match and began sobbing while attempting to give his concession speech. In professional tennis, both finalists make public remarks after the championship match. It's a difficult moment for the runner-up, in particular. Federer couldn't quite pull it off until Nadal stepped in to encourage him. A friendly gesture, pretended or not, can lift us up. A gracious winner can make it a little easier to swallow a hard loss. That's another social function of manners: to soften the hard edges of our social interactions. A smile creates more goodwill than a frown.

What tips things over the edge from a display of cunning that we find acceptable to one that inflames us with indignation? Perhaps a study of capuchin monkeys can help explain it. Brosnan and de Waal placed two female monkeys in side-by-side cages and had them do simple exchange tasks for food rewards.[13] Each of the monkeys could see what was happening in the other cage. At first, both monkeys were given cucumber slices as their reward when they successfully exchanged a token. Everything went fine until one monkey received a grape instead of a cucumber. Grapes are a favorite food of capuchins.

The one who received a cucumber instead of a grape after the next exchange screamed and threw the cucumber back at the trainer. She would not accept the cucumber because she saw that the other monkey was receiving a better reward. This seemed to violate her expectation that they should both get the same reward for the same task. Apparently, capuchin monkeys have a sense of fairness, and they react strongly when it is violated. We might say that the one who kept getting cucumbers instead of grapes felt *cheated*, and she let everyone know it.

We have a similar aversion to being cheated, even vicariously as sports fans. It inflames us with indignation because our expectation is that the playing field should always be level. We have a keen eye for unfair treatment, just as we do for lying and other forms of misbehavior. It's part of the unconscious mental background of our moral lives. When we notice something that violates our sense of fairness, it bursts into our consciousness as a strong feeling. We point and scream, "He cheated!" We want everyone to know about it so that the cheater will be punished. We are vigilant watchers, making sure that no one takes unfair advantage of us.

The problem with our sense of fairness is that it is biased toward our own interests first. We are not naturally impartial. There is a difference between watching out for cheaters and being fair-minded. The self-protective instinct (watching out for cheaters) is naturally stronger. It is harder for us to be concerned about others than it is to be concerned about ourselves. That is a limitation of our morality, and it is something we have been working to improve for tens of thousands of years.

Given the subjective nature of our sense of fairness, it is understandable that we often find it difficult to pinpoint the difference between bending the rules and breaking them. Cheaters break the rules of the game. Who would want to argue with that? The problem is getting everyone to agree that the rules were broken in a given case. If my team is being accused of cheating, I will see things differently than someone from the other side. It can't be helped. The Deflategate hullabaloo regarding air pressure in footballs used during the first half of the 2015 AFC Championship Game is the perfect illustration.

The Patriots destroyed the Colts, 45–7, in that game. The controversy began in the second quarter, when the Colts intercepted a Tom Brady pass.[14] The ball seemed light, so an intern on the Colts team measured the air pressure. It was less than 12.5 psi (pounds per square inch), which is the minimum standard required by the NFL. So the refs were notified, as was the league. Many believe that an underinflated ball is easier to catch.

Thus began an 18-month saga of intrigue, special investigations, accusations, counteraccusations, conspiracy theories, punishments, lawsuits, arbitrations, appeals, overturned judgments, more appeals, scientific disagreements about gas laws, and endless sports radio and television debates. Let me mention just a few salient facts and back stories to help fill in the Deflategate picture.

The weather was cool and rainy on that January evening in Gillette Stadium. If a ball had been inflated to 12.5 psi in a heated locker room (normal procedure) it would naturally lose pressure when it was taken outside for the game. The pressure of a gas in a contained space changes according to temperature. That is the gist of Gay-Lussac's law. The NFL has no provisions in its rules regarding variability in ball pressure due to temperature changes.[15]

Apparently, two different types of gauges were used to measure the pressure in the Patriots' balls and some of the Colts balls at halftime, which makes it impossible to interpret the results consistently. Moreover, the gauges in question are not precision instruments that would pass a rigorous scientific reliability test.

The Patriots had been disciplined in 2007, for videotaping Jets coaching signals during a game. Spygate, as that incident was called, set a precedent that accelerated the suspicions of Patriot haters, conspiracy theorists, and football fans when Deflategate came along.[16] Do the Patriots play fast and loose with the rules? Is that why they have been so successful?

Tom Brady performed better in the second half using balls that had been reinflated to the proper pressure level.

The NFL hired Ted Wells to conduct an independent investigation (the same Ted Wells who investigated the Miami Dolphins regarding Richie Incognito). The 234-page report concluded that it was "more probable than not" that Brady was "at least generally aware" that two members of the Patriots organization carried out a plan to slightly underinflate footballs.[17] It was a judgment based on circumstantial evidence. No direct proof was found.

Within a week after the Wells report was delivered, NFL commissioner Roger Goodell determined the punishment for breaching the integrity of the game and failing to cooperate fully with an investigation. Brady's punishment was a four-game suspension. In accordance with the collective bargaining agreement between the National Football League Players Association and the NFL, Brady appealed. The commissioner upheld his own decision after the arbitration hearing.

Both the NFL and Brady filed lawsuits in different federal court districts. Judge Richard Berman of New York decided the case, vacating the Goodell ruling just as the 2015–2016 season was about to begin.

Tom Brady didn't serve his four-game suspension until the fall of 2016, after the suspension had been reinstated by a federal appeals court. Brady had considered appealing to the Supreme Court, ultimately deciding against it.

What is the takeaway message from this bizarre case? One thing we learned is that Tom Brady, like Robin Hood, is more popular than the "bad sheriff" commissioner. Public opinion slants in Brady's favor. That's a little surprising given the level of hate that the Patriots organization inspires. A scientific study commissioned by Ted Wells notwithstanding, the gas laws of science appear to vindicate the Patriots.

Did the Patriots organization cheat? Did Tom Brady? After millions of dollars were spent investigating and litigating, I don't think we are any closer to resolving those questions. What is cheating? It is easy to define, yet hard to determine sometimes. That paradox encapsulates Deflategate.

We have a strong cognitive tendency to persist in our convictions even in the face of contrary evidence. Psychologists call it bias confirmation. We seize upon evidence to support our biases, ignoring or belittling evidence that contradicts them. This all comes into play when fighting words like "Cheater!" get thrown around. We are a litigation-prone society because our basic moral tendency is to go easier on ourselves and harder on others. That bias runs deep into our core. When threatened, we tend to see villains across the way from us.

Finally, let me mention gamesmanship as a form of deception that stands somewhere between the gentle pretending of good manners and the kind of behavior that borders on cheating. Calling a timeout to ice the kicker in a football game is an example of gamesmanship. It's not cheating, or breaking the rules. Instead, it is a mild abuse of them. The rules were not intended to disrupt the normal play of an opponent, but they can be used (misused) in that way. Another example would be a tennis player who takes a bathroom break to slow down the momentum of her opponent who is playing lights out tennis. It's within the rules, but the timing of the break is a little suspect. Stalling tactics in wrestling is another one. One wrestler gets ahead, then stalls (quits trying), hanging on for the win.

In the next chapter, I continue to explore the dynamics of deception in sports by focusing on the polarized relationship between coaches and referees. Coaches are natural tricksters, forever tempted to bend the rules to surprise the competition. Referees are the embodiment of rules, forever attempting to apply rigid standards to a fluid game that constantly creates never-before-seen circumstances. The mixture of these two characters in the narrative of sports is like gasoline being poured on a fire. At least it seems that way sometimes.

3

COACHES AND REFEREES

My earliest memory of a sporting event is the Jackrabbit Stampede of 1960. It was the annual rodeo for South Dakota State College (now South Dakota State University). We lived on campus in married student housing while my dad completed his civil engineering degree. The reason I remember that particular rodeo is because it had to be postponed due to severe weather. I was five years old and had never heard the word *postponed* before. A man in a dusty station wagon drove around town announcing the postponement over a loud speaker. I couldn't quite comprehend the concept. I wasn't going to go to the rodeo until later anyway. So what's the difference? I guess my mind hadn't developed a linear sense of time consciousness yet.

South Dakota State was a land grant college, meaning it was founded using money from the sale of federal lands. The government required land grant schools to teach practical sciences to support agriculture and a few other important industries. Living on campus was like living on a giant farm, a wonderland for a young boy. I was a frequent visitor to the numerous barns and pens where cows, horses, pigs, sheep, chickens, and other assorted animals were kept. I was fascinated by the cows, with shiny brass caps surgically implanted on the sides of their torsos. I always wondered if the animal scientists took things out of the cow through those portals, or put things in. Probably both. I also wondered if it hurt.

The rodeo was the biggest event of the year, which seems surprising today. There hasn't been a Jackrabbit Stampede for decades. At my first rodeo, I sat on my dad's shoulders so I could see over the high fences and chutes into the ring where all the action was. It was frightening to be that close to thousand-pound animals bucking with such ferocity. I had second thoughts about wanting to become a cowboy when I grew up.

Bronc riding was the most popular event, bull riding the most dangerous. A bronc rider had to stay on the horse for eight seconds to finish the ride and obtain a score. Scoring was based on two things—staying in your seat while raking your spurs up and down the horse's shoulders, and holding one hand high in the air away from the horse. These are not easy things to do when the animal you've clamped your legs around is twisting, kicking, and doing everything it can to get you off its back. In that sense, bronc riding is a typical sport: You win by doing something that the rules make it extremely difficult to accomplish. Golfers don't just waltz up the fairway and place their ball into the hole. No, they must hit it with different-sized sticks, then putt it on a slick surface. It's not supposed to be easy.

There is at least one thing that makes bronc riding different from most other sports. The horse also receives a score, and that gets added to the rider's score. So it's a team sport, with one of the team members being an animal. It's not like dressage or horse racing, either, where you get to train with the same horse. In the rodeo, you draw your partner by chance. That gives the sport an element of arbitrariness (or luck), like the weather in a regatta.

My uncle, Red Severson, was the basketball coach at St. Cloud State. When he brought his Huskies to play South Dakota State in 1960, I attended the game with my dad. It was played in the "barn," an old-style gym cramped with bench seating that reached clear up to the rafters. It was a loud and intimidating place for the visiting team. We won that game, but it was a bittersweet victory for dad and me.

We waited outside to say hello to my uncle. It was awfully cold, and exhaust from the St. Cloud State bus swirled around us, mingling with our own visible breath. When Red finally came out, he and my dad talked briefly. "We'll get them at our place," he said ruefully as he boarded the bus for home. It was after 10:00 pm, and they had a four-hour drive ahead of them. The barn was only about 100 yards from our house.

Coaches have different styles. There is no one-size-fits-all formula for success in coaching. You have to find the style that works for you. My Uncle Red was a histrionic coach. He would jump up and down, wave his arms, scream, and stomp his feet. He had a habit of grabbing the water bottle and squirting it toward his mouth. Invariably, some of the water missed the mark and hit people sitting behind the bench. He carried on like a man destined for a coronary. Bud Grant—the sleepy-eyed Minnesota Vikings coach—he was not.

The most intense coach I ever observed in person was Dan Gable. When I was a graduate student at the University of Iowa in the 1980s, I attended many wrestling matches. Gable was the coach at Iowa from 1976 to 1997. His teams won 15 national championships. It's an unbelievable record. An Iowa native, Gable attended college at Iowa State University, where he compiled a 117–1 record. The only collegiate match he lost was his last one. He won a gold medal in the 68-kilogram weight class at the 1972 Munich Olympics. In his six matches, he never gave up a point.

Coach Gable defied the observation that superstar athletes make poor coaches. Has another coach in any sport ever won 15 national championships? Carver Hawkeye arena was usually filled to capacity for Iowa wrestling matches. Gable would be sitting in a chair on the edge of the mat next to his assistant coaches, hunched over with one hand on his chin. When things on the mat got interesting, he prowled back and forth like a captive leopard. I don't know what was more captivating, watching the actual match or watching Gable watch the match. His body twitched and moved as if he was the competitor. If an Iowa wrestler was in trouble, he would get down on the mat and demonstrate which move to make. Wrestling isn't like tennis, where you aren't supposed to coach from the stands.

Referees have their own styles, too. Most shy away from behavior that draws attention to themselves but not all of them. Ted Valentine was a flamboyant referee who became famous for ejecting Bobby Knight from an Indiana basketball game by calling an erroneous second technical foul on him.[1] Actually, that took guts given Knight's reputation as the most mercurial coach of them all. He was the mad scientist of basketball coaches: undeniably brilliant, unfailingly quarrelsome with referees.

Sports are rule-governed activities, and the rules are designed to make it difficult to excel. That is a recipe for intrigue as coaches scheme to push their deceptive practices to the limit of the rules and referees scramble to keep everything within those limits. Coaches are tricksters who must match wits with the other team's coaches. They also match wits with the referees, but that is a different kind of contest. It is a game within the game, a metagame, and the stakes are different than winning and losing on the field.

Coaches invent plays that follow one of two patterns. They are either strategic or tactical but usually not both at the same time. Strategic plays are contests of power and execution, whereas tactical plays are contests of trickery and surprise. In college football, usually it is the blue-chip teams that become strategic juggernauts because they have the ability to recruit the best athletes. They want to line up, hike the ball, hand it to a running back, and let him run it down your throat. End of story. They don't care if you know what play is coming. They know that you can't stop them if they execute properly. That's the Alabama Crimson Tide formula under Coach Nick Saban, who often complains about the up-tempo trickery of spread offenses run at schools of less sterling pedigree. And why wouldn't he? At Alabama, the recruiting advantage alone goes a long way toward winning championships.

In strategic games, the fight is about space on the field and who controls it. Usually, it's the bigger and stronger team. Not even Nick Saban plays the strategic game all of the time, however. Coaches also employ tactical maneuvers. They mix it up, throwing in a surprise once in a while. Or, they take a tactical maneuver and build their entire identity around it. No one did that better than Chip Kelly in the six years he was at the University of Oregon, the last four as head coach.

Kelly added two innovative wrinkles to the fast-strike spread offense. One was the inside zone read. That means the quarterback waits to hand off the ball until the defensive end commits to holding his ground or chasing the running back. The quarterback "reads" the defensive player's intentions, then decides what to do accordingly. From that one basic play—a zone read run up the middle—Oregon operated its entire offense. The difficulty in defending them was that every play used the same formation. If the defender chased the running back, the read option quarterback could keep the ball and run around the edge. Or he could throw a bubble pass after faking the run. And so on. No Pac-12 team had more plays stopped at the line of scrimmage for no gain than Oregon. If you could disrupt the zone read, you could stop them. On the other hand, no team had more plays go for 30-plus yards either. They were masters of the big play.

Speed was the second wrinkle in Kelly's spread offense—not just foot speed, although that was a key ingredient. Kelly liked fast running backs. (What coach doesn't?) Oregon's LaMichael James won the Doak Walker Award for top running back in 2010. Their Heisman trophy quarterback, Marcus Mariota, was an extremely fast runner as well. The Pac-12 conference is known for speed, not size and power like the Big Ten and SEC. Speed can neutralize power. The no-huddle offense was Kelly's speed innovation. They called their plays from the sidelines using giant poster boards with pictures of Elvis and Mickey Mouse. Their offense was so fast that the defense was often caught unprepared. When that happened, it usually cost them a big play. Fittingly, Oregon called it the blur offense.

In tactical games, the fight is not about controlling space, as in strategic games, but exploiting time. It is about quick strikes, unexpected plays, unrelenting pace—taking time away from your opponent rather than controlling the field of play. To expect something is to anticipate what is going to happen next. To be taken by surprise—tricked—means that expectations have been foiled. Trickery is always a sneak attack, the deceived person invariably the last one to know what happened. Tactics are meant to confuse the opponent's sense of time management.

Here is where it gets interesting with the referees. They too were subject to the trickery and tempo of Oregon's offense. I can recall many occasions when they appeared to be as gassed as the defense. Sometimes the linesman would trip or the ball would fall out of his hands as he scrambled to place it at the line of scrimmage in time for Oregon's offense to go again. It was like a vaudeville routine. The referees were so intent on keeping up with Oregon's pace of play that it detracted from their other responsibilities. The game within the game, pitting coaches against referees, tilted in Oregon's favor. They were following Oregon's script, not the other way around.

Rules are strategic by nature, not tactical. They delimit the geography of play first of all, whether it is a court, field, course, ring, track, or some other configuration of space. They also define the purpose and extent of play: what skills are necessary (kicking a ball through the uprights, for example); what counts in scoring (making a touchdown); what is forbidden (blocking in the back, holding, etc.); how long play lasts (four quarters of 15 minutes). In short, rules create an artificially contrived world. When we enter such a world, the troubles and cares of everyday life are set aside. What really matters in the stripped-down (stark) realities of sport are elemental things: space, time, play, competition, cunning, excellence. It is an irresistible experience, morally compelling and vital.

The reason why rules can't be tactical is because tactics are, by definition, unexpected. How can you promulgate rules about matters that you can't possibly anticipate? Tactics come out of the blue, not the rule book. They are emergent, not algorithmic. There is no step-by-step process for making a sneak attack. If there were, it wouldn't be sneaky. Everyone would know what to expect. Roger Federer's SABR move is instructive. SABR is a playful acronym for Sneak Attack by Roger. He began employing it during the 2015 U.S. Open series. He would rush up on an opponent's second serve and hit his return from within the service court. It surprised his opponents and put them at a disadvantage. Federer usually won the point as a result. But then other players got accustomed to it—they began to expect it—and it was no longer quite so sneaky and effective. Tactics have a short shelf life compared to strategies. They require constant innovation.

Rules must be timeless, or at least stable and predictable, to be effective. They can't be about tactics, although tactics put pressure on governing bodies to tweak the rules and evolve the game. Stealing bases wasn't part of the "original" game of baseball, but it was a popular tactic and eventually became a normal part of the game and its rules. To devise a set of rules that could anticipate innovations down the road would be impossible—or perhaps akin to creating a new life form with human powers of foresight, like Data from *Star Trek: The Next Generation*. Only moral creatures like us can imagine (anticipate) future responses to our tactics and strategies. There are more possible moves in a chess game than there are electrons in the universe. The tactical options are limitless as well. But the rules of chess only need to define the board, the pieces, and the moves that the pieces are allowed to make. They can't concern themselves with infinite possibilities.

The stolen base in baseball is an example of a tactic that has become part of a larger strategy. "Small ball" is a common managerial strategy (baseball has managers, not head coaches). It emphasizes the advancement of baserunners using various tactics, including stealing bases, bunting, and hitting sacrifice flies. It is a very deliberate method for "manufacturing" runs, especially in the National League, where they don't have the designated hitter. In the American League, there is more emphasis on scoring runs by aggressive hitting rather than aggressive baserunning. Ironically, the American League's Kansas City Royals have been one of the most successful small-ball clubs. They won the 2015 World Series relying upon that philosophy.

Perhaps no sport blends strategy and tactics so effortlessly as basketball. It's a fluid game, mime-like in the split-second responses of offenses to defenses and vice versa. A point guard dribbles into the paint. He's not necessarily looking for a layup, although he will take it if it's there. It's a probe, a strategy. What's the defense going to do? If they collapse, overreacting, the point guard passes to an open shooter in the corner. The possibilities are almost limitless. Tactical opportunities—little surprises—constantly emerge from strategies employed by both the offense and the defense.

Basketball is a game of interpretations and adjustments. As my Uncle Red would say, "You play offense by reading the defense, and you play defense by reading the offense." Knowing what tricks might be coming is the surest way to fend them off. In that sense, basketball coaches are like chess grand masters. They don't just see pieces on the board. They see meaningful patterns and gambits for future moves and countermoves. That ability to size up a situation in a glance is called "chunking" by psychologists who study how experts acquire skills.[2] It is a heightened sense of awareness about what is happening in the game and how best to respond. Basketball coaches don't just look at what individual players are doing. They see the entire game as it unfolds, sensing momentum shifts before they happen. Maybe it's time to execute a sideline trap against the triangle they are having success with. Coaches recognize what's happening quicker than anyone else in the building. That is the tactical advantage of being adept at chunking.

The strategic and tactical conundrums of referees are different. They have the task of ensuring that the rules are followed in a real game. Games are complex systems, like living things that often behave unexpectedly. Once they begin, a million different turns of plot are possible. Referees are forced to apply static rules to a fluid, sometimes chaotic set of circumstances. There is no easy formula for doing that. It is a matter of creative interpretation. A common observation about football games is that the refs could realistically call a foul on every play. There is always a lot of holding and grabbing going on. When does it merit a flag? That is a judgment that requires experience and practical wisdom.

Referees must decide if a hold, for example, or a bump, is merely incidental. Or, did it change the probable outcome of the play? They make multiple decisions of this kind in the blink of an eye, on every single down. The speed of the game doesn't allow for hesitation. There is so little time that being decisive—*overly* decisive—is a necessity for survival. It's a contributing cause of many bad decisions. As a ref, you don't have time to wonder, Should I have blown the whistle? And yet those sorts of niggling second guesses do work their way into the back of their minds. Zebras are human, just like the rest of us. They feel pressure not to interrupt the flow of the game needlessly. Calling ticky-tack fouls can turn an otherwise entertaining contest into a series of boring interruptions, frustrating everyone. On the other hand, missing an important call could determine the outcome of the game. Referees are well aware that they sit on a razor's edge. It's why coaches find it productive to work the refs (scream at them) early and often as a strategy for planting a smidgen of guilt that might result in a noncall or a makeup call later on.

Referees also feel pressure to call the game in a balanced way. The biggest complaint coaches make about referees is bias. Like all primates, coaches have a keen nose for what's unfair. What sets them off regarding referees is the sense that their team is being called for something that the other team is allowed to get away with. Coaches know that it is impossible—even undesirable—to catch every little infraction. But they want consistency across the board. If it is a foul on one end of the field, it has to be a foul on the other end. That sounds so reasonable—who could object? It is also *laughable* coming from coaches because they are probably the most biased individuals in all of sports. They are naturally prone to spot unfairness only if and when it applies to their own team. As we have seen, it is part of our moral experience to be more concerned about ourselves than others. It's the reason we have referees—to make an effort at holding back on the partisanship.

Like all authority figures, referees want to keep things simple and about the rules. Yet, they are bombarded by novel situations that catch them by surprise. Their strategy is to keep the game flowing in a predictable narrative arch. The reality is that they are (or can be) plunged into tactical darkness the minute the game starts. Games are terra incognita to referees because of their potential to be disrupted. Not every game follows the script. There are too many moving parts and variables to control. Referees are control freaks. They have to be to do their job. In real life, however, everything changes when you get hit in the mouth.

Conspiracy theorists love to harp about referees deciding the outcome of games. It happens, but it is mostly an unintended consequence of bad calls and unfortunate circumstances. Calling a game as it unfolds in real time is difficult. Ideally, zebras try to be an invisible presence, hidden in plain sight by the flowing nature (and beauty) of the game itself. Like a moral conscience that does its heavy lifting in the secret recesses of the mind, they want their work to be unnoticed by others. Sometimes it doesn't transpire that way, and referees become the subject of the story instead of its facilitators. At the 1972 Munich Olympics, officials handed the Soviet Union's basketball team the gold medal.[3] That's what the Americans believed, and they refused to accept their silver medals as a result.

Team USA lost the game 51–50. Their record ever since basketball had become part of the Olympics in 1936 was a perfect 63–0 up to that point. Compared to the Soviet team in 1972, however, the Americans were very young and inexperienced. The halftime score was 26–21 in favor of the Soviets. With just three seconds left in the game, American Doug Collins was sent to the line for free throws. He tied the game at 49–49 when he made the first one. That's when the controversy began.

The referee handed Collins the ball for his second foul shot, then the horn sounded while he was in the act of shooting. The Soviets claimed they had called a timeout. After consulting at the scorer's table, no time out was granted, and Collins's second free throw (which went in) was allowed to stand. That gave the Americans a one-point lead with just three seconds left. The Soviets inbounded the ball. Play was interrupted before time expired, and another debate ensued at the scorer's table. The three seconds were put back on the clock, and the Soviets were given a second opportunity to inbound the ball. It resulted in an errant pass. The horn sounded, and the Americans thought they had won, 50–49.

After conferring yet again, the referees and officials put three seconds back on the clock once more. The Soviets were granted a third opportunity to inbound the ball. One of the referees purportedly gestured at the American player who was guarding the inbounds pass to step back and give the Soviet player more space. It allowed Ivan Edeshko to throw the "golden pass" to Aleksandr Belov, who was waiting at the other end of the court, along with two American defenders. Belov caught the ball and scored the winning basket as time expired.

A series of blunders scarred the ending of that game. Questionable judgments were rendered regarding the three opportunities to replay the last three seconds. A FIBA official (International Basketball Federation) came down from the stands and inserted himself into the controversy, which was against the rules. Calls were missed, too. Edeshko had apparently stepped on the line when he threw his fateful pass the length of the court. Not only that, he shouldn't have been in the game. Since no timeout had been granted to the Soviets, they weren't allowed to substitute players. Yet, the taller Edeshko did replace another player during one of the lengthy consultations. No one noticed. Head referee Renato Righetto, a Brazilian who spoke only Portuguese, admitted later that a language barrier exacerbated the problems that officials faced (created).

What lessons, if any, can be drawn from fiascos such as this? That referees are corrupt? That games are fixed? On the contrary, I think the lesson is that refereeing, like morality itself, is an imperfect system that works well enough most of the time. To expect perfection from either refereeing or morality would be to misunderstand our existential limitations and constraints. To call a game as it unfolds in real time is fraught with potential for making errors of judgment, whether of the commission or omission variety. It can't be helped, although we are obligated to strive for improvements. Isn't that what we all do—work at becoming better people?

Referees are a reminder, or a *symbol*, of our fallible moral agency. In a similar yet completely different way, so too are coaches. Taken together, as a dialectical pair, referees and coaches represent the full extent of our moral experience: the good, the bad, and the ugly of it. We loath liars and cheaters, yet admire a good trickster. How can that be? I think it is because there is a coach and a referee inside all of us. Our morality has cross purposes that come together in those two personifications. Coaches are wily tricksters, but they are also moralistic preachers. At their finest, they draw the very best out of their players. Something similar can be said for referees. They are rule mongers by definition. Yet, at their finest, they become an invisible presence and draw the very best out of a game.

Scientific studies of bias and malfeasance among referees do not support conspiracy theories about rampant corruption. Several economists employed a mathematical model to investigate referee bias in the NBA.[4] They found evidence of several kinds of bias, none of which was particularly surprising. The model underscored the long-suspected home court advantage that referees typically confer, plus a close game bias wherein they slightly favor the team that is behind and a playoff bias favoring teams trailing in a series. Sticking with the NBA, there is one case where a referee was actually convicted of a crime. Tim Donaghy served time in federal prison for placing bets on games that he refereed and sharing insider information with bookies. The Pedowitz report to the Board of Governors of the NBA concluded there was insufficient evidence that Donaghy faked calls during games to increase the chances that his bets would pay off.[5] I find that hard to believe.

The distinction between strategies and tactics that I have been discussing is inspired by Michel de Certeau.[6] *The Practice of Everyday Life* is a fascinating book that helped make culture studies a popular major at many colleges. Culture studies often turns traditional scholarship on its head—for example, using the skills of literary critics to study less lofty "texts," like comic books, soap operas, and graffiti. According to Certeau, what we find when we pay attention to what people actually do in their everyday lives are hidden practices that subvert rules and authority.

We are resisters by nature, moral protestors who take pleasure in getting around the constraints that are imposed on us. In the workplace, we don't just work for the company or boss. We take liberties and make work a place that meets our own needs. We decorate our offices, use the phone to make personal calls, shop online, "borrow" tools to fix things at home and forget to return them, call in sick when we don't feel like going to work even when we aren't sick, and so on. We are good at paying lip service to the authorities who make the rules, then doing what we want to make the rules work for us. This subversive tendency has been part of us from the beginning. We saw it in the resentment of hunter-gatherers to being bullied. We like to outsmart the powerful who think they have control over us. We know how to get away with things.

It isn't just coaches who use sneaky tactics to surprise opponents and subvert referees. Players do it too. A defensive back grabs at the wide receiver who just faked a curl route and then streaks by him heading for the end zone. It's not an obvious assault. He only wants to interrupt the receiver's stride momentarily so that he can recover and stay with him. Naturally, he doesn't want to get flagged for interference. So after a quick hand check, he raises his hands up in the air, as if to say, "I didn't touch him." It's the gesture of a victim who is being robbed at gun point: the universal sign of surrender. But in this case the football player is using a trick as old as the hills: He's *flipping the script*, pretending to be an innocent victim even though he is guilty as hell. He sells the referee and the audience on his innocence, hoping to avoid the flag. Such cunning practices are pervasive throughout sports.

Coaches and players use the rules to their own advantage when they can. They take creative liberties. A basketball player falling out of bounds with the ball in his hands turns and throws the ball at a nearby opponent. That way the ball will go out of bounds last touched by the other team. It's a cunning use of the rules to take advantage of a bad circumstance. The opponent didn't have control of the ball or even actually "touch" it. It bounced off his torso, and that counts as a touch, technically. It's not a practice ever imagined by the authorities who made the rules. But it is part of the game that was created by players making their own use of the game and its rules. Players and coaches often find ways to outsmart the powerful strategists who sponsor and oversee their play.

Rules represent the interests of the powerful. It is part of our moral nature to resent being lorded over by others. We have strong egalitarian predilections, and we enjoy putting one over on those in authority. It's why we root for underdogs. We like to see the powerful get their comeuppance. We also like to see tactical maneuvers that surprise and entertain us. Watching the strategic domination of a more powerful opponent is too predictable and boring. It provokes our distaste for unfair contests. It's unfair when a bully beats up on a weakling. We don't like it. We relate to Robin Hood more than we relate to the Sheriff of Nottingham.

Is a referee something like a sheriff? In many ways, yes. Both represent authority and make decisions about how to sanction misbehavior. Sheriffs have a much broader legal mandate, however, and that makes their power more substantial. They can throw you in jail. Referees can only throw you out of a game. Their mandate is more of a moral one linked to the integrity of the sport and its rules. Originally, laws evolved to put more starch into our morality by defining often-severe punishments for such things as theft and adultery. The Code of Hammurabi dates back almost 4,000 years. It is one of the oldest writings ever recovered by archaeologists. Hammurabi was a Babylonian king, and his code included 282 brief edicts or rules about things ranging from how much money an ox driver should be paid to the conditions under which a woman could seek divorce. Here is the code regarding theft: "If anyone is committing a robbery and is caught, then he shall be put to death."[7]

In modern civilizations, the similarities and differences between the law and morality are much more complicated. In many ways, legal systems have diminished the public role of morality, relegating it to the private sphere. We turn to the law to settle disputes that would have been resolved differently in the past. I wasn't overly surprised to read about the parents from upstate New York who went to court to get their 30-year-old son evicted from their home.[8] In a hunter-gatherer society, the group would have taken care of that problem with alacrity. There aren't many places left in our society where the old ways of our moral heritage still hold sway. I have been arguing that sports represent one of those places where a relic of hunter-gatherer morality has survived.

It would be impossible to turn back the clock and try to live our lives as if we were hunter-gatherers again. We need our legal system and other modern institutions to maintain order. But I also think it is important to be reminded about the moral nature of our species. The law can't replace morality, it can only buttress it. Garrett Broshuis makes a distinction between traditional cheating in baseball and new age cheating in an article that warns about what can happen when our legal system loses touch with its moral roots.[9] Traditional cheating includes such hard-to-weed-out activities as throwing a spitball or stealing signs. Outlawing them in the rules hasn't diminished their practice. Steroid use is the archetypical example of new age cheating. It hurt the public perception of baseball and caused the record book to become a thing of distrust. Outlawing PED use and putting in place a system for monitoring players became a necessity.

Broshuis believes that the culture of cheating in baseball—whether traditional or new age—will never be fully addressed until the moral basis for the rules of baseball is adequately appreciated. He reviews two competing legal traditions to make his point. Legal positivism interprets rules as entities in themselves, without reference to moral underpinnings. Breaking a rule has no moral weight or consequence. It's just something you don't want to get caught doing. On the other hand, natural law tradition focuses on the moral reasons for rules, making it clear that breaking rules actually does harm the integrity of the game. Broshuis's point is that the positivist view of cheating and rule-making has harmed baseball. To fix it, we need to invoke a natural law interpretation of the rules.

I agree with Garrett that positivism diminished the importance of morality in our understanding of rules and laws, which led us to take them too lightly; however, I think his view of morality is of the goody-two-shoes variety. It is a view that has shorn morality of its more cunning side. It is not just about being good and honest, important as they are. It is also about trickery and getting away with things when you can. Until we appreciate the full-bodied complexity of our moral experience, we will continue to despair about cheating as if it were a symptom of recent moral decline. Trickery in all of its forms—including the extreme form of cheating—is an endemic part of our moral experience. It's not the only part, but it is a very real aspect of conscience and the ongoing struggle to be generous and kind that has distinguished our species for hundreds of millennia.

Mythical stories from our ancestral past are one of the most important sources for our tactical repertoire of tricks and cunning maneuvers according to de Certeau. The biblical story of David and Goliath is a popular example that is often used to frame sporting contests.[10] David was the spindly shepherd boy from Israel who faced the giant Philistine champion named Goliath in a proxy fight. Against all odds, David killed Goliath with a stone thrown from his sling. It was a common practice in ancient warfare to settle disputes by pitting the best fighter from each army against one another. No one on the Israeli side wanted to face

Goliath. Finally, a shepherd boy with guts and faith in God stepped up. The best David and Goliath sports story that I recall was the 2007 Fiesta Bowl won by the Boise State Broncos.[11]

It was the first year of Chris Petersen's tenure as head coach of Boise State. In his eight years at the helm, they won 92 games, while only losing 12. They faced the mighty Oklahoma Sooners, winners of seven national championships, in the Fiesta Bowl. If there ever was a casting call for Goliath in college football, Oklahoma is one of the few that could play the role. Boise State, on the other hand, was only a mid-major conference champion and had never before played in such a prestigious bowl game. They easily fit the role of overmatched David. It was supposed to be a blowout.

The game was close and well played throughout. Boise State had a reputation for trickery, and they saved two of their best tricks for the ending. As time was running out, they needed a touchdown and an extra point to force overtime. They called their hook-and-ladder "Circus" play from midfield and scored with seven seconds remaining. In a hook-and-ladder play, a wide receiver runs downfield 10 yards, then hooks toward the middle. The quarterback delivers the ball, and the receiver laterals it to another player who is running full speed in the opposite direction. The defense is focused on the original receiver, so the lateral takes them by surprise. The story gets even more miraculous in overtime.

Oklahoma got the ball first in overtime and scored a touchdown. Boise State responded with a touchdown of their own. They needed to kick the extra point to tie and force a second overtime. Instead, they went for two, calling yet another trick play, "Statue Left." The Statue of Liberty is an exceedingly rare play in football, but the Broncos managed to pull it off. Quarterback Jared Zabransky held up the ball in preparation for a pass. Instead of passing it, as the entire Oklahoma defense expected, he slipped it behind his back and handed off to Ian Johnson, who raced into the end zone untouched. It was an improbable victory for the ages. David beat Goliath—again.

In the next chapter I will shift away from cunning and trickery to investigate the roles of imitation and ritual in morality and sports.

4

IMITATION, RITUAL, AND TRANSCENDENCE

Morality and sports intertwine our lives like twisting peptide chains in a DNA molecule. Because of their intimacy in our evolutionary heritage, the stories of sport touch upon the most significant aspects of our moral existence. That, in a nutshell, summarizes what this book is about.

In recent decades, moral psychologists have steadily pried our understanding of morality away from philosophical and theological traditions that stretch back thousands of years. They are not the only ones who have expressed disappointment with the abstract methods of modern ethics, however. Following an essay by Elizabeth Anscombe in 1958, many philosophers began to look elsewhere for a fresh start in ethics.[1] The long-disregarded virtue tradition caught their eye.

By the time Alasdair MacIntyre published *After Virtue* in 1981, virtue ethics had become a leading voice in philosophical moral theory.[2] As evidenced by the popularity of Stephen Covey's *The 7 Habits of Highly Effective People*, the reprisal of virtues (or habits of character) and their relevance to everyday life was not confined to academic philosophers.[3] Covey studied the success literature in the United States that began with Benjamin Franklin's autobiography, in which he famously listed 13 virtues that enabled him to achieve "moral perfection."[4] Covey noticed that prior to World War I, success literature focused on what he called a "character ethic." Success comes from living a principled and virtuous life according to that perspective. After the war, however, the focus shifted toward a "personality ethic," where sunny gimmicks like positive thinking became the ticket to success. The purpose of *The 7 Habits of Highly Effective People* was to bring back the character ethic formula for success in life. It struck a chord with people.

Covey's basic idea was that we become what we do repeatedly. By intentionally doing the same things over and over again—making them into habits—we can reshape our character. If you want to become a good citizen or a successful team player at work then, according to Covey, you must develop the seven habits that he identifies. The first three pertain to self-mastery (be proactive; begin with the end in mind; put first things first), the next three to cooperation (think win-win; seek first to understand, then be understood; synergize), and the last one to revitalizing the entire process of good character development (sharpen the saw).

In this chapter, I want to follow the same thread that Covey, MacIntyre, and others followed in their rediscovery of the significance of virtues. It led them back to Aristotle, whose *Nichomachean Ethics* is still the best resource we have for understanding virtues and habits.[5] But Aristotle is only the first stop for me. Virtues and habits are a form of imitation, as are many of the training practices in modern sports. Imitation is the basis for learning and play among a wide range of animal species, especially primates. Eventually, the thread leads back to our own biological and cultural origins. Following it the whole way back will make the connections between sports and morality even more compelling.

There are many reasons why virtue ethics became appealing once again in the latter half of the 20th century. Let me mention three of them for now. First, it restored the importance of moral character to ethics. Being a certain kind of person is more important to the moral life than the use of reason, rules, and principles to resolve contrived dilemmas.

Second, the focus on character lines up well with modern psychology. The traditional distinction between psychology and psychiatry is instructive here. Character traits were considered the subject matter of psychology, problems of temperament the subject matter of psychiatry. That distinction has often been blurred to the detriment of psychology. The positive psychology movement founded by Martin Seligman has fought back against the "medicalization" of life's normal and near-normal challenges. Rather than focusing on what's wrong with us (the psychiatric disease model approach), positive psychologists focus on happiness, flourishing, grit, flow, and other positive aspects of our lives and character. Seligman and colleagues published a handbook about character traits and virtues that serves as an antidote of sorts to the cheerless diagnostic and statistical manuals of the American Psychiatric Association.[6]

Third, virtues don't slight the significance of feelings the way rational principles and rules tend to do. Virtues enable us to act *and feel* appropriately in any given situation. A virtue ethicist would be comfortable with the idea that it is impossible to think or reason well without the guidance of feelings. Our mental capacities work together, not separately. Feelings do more than motivate and shape our thoughts. It is probably closer to the truth to say that our feelings and thoughts represent different aspects of the same mental experiences. Granted, feelings are less subject to conscious manipulation than thoughts. We don't construct feelings like we do thoughts. Yet, every thought has its feeling, every feeling its thought potential. I like to imagine that my thoughts are unmoored feelings that have grown legs and can more easily walk about as a result (like picturing animals as mobile plants). Words give thoughts their mobility, but it is symbols and feelings that root us to the world and give rise to our thoughts.

Aristotle was a Greek philosopher who lived in the 4th century BC. He studied under Plato at an academy in Athens. Plato had himself been a student of Socrates. That brief lineage—from Socrates to Plato to Aristotle—represents the high-water mark of ancient Greek philosophy. Some would say it is the high-water mark of philosophy, period. Like a modern encyclopedist, Aristotle systematized the entire terrain of ancient knowledge in his writings. Unlike Plato, he was more of a scientist than a mystic. It has often been said that every person is born either an Aristotelian or Platonist in their temperament.[7]

Nichomachean Ethics is a textbook or primer on how to live well. Aristotle begins by suggesting that the attainment of *eudaimonia* is the purpose of life. *Eudaimonia* is usually translated as happiness, or well-being. A more literal translation would be "good spirit." The happy life is a life in conformity with virtue according to Aristotle. Virtues, he said, are settled dispositions to act and feel a certain way. They are praiseworthy characteristics.

Aristotle mentioned 10 different moral virtues: courage, generosity, magnificence, high-mindedness, gentleness, friendliness, truthfulness, wit, tact, and justice. He thought justice summarized them all. Almost seven centuries later, by contrast, St. Augustine would claim that love is the epitome of all virtues, not justice.[8] We acquire moral virtues by habit or by practicing them. It is never easy. "Anyone can get angry," Aristotle said, "or can give away money or spend it; but to do all this to the right person, to the right extent, at the right time, for the right reason, and in the right way is no longer something easy that anyone can do."[9] Only a virtuous person knows how to behave properly in any circumstance.

Acquiring virtues is difficult because they represent the mean between two vices. Every virtue is surrounded by a vice marked by excess and a vice marked by deficiency. Take courage in the face of danger, for example. Too much of it leads to rashness; too little of it leads to timidity. To be truly courageous, it is necessary to find the right balance between being rash and being timid. How does one find the mean between the extremes of too much and too little?

We also have two intellectual virtues in addition to the moral virtues of character. They are practical reason, or prudence, and theoretical reason, or wisdom. It is through the exercise of *prudence* that we find the middle ground between the vices that envelope every moral virtue. Without prudence, it would be impossible for me to achieve real courage in the face of danger because I wouldn't know how to discern the difference between an excess of courage and an insufficiency of it. Judging correctly about when courage is called for, in what measure, and for what duration, is something that requires the use of reason. To live virtuously amid the hubbub of everyday life, both character and intellect must work hand in hand.

How can I acquire courage if I don't have any in the first place? The Wizard of Oz, you might recall, gave the timid lion a medal to boost his confidence. Well, that's not exactly what Aristotle would have recommended. He would advise us to watch what a courageous person does and do likewise. Practice being courageous and acquire the settled habit of courage by imitating how courageous people behave. That's how it's done.

Courage isn't a matter of being fearless. (The Wizard should have mentioned that to the lion.) Fear is a helpful feeling in the sense that it warns us of imminent danger. To be brave in the face of danger because you have no fear is not the same as being courageous. The person of courage is one who manages her/his fear appropriately, not allowing it to dictate how to act in response to danger. Running away from danger would be imprudent if the better recourse would be to stand and fight. On the other hand, running away might actually be the prudent option if finding help would improve the odds of overcoming the threat of danger.

Knowing when to exercise courage and when not to exercise it is part of what it means to be courageous. This is an important point about virtue ethics. Virtues are not like rules or principles. There is no simple formula for how or when to exercise them. Judgment is always a crucial factor. It makes for a very personalized and imprecise form of ethical reflection, much closer to the realities of our often conflicted and ambiguous moral experiences. No two people will exercise their virtues in precisely the same way. To be virtuous is more art form than exact science, unique to each person. Each one of us could follow Benjamin Franklin's example and come up with our own customized list of virtues.

According to Aristotle, to be virtuous is a gestalt experience where the whole is more significant than the individual parts. A truthful person will also most likely be courageous, prudent, friendly, generous, and so forth. It's a package deal. When we master one virtue, in effect we become masters of the virtuous life as a whole. There is an advantageous feedback loop at work; improvements occur across the board, not just in one area.

The practice of virtues is a sure-fire method for self-improvement, which is why virtues attracted Franklin, Covey, and many other American self-help authors. "Practice makes perfect" is an apt mantra for self-improvement in both morality *and sports*. To become a mature person with a full measure of praiseworthy characteristics is every bit as arduous as becoming a good baseball pitcher, for example. But they are not exactly the same thing. No doubt an elite pitcher must possess many virtues to attain mastery in pitching. It takes dedication, self-discipline, patience, and a willingness to listen to the coach and follow his directions. Those attributes are virtues, or very much like them. But the actual pitching is an athletic skill, which is not the same thing as a virtue. There are similarities and differences.

How do you become an elite baseball pitcher? According to Anders Ericsson, an expert on how people become experts, it can take a decade or more of *deliberate practice*.[10] Deliberate practice requires the tutelage of a coach or mentor. You can't just go off on your own and become a professional baseball pitcher. The first thing the coach will do is push you outside of your comfort zone. If you don't reach for what might seem beyond reach at first, you can't improve. Feedback is also essential. You must know what you did wrong if you want to correct it and keep improving. Most importantly, you must develop better mental representation capacities. Some of Ericsson's colleagues called this "chunking." I mention it briefly in chapter 3, when I suggest that basketball coaches are good chunkers. All coaches and professional athletes are good at it, actually.

Chunking is the ability to see meaningful patterns at a glance. It comes with extensive practice. The odds that a person off the street could hit a 90-mile-per-hour fastball out of the park are precisely . . . nil. It takes years of practice to hit a major-league fastball. The key to being able to achieve it is chunking. With practice, the batter develops mental cues about how to read the pitcher and get a sense for what pitch he is going to throw. Expert batters quickly see things that the average person can't see in the posture of the pitcher: how he grips the ball; how he winds up for delivery. This happens unconsciously as the mind makes use of its extensive experience to anticipate where the ball will be when it crosses the plate and what needs to be done to get the bat there to meet it.

Chunking is the mind's ability to tell you what is about to happen before it happens. It is like prudence for elite performers, an intellectual virtue that is built up after countless hours of practice. As a habit of mind, chunking often involves rewiring and/or building up different parts of the brain. A British neuroscientist studied MRI brain scans of London cabbies.[11] She found that they have bigger hippocampuses than average people do. In the posterior region of the brain, the hippocampus helps with spatial navigation and memory. It turns out that becoming a taxi driver in London is extremely difficult because the streets don't follow any recognizable grid pattern. After years of practice, taxi drivers develop enhanced navigation abilities, and the relevant part of the brain is enhanced accordingly. In many instances, the brain responds to training just like the body does: It builds itself up. Instead of creating more muscle, it creates more neurons.

Chunking is what a quarterback does when he surveys the defense before barking out play signals. In a glance, he sees a specific formation that he recognizes from prior film study—relegated to his memory as a chunk of information—and because of it knows what they are planning. At least he thinks he knows what they are planning, because the defense naturally does its best to disguise schemes and trick the quarterback into reading the situation wrongly. After reading the defense and acquiring a sense for what they are expecting from the offense, the quarterback might change the play on the spot to exploit what he sees. Of course, nothing stops the defense from changing its coverage in light of what they think the quarterback is up to, either. It's a cat and mouse mind game centered around what each side thinks is about to happen. The chunking and reverse chunking part of sports (the mental game) is the most important part of it. Calling the right play at the right time, with the appropriate disguises and false leads, is very difficult. Good play calling is like a moral virtue in every respect. How do you become good at it? By practicing and imitating what great play callers do.

Many authors have used Ericsson's research to comment about sports and athletic training. Malcolm Gladwell referred to Ericsson's work with violinists when he claimed that it takes 10,000 hours of practice to become an expert at something.[12] That's how many hours of practice the average elite violinist puts in by the age of 20. But it usually takes another decade of practice for a violinist to become truly great, so Gladwell's 10,000-hour rule is a little arbitrary. His point is well taken, however: Practice and opportunity are more important than talent in deciding who will excel at something.

Matthew Syed, a former elite table tennis competitor from Great Britain, believes that sports have become a battle over training methods rather than a fair competition between equal competitors.[13] He explains how Chinese training methods have made their table tennis players the best in the world. They practice playing with multiple balls all at once to enhance their abilities to chunk information at a faster rate than everyone else. If you are accustomed to being able to hit several balls simultaneously, then when you play a match where you only have to hit one ball, you are quicker and more decisive than an opponent whose practice revolved around hitting just one ball at a time. After extensive practice with three balls instead of one, the awareness and reaction times of the Chinese players became greatly enhanced. Competing against players who hadn't trained up to their standards was like child's play as a result. Chinese athletes are playing a different game because of the way they exploit the insights of deliberate practice. They see and feel what's happening quicker than everyone else. It's not the better athlete who wins; it's the athlete with the better training methods. Enhanced mental quickness gained through training is more important than having naturally quick reflexes.

The purpose of practice is to make playing a game like table tennis effortless. It must become instinctive so that it can be done without thinking. Syed calls it "expert induced amnesia." You play unconsciously, freely: without self-awareness getting in the way. When self-awareness intrudes upon performance, choking is the result. Choking is usually caused by pressure. It is a reversion from the freewheeling play of unconscious instinct back to the deliberate mental state that is so important to the beginner who is learning how to play the game. Beginners are self-conscious because they haven't yet mastered the movements that become second nature with practice. There is no time to think about how to hit a ball in the heat of battle, however. To fall back into that kind of mentality in the middle of a competition is disastrous.

Virtues pertain to a person's moral character while athletic skills pertain to a person's performance abilities. Character and performance are different, obviously, just as virtues and skills are different. Nevertheless, there are many parallels. Both require mental participation, as we have seen. Athletic skills are to chunking what moral virtues are to prudence. Mistakes in performance are like moral vices, things that we must navigate around to find the middle ground that represents the sweet spot of excellence.

The athlete strives for virtuoso performance, the moralist for a life of virtue. The two often go hand in hand. It takes perseverance and other praiseworthy characteristics to practice long and hard enough to become a virtuoso performer. Both kinds of practice—the practice of an athlete honing skills and the practice of a moralist acquiring virtues—represent different forms of imitation. Imitation is the bedrock of learning in the animal kingdom. We learn by imitating what others do, acquiring their perspective by trying it on for size, and then making it part of us. This basic human practice is actually a form of play that evolved from the parental care habits of hunter-gatherer bands.

Before I discuss the significance of play in the ancestral environment, let me recap where the thread I have been following has gotten us. It isn't just psychologists who have been disillusioned with the theoretical nature of modern ethics and the resultant disconnect from our moral feelings and instincts. Philosophers and self-help gurus have likewise been dissatisfied. Many of them have focused on virtues as a more satisfactory way of understanding how to build up and improve the moral life. Virtues pertain to our character, which we shape by practicing good habits.

When we discuss virtues, it is more like storytelling than abstract thinking. That is one of the key benefits for reprising the virtue tradition. We naturally tell stories about the struggles in our lives, the goals we have, and the progress we make in attaining them, as well as the backsliding that impedes our efforts. This is how we understand ourselves: through stories with discrete beginnings, middles, and ends. Virtues accommodate that narrative structure more than abstract thinking does. Thus, Aristotle began his discussion of virtues by saying that happiness is the goal of life that everyone seeks. In *A Theory of Justice*, by contrast, John Rawls began with an abstract thought experiment he called the "original position."[14] He says that we must imagine not knowing anything about our own condition—rich or poor, happy or wretched, male or female, and so on—and on the basis of that "veil of ignorance" build a society where everyone is treated fairly. It is probably impossible to live in a complex modern democracy without a Rawlsian framework for justice. But that kind of abstract procedural (legal) fairness is the antithesis of the personalized stories that enliven discussions of virtue—and sports.

It is hard to imagine an activity less theoretical in its nature than a sporting contest. Sports are often overlooked as a result, considered lightweight and incidental. Often cast as mere leisurely pursuits, sports are similar to virtues in their narrative significance. Just because they lack theoretical rigor doesn't mean they don't touch upon the most important issues of our existence. Narrative thinking is more primordial than theoretical thinking, a throwback to archaic times before agriculture and civilization arrived on the scene. Sports are deceptive in that sense of appearing to be nothing more than childhood games in comparison to the great issues of justice and freedom that preoccupy our politics. We shouldn't be fooled by their theoretical paucity. Such mimetic (imitative) practices as sports and morality have a much more ancient heritage, and their significance for our well-being should not be underestimated.

In the ancestral environment, hunter-gatherer bands cooperated in their child-rearing responsibilities. All the children were allowed to play together, which freed at least some parents to pursue other activities part of the time. The longer that parents shield their children from the harsh necessities of survival, the more important the role of play becomes in creating new capacities for the entire group. Play is something that is done for no other purpose than to play. It is a biological luxury. Yet, the results of play are far reaching. Most importantly, play teaches us how to live in imaginary worlds, which doesn't stop when we leave childhood behind.[15] What would life be like without television, movies, daydreams, music, sports, and myriad other imaginary pastimes that occupy us and enrich our days? Playing a game like baseball represents an imaginary world that people learn about as kids but continue to care about for as long as they live.

Play teaches us to be careful around others by handicapping ourselves: to be a little gentle when playing with someone who isn't as big as us, to be a little patient when playing with someone who isn't as skilled or sharp. That's how we learn to be fair-minded (little Rawlsian moralists). Play is our first school, where we actually learn how to learn by imitating our playmates while they imitate and learn from us in turn. Learning, as we know, is the beginning of knowledge and expertise, the fountainhead of our incredible cultural and scientific achievements. It all begins with the simple luxury of childhood play.

Anyone who has visited a zoo or a dog park knows that humans aren't the only species that engages in play. All social animals love to play. It helps them learn how to get along as a group. When dogs want to play with one another, they often do a play bow where they bend down on their forelegs with their rumps in the air and look at one another expectantly. They know what's acceptable and what isn't. They are careful not to bite too hard. Occasionally, a real fight breaks out, but it is surprising how infrequently that happens. To become vicious and cruel fighters, dogs must be trained. Even rattlesnakes restrain themselves from biting one another when they fight. For most species, fighting is a ritualized exercise—a form of serious play—that enables them to discern who the winner is without incurring lethal injury.

Rituals are another form of habitual behavior that have similarities and differences to skills and virtues. All three have evolutionary ties to play. Like skills, rituals tend to be performance enhancing. A baseball player goes through an entire series of ritual practices as he prepares to step up to the plate. He puts on his hitting gloves just so and adjusts his batting helmet. He examines his bat, taking a number of test swings. He digs his cleats into the dirt, adjusts the cup that protects his privates, and so forth. Free throw shooters do the same sorts of things in basketball. So do golfers on the tee. Preparatory rituals imbue every corner of the sports world. They are idiosyncratic habits that help manage the anxiety of high-stakes performance. They probably qualify as OCD (obsessive-compulsive disorder) symptoms. They have long been categorized as superstitions.

Superstition is ubiquitous in sports. Some players eat the same meal before every game. They wear the same socks and underwear. They refuse to shave if they're on a winning streak. Tiger always wears red on Sundays. Nadal carefully places his water bottles along a precise imaginary line in front of his courtside chair. An opponent once kicked them as they were changing ends. He was probably frustrated by the beatdown he was receiving. Nadal was surprised, then he smiled and laughed it off.

Rituals and superstitions are often linked to religious practices. To the extent that they are attempts to control events and realities beyond our control, they are like what I would describe as informal folk religions. Religions as we usually understand them today are organized institutions that hearken back to the dawn of civilization. Judaism, Christianity, and Buddhism are examples. They didn't exist in the ancestral environment, although our hunter-gatherer ancestors had plenty of rituals and spiritual practices. Institutional religions are to spirituality what ethics is to morality. Just as ethicists have made a concerted effort to civilize our morality, institutional religions have made a concerted effort to civilize our spirituality. Many people today claim to be spiritual but not religious (SBNR). They want to honor our natural spirituality but distance themselves from institutional religions. It's similar, perhaps, to the psychological recovery of morality from ethics.

Rituals are also similar to virtues in some ways. Washing your hands before a meal is a ritual practice that has virtuous qualities. Brushing your teeth before bed is another one. But rituals normally serve a different purpose. They are repetitive behaviors that help create entire moral worlds rather than personal moral characteristics like virtues. When they lived in their traditional ways, Native Americans often prepared for a hunt by undergoing a sweat lodge ritual. The ritual didn't make them more skilled or virtuous. It purified them and prepared them for the hunt. It made them worthy of the task. In a hunter-gatherer society, taking the life of an animal for food was a moral issue. The animal's spirit had to be mollified.

At powwows that I have attended, Native American dancers dress up in costumes that resemble bears, eagles, and other animals. Their dances are meant to be imitations of how those creatures behave. As an outside observer, my first thought was that they were like actors in a play. They were performing for the audience. Perhaps that is what a modern powwow has become. Later it occurred to me that the dancers were not like actors putting on a play. They were actually attempting to transform themselves into the animals that they were imitating. Rituals of this kind are spiritual performances. The ritual transforms the performer into something different than he was beforehand. It is what distinguishes rituals from other forms of imitative behavior.

Skills and virtues are matters of habitual learning; rituals are matters of habitual transformation. That's what the superstitious athlete really wants—to be transformed into an efficient performer beyond any self-doubt or cosmic interference. To be fully in the moment without distractions is the dream of every athlete. There is no specific virtue for attaining that elusive state of mind. It is one of those paradoxes, like happiness, that comes unbidden in its own time. Seek after it and you never find it.

Players who achieve a state of mindlessness are said to be in the zone, or in the flow of the game, or unconscious. It's not a skill we can practice. Nor is it the norm in athletic competition. Most of the time, athletes get by with their B game. In a television interview, I heard Jack Nicklaus say that Tiger was the best golfer he ever saw who won even while playing poorly. That's what winning ugly means. To perform at an A+ level is rare. It's like being in a state of grace. Most of the time we muddle through as the mere mortals we are. We are not superheroes.

Muhammad Ali said that fighting Joe Frazier was sort of like dying. It took everything he had to enter into the performance. Rituals prepare us for that.

What does it mean to be in the zone? That's a million-dollar question. I suspect it is a lot like what happens in meditation. Meditation is a breathing ritual. Watching your own breath come and go helps settle the body down, followed by the mind. When thoughts intrude, as they always do, you let them go and return to watching the breath. On a good day, the meditation enables you to experience the absence of time consciousness. There is no past, no future, no distractions—just the body and its breath in the present moment. Self-awareness becomes irrelevant, nonexistent. There is only the body's breath. It is likewise for the athlete in the zone. There is only her/his body that has merged with the game, nothing else. It is a seamless, unifying, all-encompassing experience.

I think experiences like that are a way of recovering what we once were before we attained self-awareness and the many burdens of moral responsibility that come with it. It comforts us to let go of ourselves and just be in the moment. Our bodies seem to know (remember) what it was like to live without a sense of time consciousness. Rituals are capable of transporting us back to that original existential condition. It's a transformation that we prize dearly. Like meditation, tribal dance, and similar rituals, sport represents one of the ways we can recall that ancient heritage of simple embodied existence. Athletes are often criticized for being muscle-bound apes. Ironically, that's what rituals help all of us to achieve—respite from ourselves by returning briefly to what we once were.

The purpose of ritual is to recover what we once were. That is why there is such a powerful sense of nostalgia surrounding sports. Fans love to reminisce about the greatness they witnessed, for instance, Reggie Jackson's World Series heroics. He wasn't called Mr. October for nothing. Or they tell the story for the millionth time of how they met someone special at the high school gym after the basketball game. And so on. Fond remembrances bloom upon the landscapes of sport like tulips on the reclaimed soil of the Zuiderzee. Every professional athlete I have ever listened to has talked about what playing the game meant to them as a kid growing up. It is the barometer they use to assess their own authenticity for the rest of their lives.

Play is like practice, an activity rich in habitual repetition. We like to repeat things in exactly the same way. That obsession is the beginning of ritual—and of games. Games like baseball are a form of ritualized play. Rules that are informal and intuitive at first become codified over time. The purpose of play is to create imaginary worlds. The purpose of ritual is to help transport us to those worlds. The purpose of practice is to help us achieve excellence in performance. The purpose of virtues is to help us achieve happiness in life. These things are interconnected. None would be possible without play. Both morality and sports emerged from the same hunter-gatherer playground. That is why their intimacy remains so significant.

One of my favorite sports movies is *Bull Durham*.[16] Kevin Costner plays the role of Crash Davis, a veteran Minor League Baseball catcher who gets called up by a lowly North Carolina club. His job is to mentor a young pitching talent who is clueless about how to be a professional ballplayer. Tim Robbins plays the role of Ebby Calvin "Nuke" LaLoosh, the guy with the "million-dollar arm and the 10-cent head," as Crash described him. The first time they met, the two players got into a fight about a woman, Annie Savoy, played by Susan Sarandon. A believer in the Church of Baseball, Annie is a groupie who chooses LaLoosh as her season-long apprentice in the arts of love and poetry.

Nuke ends up with two very different mentors in Annie and Crash. They are like oil and water—or, Plato and Aristotle. Annie taught Nuke the importance of superstition and the placebo effect. To reign in the wildness of his pitches, she convinced him to wear a garter belt under his uniform and focus on his reptile eyelids. Miraculously, it worked. Crash taught him the importance of attending to the details. When you sing a song, use the correct words, he scolded LaLoosh when he caught him making up words to a popular song. To break him of the habit of always wanting to throw heat (fastballs), Crash revealed to the opposition's batters what pitch to expect. After they hit home runs, he would amble out to the pitcher's mound. "Isn't this fun?" he said.

Crash emphasized down-to-earth matters with Nuke. When someone from the media asks you a question, for example, give them platitudes about just wanting to help the ballclub win games. Whatever you do, he warned, don't talk about your feelings. They don't want to hear about that crap. On the other hand, rituals can transport us to places that enliven the soul. That was Annie's forte. She read Walt Whitman to

Nuke, who was forced to listen before they could enjoy the pleasures of sex. By the end of his apprenticeship, when Nuke got called up to the majors, he sort of understood what both mentors had tried to teach him.

With the discussion of ritual, I have been dancing around the topic of religion, or spirituality. I want to close this chapter by distinguishing morality and spirituality. At least a dozen books have been written in the "sports apologetics" genre that celebrate sports as an American civil religion, with its own sense of the sacred.[17] It seems more than coincidental that as the reach of institutional religions continues to decline, the significance of sport-related rituals and symbolisms grows stronger. But not all rituals and symbols are exclusively religious or spiritual in their meaning. Some have moral connotations. I think it is important to understand the difference even though I would be the first to acknowledge that our moral and spiritual concerns often overlap. I am not opposed to interpreting sports religiously or spiritually. This project focuses on moral interpretation, however.

I have made the claim that rituals are basically transformative in their nature. We participate in them expecting to be changed or transformed in some fashion. Like symbols, rites, sacraments, and so on, rituals provide the opportunity to glimpse an alternative reality. The Christian sacrament of holy communion, for example, purports to offer a foretaste of the everlasting life to come. In the modern world, it is often hard to appreciate such metaphysical aspirations. We tend to think that reality is always cut from the same cloth, whereas traditional religions teach us that there is a higher reality that we must aspire to reach. Transcendence—reaching beyond ourselves and this world—is a more traditional concept for what I mean by ritual transformation.

I think there are two basic forms of transcendence. One is more in line with morality, the other with spirituality. Transcendence that *extends* the natural order of human feelings and expectations is of the moral type. The seventh-inning stretch in baseball is a moral ritual because it extends our feelings of being part of the group. When spectators sing "Take Me Out to the Ball Game," they become a transient community (tribe) of like-minded people. They extend empathy to one another that would normally be reserved for their own friends and family. Most sports rituals are of this moral kind, I believe.

Sitting next to a stranger in a church pew and singing hymns together is similar to sitting next to a stranger in a stadium and singing the national anthem. They are both examples of what I am calling moral transcendence. Just because something occurs in a church or temple doesn't mean it only has "religious" significance. Institutional religions like Judaism and Hinduism emerged at the dawn of civilization for mostly moral reasons. The great crisis people faced was how to get along with strangers.

For more than a hundred thousand years, humans lived in small bands of 20 to 30 people. Obviously, they knew one another very well. Morality evolved to help us get along in groups of that size. Within a few thousand years after we began experimenting with agriculture, people were living in towns and cities with populations reaching tens of thousands. Most of them would necessarily be strangers to one another. How did they learn to get along? Institutional religions helped solve that problem (crisis) by extending our moral feelings to strangers. The command to "love thy neighbor as thyself" is a good example of this. Institutional religions offered a brand of moral transcendence that helped make the transition to living in large civilizations a success. Of course, that isn't all they offered. Spiritual transcendence was also part of their package.

Transcendence that *overturns* the natural order of human feelings and expectations is of the spiritual (religious) type. The Native American dancer who tries to become one with the animal he imitates is seeking spiritual transcendence. He is trying to become something other than what he is. He overturns the normal range of human emotion and moral concern. We don't normally share human feelings with other species. Pet animals are an exception, although I think domesticated farm animals that we raise for slaughter abide only partially within the human moral circle.

Perhaps the most obvious instance of spiritual transcendence is the resurrection of the dead. To come back to life after having died represents a classic reversal of the natural order. It is a miraculous occurrence. Many religious beliefs embrace the miraculous. References to miracles abound in sports as well. Almost without exception they are tied to plays or outcomes that are so improbable that their success is deemed a miracle. Football's Hail Mary pass is the standard bearer. The "Miracle on Ice" at Lake Placid in the 1980 Winter Olympics is especially memorable because it had Cold War implications. The USA men's hockey team beat an "unbeatable" Soviet Union team for the gold medal. That miracle seemed to foreshadow a decade of near-miraculous world events, including the fall of the Berlin Wall and the dissolution of the Soviet Union.

Miraculous rituals of the holy communion kind are not common to sports except in fictional contexts. *Field of Dreams*, another baseball movie starring Kevin Costner, is a good example.[18] Costner plays the role of Ray Kinsella, a not-so-good Iowa farmer who hears voices and has visions that lead him to create a baseball diamond in the middle of his corn field. His wife Annie, played by Amy Madigan, tries her best to be sympathetic to Ray's fantasy. But it is hard, and they come within a hair's breath of losing the farm.

After Ray builds the diamond, Shoeless Joe Jackson miraculously appears as if he were in the prime of his life. He was banned from baseball after the 1919 Black Sox Scandal. The real Joe Jackson died in 1951. Other dead players reappear in Ray's corn field as well. Like so many spiritual stories, *Field of Dreams* is about redemption and reconciliation. The eight banned Black Sox players get to play baseball again, and Ray gets to play catch with his estranged dad, who died before the two could be reconciled.

Belief in miracles is common in sports, as is the sentimental attachment to stories of triumph over tragedy, or hope against all odds, that we often associate with miracles and sports. The University of Iowa has a new ritual with spiritual overtones of this sort. At the end of the first quarter of Iowa football games, everyone in Kinnick Stadium—including the opposing team and their fans—turns to the east so they can wave to the children who are watching the game from the 12th floor of the Stead Family Children's Hospital. It is a new addition to the university hospitals and clinics, looming over the stadium and providing a bird's eye view of the field. Krista Young, from Anita, Iowa, came up with the idea for the wave as a way to encourage and remember the kids who are fighting terrible diseases.

In a beautifully written essay titled "Roger Federer as Religious Experience," David Foster Wallace painted a compelling picture of what an honest to goodness religious experience could actually look like in sports.[19] Fans are dumbfounded by the Swiss maestro's grace on court. The game seems effortless to him. He moves as if the laws of physics don't fully apply. He has plenty of power and topspin to play the contemporary power baseline game. But he transcends that game with his kinesthetic touch and beauty. That is what takes our breath away and inspires us. Watching Federer play, Wallace concluded, helps us feel reconciled. To be reconciled is a peaceful acceptance of fate and the vulnerabilities that attend it. It is a moment of grace. Imagine that a tennis match could bring us to such a state. I would call that an instance of spiritual (religious) transcendence.

Wallace zeroed in on beauty as the catalyst in Federer's game that triggers a sense of religious awe in spectators. I think the same argument could be made for Rafael Nadal's suffering, especially on the red clay. Nadal's body visibly absorbs punishment even as he administers a spirit-crushing assault on his opponent. The physicality of his game inspires the kind of fearful awe that we reserve for Sisyphean predicaments. It is inspiring and transcendent nonetheless. It is fitting that these archrivals, Federer and Nadal, could embody such opposing pathways to the sublime. Beauty is the mellifluous way, suffering the willful way. There is enough diversity in the human condition for both to be true.

In the next chapter, I will continue the discussion of virtue and excellence. Is it possible to take our virtues too seriously, going too far in the pursuit of excellence? That is the question I will explore.

5

EXCELLENCE WITHOUT END

Bowen McCoy, a Morgan Stanley executive, spent several months trekking through Nepal with a friend while on sabbatical from work in 1982. The highest point in the Himalayas that they traversed was an 18,000-foot pass. On that day they encountered a gravely ill Sadhu, or holy man, lying practically naked in the snow and ice. How they and other climbers responded to that encounter haunted McCoy afterward. He wrote an essay about the ethical implications of the experience for *Harvard Business Review*.[1] It has been a popular addition to reading lists for business ethics classes.

There were other climbers attempting to make it over the pass that day as well. They were all strangers to one another. A New Zealand group had been first up the mountain that morning. One of them carried the Sadhu back down to where McCoy and his group were. "You take care of him," he said. "You have Sherpas." After a brief consult, McCoy kept climbing while his friend and the Sherpas attended to the holy man.

The Sherpas didn't want to carry the Sadhu down to the shelter where they had spent the night. It would be too exhausting to do that and then make it over the pass before the afternoon sun melted the ice steps. A Japanese group with a horse stopped to see if they could help on their way up. They refused to give up their horse to transport the Sadhu down the mountain. Finally, the Sherpas agreed to carry him halfway to the shelter, with the hope that he could muster enough strength to make it the rest of the way on his own.

What troubled McCoy afterward was how everyone was willing to do a little bit to assist the Sadhu, but no one was willing to let his predicament stop them from achieving their goals. He was never able to find out if the Sadhu actually made it back to safety.

McCoy believes that we encounter dilemmas like the Sadhu all of the time. At what point do I have a moral obligation to stop what I am doing to help someone in distress? Does an organization have a different set of obligations than an individual when it comes to handling moral interruptions? These are the kinds of questions that McCoy asked himself as he sorted through his guilt for not doing more to help on that very stressful day when everyone—not just the Sadhu—was feeling the effects of altitude sickness.

My interest in the story of the Sadhu is a little different than Bowen's. I think it illustrates what I am calling "excellence without end," which is the subject of this chapter. Many of us have the luxury of pursuing personal goals with a single-minded zeal that shuts out any and all distractions. Call it the bucket list gaze. We become so focused on our own experience that what happens around us is irrelevant, or merely inconvenient. An avalanche buries the village where I am headed for my once-in-a-life-time mountain retreat? Just my rotten luck.

Bucket list solipsism is just the tip of the iceberg. We also pursue unabated excellence in our work lives. Organizational success literature is full of advice about how to create a business dedicated to excelling in everything it does. Good is no longer good enough. You must strive to become greater than that.[2]

Ours is an age of specialization and expertise. Modern economies are so nuanced and competitive that the best chance any of us has at success is to drill down and become an expert at one little thing. Every field has a growing list of subdisciplines to which we can dedicate our entire lives. Want to become a bird biologist? Study one minor subspecies—McKay's bunting, a plump white bird that inhabits only the western shores of Alaska—and become the world's expert. The scaffolding of our knowledge is a complex maze beyond the understanding of any individual. Even Google algorithms can't fathom the entire edifice of human inquiry. The output of scientific research doubles every nine years, and the pace is quickening.[3]

Sports are no exception. Specialization and expertise dominate there, too. It is not uncommon to spend a lifetime doing just one thing better than almost everyone else, for example, throwing a discus or hitting a ping-pong ball. When you get too old to compete professionally, you transition into the coaching role. Elite Olympic athletes in a growing list of obscure sports (synchronized swimming and curling come to mind, but there are dozens of others) are subsidized by governments and other organizations so that they can train professionally year-round.

The pursuit of perfection in performance, like Nadia Comaneci's unprecedented string of seven perfect-10 scores in gymnastics at the 1976 Montreal Olympics, is part and parcel of being a world-class athlete. Rarely do we stop to wonder if things have gone too far. Is it a good thing to devote one's life to doing just one thing? For those who come out on top, no doubt it is worth it. For every Nadia Comaneci or LeBron James, there are millions of wannabes. The dream of athletic perfection ends in disappointment for most of us, including many professional athletes whose bodies break down from recurring injuries.

Injury is probably the surest sign that doing the same thing excessively is not normally good for us. Larry Bird was forced into retirement because of his back, Rafael Nadal has had ongoing problems with his knees, and Stephen Curry has a notoriously weak ankle. Pitchers opt for Tommy John surgery as a precautionary measure *before* injury occurs. They know the human body wasn't designed to throw fastballs. Then there is the CTE (chronic traumatic encephalopathy) issue in football and other physically violent sports. Mike Webster died in a demented state of lonely isolation due to the concussions he suffered while playing football for the Pittsburg Steelers. In that sport, nothing is more revered than being a tough guy. "Don't be a pussy," as one former player succinctly put it.[4] Ignoring pain and injury is part of the culture.

It's impossible to pursue a goal with total passion and commitment without becoming myopic regarding the rest of life. That's one of the downsides to the pursuit of excellence. When failure is not an option, self-centeredness becomes a requirement for survival. People talk about the sacrifices it takes to reach elite performance levels, but they usually have in mind the hours of practice it takes, not the moral self-absorption. The day-to-day lives of many elite athletes are shepherded—perhaps "curated" is more accurate—by teams of professional helpers: trainers, doctors, coaches, therapists, nutritionists, agents, consultants, business managers, lawyers, personal assistants, and what have you. The biggest stars become CEOs of Me, Inc., corporations with lucrative endorsement contracts and social media outlets that promote their particular lifestyle brands. It is no wonder that many people feel that they are entitled egomaniacs—or, as my grandfather would have said, "too damn big for their britches." I'll explain why I don't think that is a fair judgment a little later.

I think the pursuit of excellence without end is actually a perversion of the virtue tradition. Recall from the last chapter that virtues are excellences of character. We don't master a virtue like courage by pursuing it single-mindedly. Virtue is always a middle path between extremes of excess and deficiency. Every virtue is surrounded by two vices. The pursuit of excellence in character is a matter of balance and moderation, not a headlong drive to the top. Good and beneficial things are only good and beneficial up to a certain point. Excessive courage would be a vice, call it rashness or instability, not a virtue that never ceases to improve upon itself. Virtue without end is no virtue at all. It is a misunderstanding of what virtue requires. The perfect, I suspect, has gotten in the way of the good.

Martin Seligman and his associates in the positive psychology movement focus on virtues, but they ignore the vices that accompany them. That would be negative and contrary to their purposes. Being positive all of the time has its drawbacks, however. Some researchers are finding that flexibility is more important for our mental health than always being positive or happy.[5] Repression is the denial of negative experiences. In the United States, there is tremendous pressure to be positive all of the time, particularly in sports. (Ironically, no nation prescribes more antidepressant medication.) Sometimes pessimism is more appropriate. It serves a purpose, like fear or pain—warning us about danger and risk. Flexibility blends optimism and pessimism just as virtues blend too little and too much of a good thing.

We are easy targets for marketers who hawk their blinding visions of how wonderful life could be if we followed their advice or bought their products. Call it the booster effect. Being overly optimistic can actually lead to trouble. Jonathan Raban tells the story of how the U.S. Department of Agriculture hyped the promise of southeastern Montana as a place to homestead and practice dry land farming.[6] "Rain will follow the plow," they promised in their glowing brochures. Now, almost a century later, the area is filled with tumbleweeds and abandoned farmsteads. The rain never materialized, and those who tried to make a living based on false promises failed.

Boosterism is practically a requirement in sports. In rural Texas, towns like Midland and Odessa devote their very souls—including its dark recesses—to their high school football teams. That's the poignant story H. G. Bissinger told in *Friday Night Lights*.[7] Odessa's Permian High School had great expectations for a state championship run in 1988. Then they got knocked sideways when their star running back, Boobie Miles, tore his ACL. What made matters worse is that the injury happened during garbage time of a meaningless game. The entire town was furious with the coach. The team managed to regroup without Miles, making it all the way to the semifinal game in the playoffs. (In the movie version, they make it to the championship game.) There they battled a superior team from Dallas Carter High School and came within inches of winning on the last play. To almost win is sometimes the worst kind of loss to absorb. The grief lingers as what might have been does a slow burn in the heart.

Life seems more interesting and meaningful than it actually is when a town is afflicted with championship fever. There is an air of expectancy and clarity, a vim that puts a little extra giddy-up in everyone's step. To win a state football championship in Texas is like glimpsing the pearly gates or climbing Mt. Everest. Not everyone gets the opportunity. It will become the highlight of an otherwise boring and toilsome life. That's what Charles Billingsly and many other Odessa residents believed. Billingsly was the alcoholic father of one of the Permian players. He had won the state championship when he played and thought his son was throwing away the same opportunity. It made him mean and bitter.

There is a utopian quality to the dreams we invest in sports. Everyday life never quite measures up to them. To dream big is to court disappointment. Like long-suffering Chicago Cubs fans, we do it anyway. Once in a lifetime, it could pay off—as it finally did for the Cubs when they won the World Series in 2016. Maybe that's enough. In any case, we can't seem to live without the *possibility* for glory that our favorite teams provide us. Whether it is fantasy or not seems beside the point. It's the kind of dream that keeps us vital.

Angela Duckworth is a positive psychologist who studies grit, which she defines as passionate perseverance.[8] She believes we should be encouraging kids to tackle hard things so that they develop more grit. Grit is a reliable predictor of success and high achievement. Hard work and effort count more than talent in determining how far we go. It makes perfect sense.

Grit is a moral virtue. True to positive psychology form, Duckworth doesn't talk about the vices that make the practice of grit hard to achieve. Apparently, you can't ever have too much grit, and too little of it would be a character deficiency too obvious to warrant comment. But how would I know when passionate perseverance is no longer an asset to my success? There is no discussion of the practical wisdom (prudence) that is necessary to guide me in the application of grit. What do we call a person who applies grit even after it becomes obvious that it is time to quit and regroup? "Headstrong" comes to mind. A person who gives up too easily is usually called a quitter. I can understand the desire to infuse some backbone into our kids. But there is an art to knowing when to apply a moral virtue, to what extent it should be applied, and in what circumstances. There are limits to the value of virtues, even grit. To understand them requires wisdom.

You can have all the grit in the world, but if you don't know how to apply it properly in your life it could actually hinder your success. Or it could wreck your life, as in the case of many football players who gritted it out and stayed on the field even when they were concussed and injured. Junior Seau, the first hall of famer of Polynesian descent, played in the NFL for 20 years. Sadly, a few years after retiring, he committed suicide. The National Institutes of Health found evidence of CTE in Seau's brain tissue.

Sometimes in real life it is important to be able to distinguish what is realistically possible from what is merely false hope or fantasy. It's also important to be able to step outside of our own myopic drive to assess what's going on in the world around us. What if my relentless pursuit of personal success is contributing to problems on a different level? I am reminded of the ecological collapse that occurred on Easter Island. The Rapa Nui people built a thriving civilization on their isolated South Pacific island. It is famous for the large stone statuary—called *moai*—that dot its coastline. Many of the statues are gigantic, weighing as much as a truck. Modern visitors are amazed that a Stone Age people could create such artifacts. Anthropologists are puzzled about why they created them as well. The statues probably represented protective family deities.

It turns out that Rapa Nui civilization collapsed because every tree on the island was cut down for use in hauling *moai* from the inland quarry where they were constructed. They used tree trunks as rollers so that they could pull the heavy stones across the land. An escalating competition about whose family had the biggest and most decorative *moai* drove them to turn Easter Island into a treeless wasteland. They had plenty of passion and perseverance, plenty of grit. It wasn't easy to build and haul those monuments. What they lacked was the wisdom to understand that their goals were destroying the island's ecology. We can't live on grit—or any virtue—alone. Personal success can't be the measuring stick for all things. Sometimes we need to look around and see what's happening in the world beyond our own unbridled pursuit of excellence. Even the success of our species has limits.

Jared Diamond investigated why some civilizations that faced dire ecological challenges survived when others, for instance, the Rapa Nui, did not.[9] For example, both Iceland and Greenland were settled by Vikings within the last one thousand years. Iceland's civilization has survived to this day, but the Greenland settlement only lasted about four hundred years. Greenland had two inner valleys that were farmable in the Viking style, but they proved to be too isolated and drought prone. Iceland had its problems as well. The volcanic soil was shallow and easily swept away by the wind once it had been plowed. Yet, Icelandic civilization survived, whereas Greenland's didn't. Why? It's primarily because Iceland was more easily accessed by ships from Norway, which could help sustain the colony in difficult times. Fledgling civilizations require outside assistance to survive.

Actually, there were two different settlements on Greenland, not just the Vikings. Inuit hunter-gatherers also frequented Greenland. They stayed mostly to the north, while the Vikings settled in south-central valleys. The Inuit hunted whales, seals, and fish. When times got bad, they simply moved on to other territories in the greater Arctic region. On the other hand, the Vikings tried to grow crops and raise farm animals like they did back home in Norway. They weren't flexible like the Inuit, and they refused to learn any lessons from the Inuit that might have prevented their own starvation. Hunter-gatherer societies are more self-sufficient in difficult times. They also tend to be more attuned to what's happening in the world around them. Their livelihood depended upon it.

Basking in the glow of modern civilization, we assume that agriculture is a more permanent and superior way of life than hunting and gathering. Yet, when things go wrong, the settled permanency of farm life becomes a liability, as the Greenland Vikings found out. Being light on your feet (nomadic) has its advantages. The hunter-gatherer way of life is the crucible from which our species emerged in an often unpredictable and harsh climate as the recurrent ice ages of the late Pleistocene were coming to an end. Greenland, with its Northern latitude and massive glaciers, replicated that Ice Age experience for Inuit and Viking settlers. Not surprisingly, the hunter-gatherer system of the Inuit was better adapted for perseverance in those circumstances. Farming only works when the weather is predictable for long periods of time. It's easy to overlook the fact that we have enjoyed a 12,000-year run of mostly stable weather.

I see parallels to Michael Lewis's *Moneyball* in the Vikings and Inuit of Greenland.[10] Lewis asked a simple question that helped transform baseball—and other professional sports as well. How, he wondered, could the Oakland Athletics, with a payroll of $40 million in 2002, hold their own against the New York Yankees, who spent three times as much? The answer turned out to be "sabermetrics," or the use of new forms of statistical analysis to identify undervalued players who could produce winning results without commanding excessive salaries. Billy Beane was the manager of the Oakland A's who used the new analytical approach to field a team that actually won as many games as the well-heeled Yankees.

Before sabermetrics, baseball had been mired in 19th-century methods of player evaluation, which were inefficient—even wrongheaded in some cases. Take the venerable statistic of batting average, for example. New research indicated that team batting average didn't correlate well with how many runs are scored in a game. And it is *runs* that win games, not batting averages. On-base percentage and slugging percentage are better indicators of offensive achievement because they provide more specific information concerning the generation of runs. The A's used a lot of other exotic metrics, too, for instance, WAR (wins above replacement), which compares the value of one player to another based on how much each one helped their team to win games.

You can have the most money to spend, like the Yankees did, but if you don't spend it wisely you are squandering your financial advantages. It's the same thing we saw with grit and other virtues. If you don't apply them wisely, you are probably doing more harm than good. Everyone in baseball now pays attention to the new analytics, including the Yankees; however, the 2002 Yankees personified the settled wisdom for how to construct a baseball team by using traditional scouting methods to identify talent. They were like the Vikings who went to Greenland and tried to create a new Norway in a land that was not well suited for raising crops and livestock. Neither the Yankees nor the Vikings were capable of perceiving their own insufficiencies and limitations. It made them inflexible, perhaps even arrogant. Old ways die hard in the face of new circumstances.

There is a paradox regarding wisdom—or, more precisely, the limits of its utility—in all of this. Wisdom that becomes settled loses some of its effectiveness because its reliability gets taken for granted. We fall into the trap of forgetting to notice what's going on around us—and adapting accordingly. When we think we've seen it all, we get lazy. There is nothing new under the sun except the same old same old. Baseball scouts want to see how fast a prospect can run, how hard he can throw, how well he can hit, and how well he can field the ball. That's how it's always been done. It never occurred to them to try to assess a player's impact on the team's ability to win with more precision. That's what opened the door to an entirely different mindset—a paradigm shift—in Oakland. Wisdom that doesn't reach beyond itself grows stale.

The A's proved to be more cunning and flexible because they had no other choice. Necessity is the mother of invention more often than not. That's not just a cliché. Oakland couldn't compete financially with New York, so they improvised. They subverted the strategic power of money in baseball by devising a new way to achieve and define success. Like the Inuit, the A's were more attuned to what was happening around them. They got better at "reading" (interpreting) the nuances of talent by exploiting the cumulative data of every baseball game that had ever been played. The new analytics became possible once the box scores from a century's worth of ballgames had been computer automated.

New correlations between winning and performance on the field were mined from the historical data by tech-savvy analysts. Stone Age people exploit the cumulative memory of their experience in much the same way—but without the benefit of computers. Some might say that the mind is still the best computing machine the world has ever seen.

There's a difference between doing things the same old way because the past carries you along in its somnolent wake (like the Yankees and Vikings) and learning from the past by reinterpreting it to fit new circumstances (like the A's and Inuit). There is no easy formula for how to be flexible—when to change, for example, rather than staying the course. Necessity, capability, and wisdom play their parts. So too does the moral habit of looking for new ways to take advantage of opportunities and circumstances. It strengthens the kind of mental skills needed for survival in a rough-and-tumble world that is often unfair and merciless. What the Oakland A's accomplished was akin to that.

Because our ancestors faced unpredictable conditions in the late Pleistocene, they developed an opportunistic and flexible way of life. They were born risk-takers. Built into their psyches was a willingness to cross mountains and even oceans to find food, shelter, and a better life. Their morality was equally adaptive and opportunistic. They would take advantage of others if the opportunity presented itself—provided that the risk of getting caught and punished was not too great. Conscience is an instinctive risk calculator. Prudence—the intellectual virtue that helps guide our practice of moral virtues—has its beginning in the cunning algorithms of the hunter-gatherer conscience. Like the antibodies of our immune system that present a flexible front against new diseases that are constantly emerging, hunter-gatherer morality was capable of quickly adapting to new circumstances.[11] By contrast, the rule-based morality that we are more familiar with today is not very flexible. We view morality as scripted and sacrosanct, not cunning and opportunistic. Rules are rules, not meant to be broken. It is civilization that wants everything written down in stone.

As a collection of ancient oral traditions and texts, the Bible often hints at the tensions between preagricultural ways of life and postagricultural ways of life. Institutional religions were instruments of our own self-domestication, helping to civilize us after the invention of agriculture made it possible to live in settled communities and empires. From the Sinai wilderness, reminiscent of our uncivilized past, Moses came down from the mountain with a rule-based moral system (the Ten Commandments) etched in stone. In the story of Cain and Abel, it is the latter—the farmer—who is preferred by everyone, including God. The nomadic brother—Cain—is the outcast, the murderer, the uncivilized one.

In sports, we like our leaders to be risk-takers, not timid rule mongers. Quarterback Brett Favre embodied the type. He was known as a "gunslinger," a throwback to the Wild West, where vigilante justice and gun fighting filled the void of lawlessness. Favre played with the same immunity to pressure that enabled real gunslingers to face down their enemies. He was one cool customer. He was beloved (and forgiven) for his willingness to throw bullet passes into tight spaces where they probably shouldn't have been thrown. Doubtless he had too much confidence in his arm. Favre still holds the NFL record for most pass completions. Interestingly, he also holds the records for most pass interceptions and most pass attempts. He was a risk-taker, seemingly unafraid to fail, and undeterred by his many mistakes. That is a crucial ingredient in learning how to win. The road to athletic success always includes failure. Perhaps that's where it actually begins. It's where the most valuable lessons are learned.

All my life, I've been reminded that the greatest baseball players fail two out of every three times they step up to the plate. It's part of our success mythology, a tale of persistence that pays off when we don't quit at the first sign of adversity. The attainment of athletic excellence requires sacrifice and the acceptance (endurance) of failure. Excellence without end—the subject of this chapter—is a cautionary subtext in persistence and success narratives. Sometimes, the better part of valor is to back off and regroup. Sometimes, endurance becomes a stubborn unwillingness to learn the lessons that come from failure. The difficulty is in discerning where that balancing point between persistence and stubbornness lies. It takes wisdom to find the middle way. Saying that doesn't make it easy or even comprehensible. The fumble-around method is probably the best we can do when it comes to becoming wiser. That's a lesson I learned on the golf course.

For years, I tried to correct my natural fade with the driver. I changed how I stand when I address the ball, but it often led to weird corkscrew-like hooks. I changed my grip, but that made the hook worse. I tried to hold my left wrist cocked through impact, and sometimes I would blast a perfect drive, straight and true. But the good drives were few and far between. What I have settled on is accepting the fact that I have a natural fade, and I play accordingly. It's more fun to do it that way, and wiser.

Great quarterbacks like Brett Favre react to what they see on the field, recognizing (chunking) defensive schemes instantly without thought. They play instinctively, unconsciously, mindlessly. Most of us, I suspect, wouldn't be able to abandon ourselves to the game in that way. We would hold back something, and it would be the cause of our hesitation—and our athletic demise. In that split-second—that's all it would take—the defense would pound us unmercifully into the turf. To control the game by giving up self-control and allowing the mind free reign to calculate risks and make instantaneous decisions is a skill that all elite athletes train themselves to possess. Paradoxically, it takes long, hard practice to be able to play with abandon. First, we must strip away the bulwark of self-consciousness that civilization has bequeathed to us. It is our primate instincts that enable us to perform at our best.

Addiction—like injury—is another indicator that too much of a good thing can be bad for us. Addictions are bad habits of the excessive variety (vices of excess). Smoking, alcoholism, and overeating are garden-variety addictions in our society, but it's possible to become addicted to anything. Tiger Woods underwent treatment for sex addiction after extramarital affairs destroyed his marriage and upended his image—even his career. Favre was treated for Vicodin addiction. Rehab is a requisite stopping point in the all too common sports hero redemption narrative.

Addictions are like sweet-scented bear traps. We succumb to them because we have limited experience, biologically speaking, with the task of resisting the temptation to overindulge. Prior to the 20th century, few humans had the opportunity to live in a culture of abundance. We evolved to survive the *scarcity* of resources, not to contend with a superabundance of them. Moral evolution enabled small groups of hunter-gatherers to band together so that they could share food, thus decreasing the likelihood that they might die of starvation. Generosity and humility were crucial virtues in their fight against scarcity. In modern Western cultures, scarcity is no longer the locus of our moral purpose. Now we must contend with abundance and the consumption—to our heart's content—of delicious foods, drinks, drugs, and so forth, that are specifically designed to entice our palates and desires. The modern shopaholic is a person whose conscience knows not what to do with the temptation to buy one more thing ad infinitum.

We evolved to be athletes, not couch potatoes. Evolutionary biologists speak about the "mismatch" between how we evolved to live and how we live today. Eating too much while exercising too little can lead to obesity, heart disease, diabetes, and other mismatch diseases. Our bodies evolved to crave fats and sugars because they were a good source of energy that could be quickly stored as body fat. Having a little body fat in a harsh environment with scarce resources could mean the difference between survival and starvation or exposure to the elements. Few humans became obese because animal fat and honey—the only form of natural sugar widely available to Stone Age people—were scarce. Our cravings evolved to match the scarcity of what we craved. Now, however, I can raid the cupboards 24/7. If I run out of things to eat at home, I can go to a grocery store with acres of beautifully displayed foods ready to purchase at any time, day or night. It's damn hard to say no to this constant cornucopia of temptation that could easily wear down the aspirations of an ascetic monk. Addictions and mismatch diseases are part of the travail of life in a culture with too much abundance.

Practicing the same basketball move or golf swing over and over again can be construed as a kind of "good" (nonharmful) addiction. Not all addictions and obsessions belong in the annals of psychiatry, although the bad ones surely do. They are bad because they lead to self-destruction. It's probably true that good addictions are a requirement for success in sports. If you hate to hit balls at the practice range, it's safe to say you will never become a professional golfer. It takes obsessive interest—addictive desire—to be willing to put in the hours of deliberate practice it requires to become a world-class athlete. Not everyone would agree to where the line between good and bad addictions ought to be drawn. There is some room for a gray area, as in most things.

The problem of too much abundance flipped the basic moral script that has guided us for thousands of millennia. We evolved to combat the detriments of scarcity, not the insatiability of our appetites. We have resorted to medical and psychological categories to interpret our lack of success in refraining from overconsumption because "willpower" and other traditional moral categories haven't been adequate for the task.

Constitutionally, our species is better at enduring deprivation and hardship than resisting opportunities to scarf down yet another ready-to-hand candy bar. The scarcity model of hunter-gatherer morality isn't altogether irrelevant to modern life, however. That is especially true in modern sports, where overcoming scarcity still remains essential.

Scarcity is central to the meaning of modern sports. We define games, first of all, by delimiting their spatial and temporal boundaries. A college basketball game only lasts 40 minutes, then it is over with. You don't get the opportunity to play on and on. When time runs out, your chance to score more points ends. There is a limit—a scarcity—to every team's opportunities. The basketball court is finite as well. If you happen to make a basket while standing on the out-of-bounds line, tough luck. It doesn't count. The physical and temporal boundaries of play make the chances for success harder to come by. Sporting events are designed to make it difficult to excel. If it weren't difficult, we wouldn't care to participate or watch. It's the difficulty—the scarcity of virtuoso play—that we find so beautiful and compelling. There is only Roger Federer, one maestro, in the game of tennis today.

It is moral drama that attracts our attention to sports. Winning is the ultimate scarcity that must be overcome. Only one team can win the NCAA basketball tournament. That means 67 other teams go home still hungry every year. The thrill of victory recapitulates the moral experience of hunter-gatherer societies because modern athletes, like their Stone Age ancestors, contend with challenges that are primarily based upon scarcity. The finite plays a bigger role than the infinite in modern sports; overabundance and excellence without end have limited purchase.

Lindsey Vonn, the great American downhill skier, didn't fare as well as expected in the 2018 Pyeongchang Olympics. Some Americans were rooting for her to fail because she made a comment about competing for her country, not President Donald Trump.[12] An avid golfer, President Trump has been a divisive figure for many in the sporting universe. That is particularly true in professional football. The president has repeatedly criticized the NFL regarding Colin Kaepernick and other players who kneeled during the national anthem as a way of protesting racial violence in the United States. He thought the protesters should be fired. The president's core supporters have vociferously defended him against every perceived slight coming from professional athletes. For example, some Trump supporters suggested that LeBron James—a frequent critic of President Trump—should just shut up and play basketball.

Vonn's response to the "haters," as she called them, is instructive concerning the personal meaning of morality in the United States today. She said that she was being "true to herself" when she made the comment about the president. That's what justified it in her mind—the fact that it came from her heart. I think most of us believe that being true to ourselves—being totally honest—is a sign of authenticity. To be an authentic person is our highest moral calling. The interesting twist is that most of us believe that real authenticity is rare. There is, we believe, far too much insincerity, gossip, and triviality in how we live. To be in touch with one's true self, to express the purity of heart that resides deep inside of us—to be the poets of ourselves—is what we find most admirable in our heroes. In the solidarity of being true to herself (being her own hero), Lindsey Vonn found her solace and her voice.

It seems fantastic, even ironic, that our sense of personal morality could somehow repurpose the scarcity paradigm of our evolutionary heritage. What we find so scarce in our moral world isn't food and shelter, as in hunter-gatherer societies, but *authenticity*. To be authentic is a rare achievement that places us beyond the reproach of others. Criticism is meaningless if I am doing or saying something that is truly heartfelt. That's what Vonn meant by saying that she was being true to herself: The hate couldn't touch her.

The virtues that hunter-gatherer people admired most were humility and generosity, whereas I think we admire honesty and authenticity the most. No one would say that Lindsey Vonn was being humble, or generous, in her comments about the president. But they would probably acknowledge her honesty and authenticity. Like all of us, she is searching (striving) for a heart of gold, as a song from my high school days put it.[13] That is why I don't think elite athletes are pampered egomaniacs. Yes, they can become single-minded about their quest for athletic glory. They have access to wealth and resources beyond the reach of most people. But that's only part of the picture. Tied to the quest for athletic excellence is the parallel quest to discover the depths of the heart. That's where the motivation and confidence to excel ultimately comes from. I don't think athletes judge themselves based upon how much they acquire (wealth, trophies, etc.). I think they base their judgments on how successful they are at finding their own inner strength. That's what the heart, or spirit, gives us. The quest for authenticity exceeds and sustains the quest for athletic achievement.

Even Superman—the epitome of a perfect hero and athlete—needed his fortress of solitude so that he could unwind and get in touch with his true self. Our real-life sports heroes are a little bit like that.

Too much of a good thing can sometimes be bad for us. That is the message of this chapter. When the only thing that matters is our own excellence—I call it excellence without end—it can lead us astray. I find it puzzling that self-esteem is rising among American children while at the same time more and more of them are being diagnosed with ADD, depression, anxiety, and other mental illnesses. How can that be? My suspicion is that it has to do with inflated expectations. Every kid is told that he or she could grow up to become a VIP of some kind or other. Most of them won't have the opportunity, or the temperament, to do so. The gap between expectation and reality can lead to difficulties. I wonder if we are foisting the same burdensome expectations upon young athletes.

The Inuit survived in Greenland while the Vikings didn't because they were more adaptive and flexible. The same was true for the Oakland A's compared to the 2002 Yankees. Being responsive to reality seems to work better than trying to dictate what it ought to be. Sports dynasties often collapse when their greatest players retire. Michael Jordan's Chicago Bulls are the perfect example. It actually happened twice to them because Jordan retired twice: once to play baseball after having won three NBA titles in a row, then again after achieving a second three-peat of NBA titles when he returned from his baseball interlude. Not all sports dynasties collapse in that way, however.

The New England Patriots and San Antonio Spurs are often praised for being able to withstand the loss of great players without falling apart. Why is that? I believe it is because their organizations think and act more like hunter-gatherers than other organizations do. I think that is particularly true of their coaches—Bill Belichick and Greg Popovich, whose dry-to-the-bone news conferences often sound eerily similar. They don't hang on to players or the same strategies forever. They are willing to cut their losses and rebuild their base. They seem able to learn lessons from failure without becoming stubborn and bitter about it. They don't overvalue one way of doing things, unlike Viking farmers and baseball traditionalists. They don't seem to have forgotten that virtues are adaptive because they represent a compromise between too little and too much.

In the next chapter, I will discuss the specialized brain cells called mirror neurons that enable us to simulate what other people feel and do. The implications for how we understand sports are staggering. And yet mirror neurons alone cannot explain everything about our moral experience and athletic capacities.

6

NEUROSCIENCE, MIRRORING, AND COMPLEMENTARITY

I could have included a discussion of neuroscience in the previous chapter about excellence without end. That's because it is crawling with soothsayers who foretell a future of near-miraculous improvements to the human condition. It's been that way at least since the elder President Bush declared the 1990s to be the decade of the brain. It was hoped, for example, that neurobiologists would be able to identify clear biomarkers for such mental illnesses as schizophrenia. To date, none have been found. Nor have we been able to identify a single gene as the causative agent for schizophrenia, as many had hoped (prophesied) in the euphoria leading up to the completion of the Human Genome Project.

The human genome has taught us that genes are far more complicated than we ever imagined. A typical personality trait—shyness, let's say—could never be traced to a purely genetic cause. It doesn't work that way. Certainly, there is a genetic *influence* on the kind of people we become in life. Hundreds of genes—not a few, or even a dozen—would be interacting with one another in the emergence of something as socially complex as shyness. Not only that, those genes would also be interacting with the unique experiences of each shy person's life. Genes don't dictate what becomes of us; they are only part of a larger conversation. Our experiences actually help determine which genes get switched "on." We have approximately 19,000 of them, most of which are silent, or "off." The responsiveness of genes to life experiences—

their *plasticity*—is referred to as epigenetics. Each one of us forges a unique "epigenetic" code based upon how our genes interact with the particulars of our biographies.

The same lesson regarding the plasticity of genes applies to our brains as well. They too interact with our unique experiences. They too are customizable and responsive to what life brings. For example, researchers have found that professional athletes are quicker than others at learning tasks that track the motion of multiple objects.[1] Their athletic training gives them the edge. Consider all of the film study that quarterbacks do. It enables them to recognize defensive schemes instantly and anticipate what is likely to happen once the ball is hiked. Some neuroscientists call that acquired skill "chunking," as I mention in a previous chapter. What I can add to the story is that chunking and other such acquired skills actually change the anatomy of the brain. Athletes have a thicker STS (superior temporal sulcus) region, which is crucial for motion perception. That's why they can track complex motions better than the rest of us.

Until recently, scientists thought the human brain was plastic—or changeable—only during childhood. Now we know that even adult brains can be trained and improved. The idea that we can change the structure and capacity of our own brains through deliberate practice is nothing short of mind blowing. Think about that for a second. It makes the temptation to exaggerate about what the future will bring more understandable.

Treating the brain as if it were just like a muscle that can be made stronger through exercise has become a training cliché in professional sports and elite college athletic programs. Everyone, it seems, is making use of the latest neuroscience technologies to make athletes quicker at recognizing situations on the field. A quicker mind is able to slow the game down, allowing athletes more time to absorb what's happening around them—and make better decisions as a result.

Stephen Curry is one of the more famous practitioners of new age training methods that focus on improving the brain. Several years before he became a NBA superstar—winning back-to-back league MVP Awards in 2015 and 2016, and breaking his own record for three-point field goals made in a season four times—Curry began training with Brandon Payne at Accelerated Basketball. Payne created elaborate drills that challenged and stressed Curry to the point of frustration. In one now-famous video, Curry can be seen dribbling a ball in one hand while tossing a tennis ball up and down with the other hand. He is also wearing a pair of strobe goggles that partially block his vision, forcing him to anticipate where the two balls will be at least part of the time. Payne's drills involve the use of technology designed to improve a basketball player's "neurocognitive efficiency." It works by overloading the brain so that it must adapt and learn (stretch) to make progress. It is reminiscent of the Chinese table tennis training tactic of forcing players to practice with multiple balls. When it came time to play a match with just one ball, it seemed much easier because their minds were accustomed (trained) to following several balls at once. The game had slowed down because they trained for something more arduous.

Spectators show up early to Golden State basketball games to watch Curry warm up. It's become part of the show: a new sports ritual. His dribble routine with two balls at once is like an *Ed Sullivan Show* circus act. (You youngsters can still catch the reruns.) Trying to follow both balls at the same time with your eye is almost impossible, like watching a ceiling fan as it spins. All you can see is the blur of the fan, not its individual blades.

In baseball, "neuroscouting" has become the new "moneyball" strategy for identifying talent using unconventional analytics. The Boston Red Sox drafted Mookie Betts in 2011, based on his scores on a pitching simulation program designed by a secretive company called NeuroScouting.[2] The program is like a video game that can be played on a laptop. You watch the ball as it is released from the pitcher's hand and press a button when you recognize the pitch—fastball, slider, knuckleball, whatever. Betts proved to be adept at identifying pitches early in the simulation. He made his major-league debut at the age of 21, and has become one of the best hitters on the team. The Red Sox currently require minor-league players to participate in a NeuroScouting development program. It helps train their brains to recognize pitches quicker without having to take batting practice. To be able to improve actual baseball skills without having to hit real balls and risk injury accelerates the player development process. That's the theory anyway.

In a recent book, Brandon Sneed described an entire range of neuroscience consumer products that are currently being used in professional and college sports.[3] Many employ EEG (electroencephalogram) readers that record electrical brain activity. In one such product, the athlete puts on a cap with electrodes that touch the scalp, then plays a video game on a phone app while the EEG collects data. Brain activity shows up as a series of wave lines that are interpreted by the app. In performance activities, the most important brain wavelength occurs in the alpha range (8–12 Hz). After interpreting the data, the app prescribes a training program to help optimize brain activity. Purportedly, it takes about 30 sessions to see beneficial changes from EEG training. Beach volleyball Olympian Kerri Walsh Jennings endorses the technology, as do many other athletes and trainers.

EEG training is essentially a biofeedback system. It tells you how your brain is functioning, and that knowledge enables you to become more mindful about how to manage it effectively. That's the basic concept behind any biofeedback system: As you become more aware of something that normally functions below the level of self-awareness, you are able to exercise some measure of control over it.

One of the most important attributes for any athlete is the ability to perform under pressure. Many neuroscience technology products focus on calming the brain by enhancing its ability to reach meditative states. Russell Wilson, the Seattle Seahawks quarterback, is renowned for his calm demeanor. He doesn't panic, even when he is running for his life from a blitzing linebacker. It's probably no accident that the Seahawks train their players to have that kind of mindset. They use traditional methods (yoga, meditation), in addition to the latest brain training gear and games.

It's equally important to be able to calm down *after* the game is over so that your body can rest and recover. That can be difficult to do when you are flushed with adrenaline. NFL cornerback Josh Norman wears an electrical stimulation device that helps reduce the lingering excitement effects once the football game has ended.[4]

Virtual reality training might be the most promising neuroscience technology for athletes. A baseball batter can get more practice swings at a particular kind of pitch in one virtual reality "cave" session than he might get in a year's worth of normal practice. Football players can learn tackling and blocking techniques without always having to bash heads and risk concussion or other injuries. The possibilities seem endless—even to the point of redefining what reality itself means, as such movies as *The Matrix* and *Avatar* tried to do.

A longstanding contentious philosophical issue is whether the mind is reducible to what the brain does. Progress in the neurosciences has tipped the scale toward brain–mind equivalency. Even the soul, an ancient metaphor for the most vital (immortal) part of ourselves, is vulnerable to the ascendancy of the brain as the one and only organ necessary for explaining (orchestrating) who we are. There is a new somatic ethic that focuses on nurturing the body to influence and improve the brain. Sometimes it is called neuroethics. The more we learn about the brain, the more responsibility we feel to take good care of ourselves by taking good care of our brains.

For many, the brain alone has become synonymous with their self-identities. That is unprecedented. It puts a "neuro" spin on the self-help tradition that began with Benjamin Franklin's claim that 13 virtues enabled him to achieve moral perfection. Putting our focus on improving the brain is different in scope than trying to improve our moral character. We have the opportunity—and the "neuromoral" burdens that go along with it—to embark upon a journey of self-guided evolution. "Transhumanism" is a term that often comes up in discussions of this kind. It means that we have come to a point where we can deliberately alter ourselves and become something other than what we are (transhuman). What does the future of sports and morality look like in such a context? I briefly explore that issue in the final chapter of this book. For now, I want to comment on how the turn to neuroscience relates to the moral experience of our hunter-gatherer ancestors before taking a closer look at mirror neurons.

In the ancestral environment, as we have seen, our bodies and minds adapted to the demands of traveling long distances in search of food, for instance, running down large animals. Our legs grew longer and our foot arches stiffer, we developed sweat glands and protruding noses to help cool us down, and our brains became responsive to neurochemicals that eased the pain and monotony of running for hours on end. We also developed a moral sensibility to encourage mutual cooperation and generosity.

Moral regard for others was only one motive among many in our ancestors' inner life, however. There were stronger urges to look after one's own interests first (egoism) and the interests of family members (nepotism). The basic components of self-awareness—consciousness, the unconscious, and conscience—bear the telltale signs of inner moral struggle. Early humans were cunning opportunists, capable of hiding their deceptions even from themselves by relegating them to the unconscious. That's how they learned to mask any appearance of guilt, which others could all too easily detect in them. Far from being a voice of divine goodness, conscience has always been encumbered with the more mundane task of calculating how much selfishness a person could reasonably get away with.

Because of our hunter-gatherer past, we are predisposed (preadapted) to thrive in the competitive arenas of modern sports. The best sports—the most challenging and interesting ones—test the limits of our bodies *and* our minds. The physical nature of athletic competition seems all too obvious in its importance. Yet, I suspect that matching wits is even more significant. It's the latter kind of competition that moral evolution prepared us for. Ask yourself this question: Do you get more joy from outwitting an opponent or physically overpowering one? My answer skews toward outwitting the opponent.

The evolutionary adaptations of mind and body that our ancestors experienced were driven by unconscious forces. Even though their moral habits encouraged more and more cooperation over time, like a positive feedback loop, that trend toward more cooperation was not part of a deliberate plan. It just worked out that way. That's what is different about training the brain today. It's part of a self-conscious plan to improve ourselves. It's as if the discovery of brain plasticity has thrown us back into the ancestral environment, but this time we have all of the knowledge of the neurosciences working for us. We are changing ourselves and adapting (evolving) *deliberately*, not accidentally, by training our brains.

Whether we can actually change the structure of our minds—the tensions between consciousness, the unconscious, and conscience—through deliberate practices that target the brain remains to be seen. Our minds evolved for the moral purpose of matching wits with one another. We are prone to generosity and, at the same time, selfish conniving. That moral paradox has haunted and shaped our inner selves from the very beginning. Can the neurosciences straighten out the crooked pathways of our character more ably than institutional religions did in the past several millennia? Or more ably than modern psychiatry and psychology did during the past century? It will be interesting to see.

The accidental discovery of mirror neurons in Italy is one of the landmark achievements in the neurosciences. Scientists at the University of Parma made the discovery while studying the premotor cortex of rhesus macaque monkeys.[5] Other than humans, macaques are the most widespread primate on earth. Like us, they are a social animal, typically living in groups of 20 to 50 members. Rhesus macaques have round, reddish faces; weigh about 20 pounds; and live as many as 30 years on average.

The Parma scientists used brain scanning technology to identify precisely which neurons were active when the monkeys grasped different things with their hands. After months of testing, one scientist happened to notice that the same neurons that were active in the test animals also fired in a monkey that he was hooking up for the next round of tests. But the monkey being prepped for the experiment wasn't grasping anything in his hands. Instead, he was watching another monkey grasp things. That wasn't supposed to happen.

What they accidentally discovered was that there is a subset of neurons in primate brains (including our own) that are capable of combining motor control functions with perception. Prior to their discovery, it was thought that each function—motor control, visual perception, auditory perception—was handled by a separate neuron. They called these special multifunctional neurons "mirror neurons" because they mimic (mirror) what is occurring in someone else's brain.

What makes mirror neurons so significant is that they demonstrate how mentally connected we are to one another. Seeing someone else do something, we simulate in our own brains what it would be like for us to do the same thing. When someone is hurt, for example, we really do *feel* their pain because our brains simulate exactly what it feels like. It's not a metaphor: Feeling what others feel—*empathy*—is a real biological connection in the brain. Because empathy is inherent to mirror neurons, many primatologists now believe that all primates have the potential to become morally self-aware, not just humans. Empathy is the beginning of kindness and generosity.

When mirror neurons in the Broca area are shocked using TMS (transcranial magnetic stimulation) technology, we temporarily lose the ability to speak. Broca's area is important for the use of language. It's also involved in the control of hand gestures, an ability that the same TMS treatment temporarily deprives us of as well. That has led some neuroscientists to think it is possible that gesturing with our hands to fire mirror neurons in others was actually how the use of language first began. In that sense, language is literally a shared cognitive system. It is a way for the brains of a group of people to interact as if they were one hive-like metaorganism—or one *team*.

Mirror neurons help explain why imitation is so important to learning. As children, for example, how did we learn to eat with a fork and knife? Simply put, we watched others do it and then imitated them. We didn't need to go to utensil school. Watching others eat with utensils, our mirror neurons automatically simulated how it's done. It's as if the brain were conducting its own dress rehearsal. Then, when we actually tried using a fork, the hands already knew roughly what to do because the mind had simulated it. With a little practice, and more watching, we mastered the task thanks to our mirror neurons.

We have stronger mental connections to one another than we ever realized. We are never alone in our own minds. On the contrary, we are constantly simulating (reproducing, sampling, sharing) the thoughts and actions of others. In a previous chapter, I mention the illusory presence of another person (called the "third-man factor") that some extreme athletes, for instance, arctic explorers and mountain climbers, experience. It doesn't seem quite so otherworldly or far-fetched in light of mirror neurons. Even self-identity is probably something that emerges because of our cognitive connections to others. First comes our connection to others, then our capacity to be ourselves. That reverses the standard but probably mistaken view that first we gain self-awareness, then we become aware of others.

In their capacity to simulate what we perceive in others, mirror neurons could hold the key to self-understanding. They are like a reference library to human conduct. Aristotle said that we acquire a virtue like courage by imitating what courageous people do. Now perhaps we know what he meant by that. Imitating what a courageous person does, one brain coaches another, indicating how to feel and behave. It's like a Vulcan mind meld. (Ignore that simile if you are not a Trekkie!)

Mirror neurons demonstrate the importance of the body even in the realm of understanding. Body awareness—including athletic prowess—is a kind of social intelligence. Athletes are not weak-minded or dumb, as some like to portray them. On average, I think great athletes have a better capacity for making cognitive connections with others than the rest of us do. Maybe they have more mirror neurons or more efficient mirror neurons. I don't know. Think about how close teammates often become. We call it camaraderie, bonding, team spirit, locker room culture, family, and so on. I think it involves building a cognitive hive, a shared mentality that enables the team to function with one mind instead of many individual minds. Not all of us are capable of surrendering to the greater mind of the team.

Teammates become cognitively connected through disciplined practice. They share intentions more easily and intuitively than in normal circumstances. NFL quarterbacks have an uncanny ability to know when to throw the ball to their favorite receivers. How many times did Joe Montana throw a perfectly timed pass to Jerry Rice, for instance, or Troy Aikman to Michael Irvin? There are too many memorable quarterback–receiver duos to list here. It's as if their minds were synchronized—like a pair of Western grebes dancing across the water in perfect unison—each knowing or sensing what the other was about to do. Nor is it simply because they are running routes that they practice every day, which certainly helps. Joe Montana seemed to sense when Jerry Rice was about to break away from his route and do something unscripted. Mirror neurons enable people to share intentions and even anticipate them. Quarterbacks and receivers develop a heightened capacity for doing that.

Wayne Gretzky, the "Great One," had that kind of anticipatory intelligence in spades. "I skate to where the puck is going," he famously said, "not where it has been." I think that's my favorite quote in all of sports. It's what mirror neurons help great athletes achieve: They see what is about to happen before others do because their minds are slightly more attuned to the developments, intentions, and actions occurring around them. It is the strength of their minds—their cognitive networks—that gives them an edge.

Two minds are better than one. I often hear that comment. It's a workplace cliché, meaning we are supposed to put our heads together so that we can solve problems more efficiently. I don't think it works. Two minds are not necessarily better than one. In fact, sharing one mind—being attuned to what others think and feel—might be the most efficient problem-solving strategy ever devised by natural selection. It's what enabled *Homo sapiens* to achieve unprecedented dominion on earth. There is ample evidence of this in sports. Offenses, for example, always have the advantage over defenses—no matter the sport—because they know what they are trying to do. They have one mind. Defenses are always put in the position of having to scramble and react to offenses. It's inexorable: Actors have the advantage over reactors. The latter must first interpret what the former are trying to accomplish before they respond as actors in their own right. There is a lag time that privileges offenses/actors. Defenses do their best to hang together with one mind, but their efforts are constantly foiled by the decisiveness of the offense. The best example of this that I can think of is the pick-and-roll play executed to perfection by John Stockton and Karl Malone.

Stockton and Malone played in the NBA for the Utah Jazz in the 1980s and 1990s. They took their team to the finals twice, never quite getting over the hump to win the title. Stockton was a skinny ball handler out of Gonzaga who looked too young and boyish to be an elite playmaker. In a game where offensive plays often turn on a stutter step or head fake (or some other deceptive move), to be blessed with an innocent-looking baby face confers a distinct advantage. Harmless as he may have looked physically, Stockton was ruthless at exploiting advantages on the court. He was one of the best decision makers and passers the game has ever seen.

Malone was Stockton's perfect complement and antithesis: a bruising power forward from Louisiana who went to unheard-of Louisiana Tech, a college close to home. Long before Lebron came along, Karl Malone had a Lebron-like physique and presence. Get him the ball headed toward the basket and he'd finish with a layup plus a trip to the foul line. He was so reliable as a scorer that they called him the "Mailman." As of 2019, Karl is one of only two players to score more than 35,000 points in his career. Kareem Abdul-Jabbar is the other one.

Before Stockton and Malone came along, the pick-and-roll wasn't very popular. Like the zone read in college football, the pick-and-roll is a simple play, with lots of potential wrinkles that depend upon how the defense responds to the initial move. Here's how it usually worked for Stockton and Malone: Malone raced down the court and planted himself like an oak tree on the edge of the key. Stockton brought the ball up and glided past Malone, forcing his defender to run into Malone's pick. Before the defense could switch and recover, Malone would turn and barrel toward the basket. Still dribbling, Stockton would flick a phantom sidearm pass that buzzed past a defender's ear before being snatched from thin air by Malone, who slammed home a dunk while being uselessly hacked by a slow-to-react opponent. Then he calmly went to the line to sink his free throw. Rinse and repeat a dozen or more times every game. For variety, Stockton sometimes shot a jumper instead of passing to Malone, who sometimes spotted up for a jumper of his own.

Stockton and Malone were seemingly joined at the hip, by which I mean they were mentally bonded to one another. They had the "one mind" hive thing going big time, mirror neurons firing synchronously, always one step ahead of their opponents. Their on-court teamwork was something to behold.

Mirror neurons help explain the biological basis of our morality just as they help explain the biological basis of our teamwork in sports. Empathy isn't something we must imagine or conjure up to understand and get along with others. Instead, it's an instantaneous connection that we feel when our brains simulate what is occurring in the brains of others. First, we imitate people, and only then are we capable of understanding them. In that sense, our bodies take priority over our minds. Actually, the mind is an extension of the body just as thoughts are an extension of our more basic feelings. Without the body, which includes the brain, there is no mind. Morality is an embodied way of knowing and responding to others. Mirror neurons provide hard evidence of that circumstance. Here's a fair question though: Just how far can the mirror neuron explanation of morality take us?

Granted, we have genuine moral feelings for others that are rooted in our biology. Does that mean mirror neurons are sufficient to explain the full extent of our moral experience? I think there is much more to morality than just being in synch with others. If that's all there was to morality, we wouldn't need a conscience. We don't just mimic others, although that is crucial to how we learn from them. We also seek opportunities to outwit them and get away with things. Conscience is nothing if not cunning in that sense. It calculates risks and rewards, making use of empathy and understanding to minimize the chances of falling out of favor with others for being overly self-serving. Mirror neurons, it seems, can only account for part of our full-bodied moral experience. The cunning side of morality requires something more complex from our mental repertoire.

Evolutionary psychologists have taken a different tack toward understanding morality than mirror neuron theorists. They think the brain consists of dozens, perhaps even hundreds, of semi-independent modules that perform algorithm-driven tasks beneath the level of consciousness. An algorithm is a mathematically precise set of instructions for how to accomplish something. To take one example, about 20 percent of the brain is dedicated to managing our eyesight. (Other parts participate in vision as well.) To coordinate what we see requires millions of computations. Colors must be adjusted, in addition to light, depth, contrast, shape, and so forth. The slightly different perspectives of our binocular eyes must also be blended together. In short, myriad behind-the-scenes calculations underscore the seemingly simple act of opening our eyes to look at the world around us. Our conscious selves have little to do with it. A functional brain module takes care of everything without the need for awareness.

Each major function in life—seeing, hearing, dreaming, talking, and so on—has its own dedicated brain module, according to the computational theory. That includes morality. It would be plausible to equate the moral module with conscience, or at least the part of it that is devoted to unconscious risk assessment. We are constantly weighing the risks and rewards for our behavior. For example, a baseball player may wonder whether to steal second base. His brain has already calculated the risk of being thrown out, which goes a long way toward determining the self-conscious "decision" to stay put or go for it. The brain communicates the risk to the self through a feeling. If it's too risky, the feeling is more dreadful; if it is low risk, the feeling is more hopeful. That's how the calculations of the moral module would influence our behavior.

I think our moral experience entails the workings of both mirror neurons and a computational module. One system or theory alone is insufficient to account for everything about us. On the one hand, we genuinely care about one another, especially those we are most familiar with. We want to help them when they are suffering; we feel their pain. These are honest feelings, with no ulterior motives lurking in the recesses of the mind. Mirror neurons help us to understand how such empathy arises in the brain without the need for algorithms and calculations.

On the other hand, we really are opportunistic risk-takers who love nothing more than to exploit our advantages. We have a natural predisposition to want to compete with those around us, particularly if they are not part of our small social group or team. It gives us great pleasure to outwit our competitors. That requires a calculative mind, capable of assessing opportunities and risks without having to stop and think. A computational moral module—a calculating conscience—helps us to understand how such cunning arises in the brain independently from our less devious mirror neurons.

We need a neuroscience "complementarity thesis" to appreciate both aspects of our moral experience, not just one or the other. That's something I learned to appreciate in a college physics class. In physics, the complementarity thesis says that visible light (and any other form of electromagnetic radiation) behaves like a wave *and* a particle at the same time. It's paradoxical but true. We can't appreciate the complexity of light—its full measure—without viewing it as if it were simultaneously two different things. Waves behave one way, particles (tiny objects) another. How can it be both at the same time? Circumstances, as well as the limitations of our theories, go a long way toward answering that question. In some circumstances, the wave theory is better at capturing how light behaves; in other circumstances, the particle theory is better. The same holds true for the neurobiological theories of our moral experience.

When cunning is involved, computational theory makes sense. When the synchronicity of our minds is involved, we are better off looking to mirror neurons for an explanation. Both are necessary to understand the full extent of our morality. This duality in our moral experience might actually be a consequence of how the human brain evolved. Some parts of the brain are ancient, the brain stem, for example. It probably reaches back to when mammals first appeared a couple of hundred million years ago. We know that mirror neurons are shared by all primates, so they are fairly ancient as well, going back at least 60 million years.

On the other hand, some parts of the human brain are of recent origin: the frontal lobes of the neocortex, for example. That's the part of the brain responsible for our higher cognitive functions, including self-awareness and conscience. It is more calculative in its workings, less spontaneous than the more ancient mirror neurons. It's as if we have two different brains contributing to the complicated and extensive terrain of our moral experience. Sometimes they work well together, sometimes they work at cross-purposes. That's why there is so much potential for internal conflicts, hypocrisy, and mixed motives in our moral behavior. We are riding the dragon of competing brain influences.

When did athletic competition really begin? Maybe it was when we grew those big frontal lobes. Our minds evolved for the moral game of matching wits with one another. We are prone to generosity and, at the same time, selfish conniving. As I said earlier, that moral paradox haunts every social interaction that we engage in. Only a complementarity thesis can explain the full range of our moral complexity.

7

FANDOM: WHY WE WATCH AND CARE SO MUCH

I'm a television sports junkie. It's the only thing that stops me from chucking my cable contract when I get sick and tired of watching 10 mind-numbing commercials in a row about the latest pharmaceuticals designed to improve my irritable bowel syndrome, erectile dysfunction, and every other private misfortune imaginable.

If I get rid of the cable, how will I be able to watch so many live sporting events? That's the sine qua non that has kept me paying those outrageous fees month after month. I know, I know, I should look into an internet streaming service instead. I should probably play fantasy football too, instead of caring so much about the real thing. When did I become such a luddite?

My favorite season is fall. When the leaves start turning red and the air has that frosty bite to it, I feel invigorated. Not just happy—*really invigorated*. I've often wondered why. The change of season must have something to do with it. Maybe it's the slow extinction of summertime hopes and dreams that I find so agreeable about fall. Summer is always imbued with so many expectations that it can't possibly live up to them. It's an unrequited season, all too short and invariably disappointing because of it. Then fall arrives like a soothing balm. There, there.

Let's be honest—*football* is what really invigorates me when the leaves start turning.

Perhaps March Madness has no rival in terms of American sports pageantry given its existential purity. You either win or go home. If you survive until the end you are the undisputed champion. There's no need for a poll. Football is a different kind of animal. Personally, I find the holiday avalanche of college bowl games every bit as compelling as March Madness.

You can't play football twice in a weekend like basketball teams routinely do. It's too grueling for that. There are more elements of risk and chance at play in football. Even the ball is designed to take funny bounces. On a given day, the best team might run into a streak of rotten luck. It happens. That means it's always arguable who the best team really is. Even if we had a perfect playoff system, there would be room for doubt about who the champion is. You can't always settle it on the field, with college football, in particular. How do you compare two teams that never played one another or a common opponent? There will always be an element of human judgment that can't be scrubbed from football. Arguments and polls are part of the experience. I think that's why fantasy football has become such a significant game in its own right, a fan's game that repurposes the "real" game happening on the field. I'll say more about that a bit later.

Throughout the week, I anticipate Saturday's slate of televised football games. Thursday and Friday games are mere appetizers. My favorite teams invariably include the Iowa Hawkeyes, Oregon Ducks, Notre Dame Fighting Irish, and any teams from the Big Ten, Pac-12, or Mountain West that are having good seasons. I admit it: I'm a fair-weather fan with a bias that slants toward the West and Midwest regions of the United States. Basically, all that means is that I like to attach myself to a winner. It's why I became so endeared to Oregon when Chip Kelly was their coach. (I also happen to live in Oregon.) They won a lot of games, usually in dramatic fashion. If Iowa is having a good year, I root for them—even over Oregon—because I went to Iowa. For me, loyalty to alma mater counts a lot more when we are winning. It's a sliding scale computation, loyalty. I never know what to expect from Iowa coach Kirk Ferentz's team. About the time I think he should be fired, they go 11–0 in the regular season, as they did in 2016.

Here's the funny thing about watching football games and other sporting events on television: I have a hard time actually watching the game from beginning to end. I squirm. I get my hopes jacked up. I feel inklings of despair if my team suffers any hint of a setback. So what do I do? I channel surf instead of watching the game I waited all week to see, checking back occasionally for scoring updates. It's hard to explain or even fathom. I feel compelled to watch and *not watch* at the same time, adrift in a self-imposed yin-yang twilight zone. Is that crazy or what?

What is it about being a sports fan that turns me into a superstitious television junkie? Why do we care so much? In this chapter, I will explore what makes being a sports fan so captivating. I'll start by continuing the discussion of mirror neurons from the last chapter.

Whenever Michael Jordan did something even mildly spectacular (by his standards) on the basketball court, for example, soaring to the basket for a one-handed windmill dunk, the same mirror neurons that fired in his brain also fired in the brains of his adoring fans. They felt the same feelings he did. They didn't just want to be *like* Mike, as a ubiquitous Nike ad of the Jordan era proclaimed. Even fans like me who only watched Jordan play on television instead of in person actually shared in his achievement. That's the power of mirror neurons. UCLA neuroscientist and avid tennis fan Marco Iacoboni put it very simply: "To see the athletes perform is to perform ourselves."[1]

Mirror neurons create cognitive connections that bring us so close together that we actually participate in the experiences of others.

Think about it: Why would I bother to watch if watching didn't engage me experientially? Being a fan is not a passive experience. Maybe watching soap operas can turn you into a couch potato, but being a sports fan can't. It's a full-body engagement—a contact sport, as they say—an opportunity to get a taste for what we are observing. We put ourselves into Jordan's place on the court, incorporating his actions into our own bodies, simulating (channeling) his mental activities. When he rises up for a jump shot, in my mind I'm rising up to do it with him. If I really get carried away, I'll actually jump up and imitate the shot like a shadowboxer who throws punches in the air at a make-believe target. It's not exactly a self-directed (conscious) action. In concert with the mind, the body too is capable of replicating what is being observed on its own initiative. It's like a reflex action, or a reaction. Someone smiles at me, I automatically smile back. It happens without thinking. In fact, it would take deliberate effort to *stop* the reflex to smile back. Such is the power of mirror neurons concerning our reactions to others, especially athletic heroes.

Scout bees search for pollen, then return to the hive to let other bees know where to find it. How do they do that? They *dance*. By imitating their dance, the other bees pick up geographical cues that will lead them to the pollen. In many ways, we are just like those bees. We understand one another by imitating one another. We evolved to live in close cognitive proximity with our neighbors so that we could mirror their thoughts. We are mind–body readers. We crave opportunities to observe and vicariously experience athletic performances like we crave sugar (honey) in our diet. They are satiating experiences that we enjoy repeating again and again.

Have you ever been at the ballpark and noticed that even someone engrossed in conversation will suddenly look up at the crack of a bat that sends a baseball soaring over the fence? It's involuntary, and irresistible. To witness such a marvel is enlivening. It refocuses our attention on the game, however briefly.

Vicarious experiences are not merely the work of imagination. We aren't daydreaming (fantasizing) when we see ourselves in Jordan's shoes. Instead, our bodies synchronize themselves to Jordan's body. It's like a conversation, except the language is nonverbal and ancient. What often takes great effort to accomplish verbally—a meeting of the minds—is effortlessly achieved in a glance whenever we observe one another. That's because our mirror neurons fire sympathetically, communicating a sense of belonging together from one brain to another. It's why we are predisposed to making friends. (There are other reasons why we are predisposed to making enemies.)

The harmonious firing of our mirror neurons is a moral language at heart. It begins with watching others and listening to them. It doesn't work when we are alone in the world, or when the people we watch aren't engaged in some meaningful activity. Watching someone sit still doesn't excite our mirror neurons. There has to be intentional movement that our minds are capable of comprehending. The eye is attracted to movement, but mirror neurons are attracted to the intentions that make movement possible. There is a similarity and a difference between the two kinds of attraction.

When mirror neurons fire, they are not simply registering movement that the eye has noticed. The movement has to entail some purpose, or meaningful content. Action catches the eye, but it is *drama*—meaningful action—that holds our attention. Meaning is created when we understand the intentions behind an activity. We don't ascribe meaning to random acts: a leaf falling from a tree, for example. We make sense of the behavior of others by interpreting it as a story with future ramifications. Mirror neurons represent the beginning of our capacity to care and empathize in this sense—to picture how the story might unfold when someone intentionally does something that we find intriguing.

Imagine Michael Jordan reaching out to intercept an ill-advised pass. From a fan's perspective, it isn't random action. It is chock full of meaning because of the narrative possibilities. If he succeeds in stealing the pass, then he will most likely race down the court for an easy dunk. And if the steal were to occur at the end of a close game, it could mean the difference between winning and losing. Everything that a fan cares about comes into focus in that potential stolen pass. It is a dramatic moment, compelling in its ability to capture our undivided attention, to light up our brains.

Mirror neurons promote a cognitive connection—a sharing of identity and experience—between those who watch and those who perform. That's one reason why we find being a fan such a compelling experience. There are others that are just as significant. One pass over the arena (or the cuckoo's nest) isn't sufficient to explain everything that's going on there. It's too rich and complex for that. So let's take another look from a different angle.

Forest canopies served as the first arenas, where primates could huddle together in safety and watch the dramas of life unfold beneath them. What probably began as the protective behavior of parents watching over their offspring as they played with nary a worry about the dangers around them eventually became an interesting pastime in its own right. For our species—the primate with the greatest facility for creatively rendering what we observe—the desire to watch others play eventually led to the orchestration of loosely structured performances and competitions that could be enjoyed as entertainment. That, I suspect, is how sports fandom got its start long before civilization took root. Without our natural predisposition to enjoy watching others play, there wouldn't be such modern games as basketball.

The play of games echoes (mimics) age-old competitions for survival. Even modern sports stand in the shadow of that greater game of life. Modern athletes still rely on the adrenaline-induced panic that stirred our ancestors to run for their lives from the deadly pursuit of predators. Would athletic competition as we know it today be conceivable without the motivating effects of adrenaline and other hormones that have coursed through the animal kingdom for millions of years? The heritage of our distant past still lives within us—still helps to shape what we do and why we do it. We find modern sports so tantalizing, I believe, because they embody an ancient call of the wild. They transport us back to what we once were.

In Jack London's popular novel *The Call of the Wild*, a large mixed-breed St. Bernard named Buck slowly rekindles his wild wolf nature after suffering at the hands of cruel people.[2] Buck was born in California, a happy pet with a good home until he was kidnapped and eventually shipped to Canada for use as a sled dog to service Klondike gold miners. It was a harsh life, and Buck was traded many times, each new owner seemingly worse than the last. Finally, he caught a break when a good man named Thornton rescued him. He and Buck were devoted to one another. The last tentacles of Buck's domesticity were severed forever when Thornton was murdered. Afterward, Buck became the wolf that had always been part of him from the beginning.

I think London's story is so appealing because it reminds us that the past never really disappears completely. In our bodies and genetic makeup, the memories and experiences of long ago still persist, awaiting their chance to be reawakened. The joy of running that I wrote about in the introduction is a good example of what I mean. Something aboriginal awakened in me when I took up jogging. Like Buck's wolf nature, it had always been there, a latent instinct still available if and when the right opportunity came along. This, I believe, is what happens to us when we become fans of modern sports as well. The passion we feel is a recovery of what we once were. It revives our natural instincts to watch and take pleasure in the feats of others. It also revives our ancient moral instincts to form into tribal groups that look askance at those who cheer for the other side.

Sharks have persisted practically unchanged for four hundred million years. That's a long time. Hominids like us have only been around for a few million years by comparison. Nature doesn't mess with a formula that works. It sticks with it, repeating itself until something forces it to change. That's why the experiences of our past persist in our genetic heritage and body memory. Nature privileges what has worked well in the past, out of which the future (new life) emerges on tentative legs like a newborn wildebeest. I think that's one of the reasons why we are prone to feelings of nostalgia, and to overestimating the value of the good old days. Nature itself imbues us with that instinctual bias.

Utopias come to mind as a memory of something from long ago. The Garden of Eden is the perfect example. Even science fiction tales that take place in the future find their meaning and structure from the mythologies of human memory. What is *Star Wars* but an ancient tale of good versus evil that has been told and retold since time began? We long to recover the time of innocence, the lost garden of our becoming. That same nostalgia, I suspect, is the basis for loyalties to country and sports teams. We nurture it by singing the national anthem at the beginning of athletic contests.

Being a fan is a regressive experience in the sense that it recaptures (reinvigorates) what we once were. We regress into moral tribalism as fans, feeling disdain—even hatred in some conditions—for the opposing team and its fans. Tribalism is a moral feeling of group loyalty that naturally includes a xenophobic element: a tendency to mistrust other groups. It hearkens back to the ancestral environment where bands of early humans often competed against one another for food when environmental conditions were harsh. Members of rival groups were untrustworthy because they would steal your food or, worse, to ensure their own survival. Remember that morality evolved to help small bands of humans function more efficiently, like teams, thereby increasing their chances of success. It didn't evolve to assuage the conflicts and competition between rival groups. We witness that fact in the sports arenas and stadia throughout the world, where fights and riots between rival fan bases—rival tribes—are more common than we care to admit.

Reverting to a tribal sense of fan loyalty is not a bad thing, although the potential for conflicts between rival fan bases is real enough. Most of the time, thankfully, we don't indulge those rowdy tendencies. We prefer to get along, as our ancestors did when there was enough food for everyone. Attending a sporting event is usually a form of celebration, which is a more participatory entertainment experience than, say, watching television. Pregame celebrations are welcoming rituals, full of expectation and hope. Fans get together to tailgate before football games—sharing food, drinks, laughs, and banter—with friends and strangers alike. Adopting the transient persona of a sports fan breaks the ice that too often isolates us from one another. As a result, there is less loneliness in stadiums and their parking lots. Being a sports fan provides a home-like nexus within which to relax and let go of our normal guardedness. A game—a seemingly trivial event—helps us to briefly shed the burdensome cares of everyday life. To enter into a make-believe world that refreshes the spirit has always been the purpose of play, which includes watching the play of others.

There is a dialectical interplay of remembering and forgetting (an irony of historicity) at work in the artful practice of being a sports fan. It takes us back in time to what we once were. Yet, in that very act of remembrance we exploit the opportunity to forget ourselves and become as playful as children once again. Without the recollection of our watchful heritage—the call of the wild—it wouldn't be possible to forget and let go of our worldly cares. We lose our preoccupied selves by becoming engrossed in what transpires on the field of play in front of us. It works like a salve on the soul. Memory would be irrelevant without forgetting because there would be nothing that needed recalling. Likewise, forgetting would be impossible were it not for a lapse of memory. These things belong together, a vital circle connecting what we are today to what we used to be.

Border state and intrastate rivalries between universities bring out some of the most elaborate jokes and put-downs among fan bases. It can get ugly or (much more likely) just plain silly. Growing up in South Dakota, for instance, I attended many basketball games between the South Dakota State University Jackrabbits and the University of South Dakota Coyotes. At the risk of stating the obvious, these schools didn't like one another much. On occasion, a drunken SDSU fan would heave a dead coyote onto the floor while his academic counterpart from down the road did the same with a dead jackrabbit. The reaction was a predictable mixture of moans, jeers, chuckles, and head shakes. The public announcer would admonish the crowd using blatantly ineffective reverse psychology: "Thank you for not throwing things onto the court!"

How do you sneak a dead carcass into an arena? Who does such things? Being an animal lover, I never appreciated the intended levity.

More recently, while I was walking my dog at a state park in Oregon, a stranger asked me if I knew why Oregon State University Beavers fans wear orange clothing. The state of Oregon divides along the "civil war" fan bases of the UO Ducks, who used to wear green and yellow before Nike created ten thousand Ducks uniform color variations, and the

OSU Beavers, who wear orange and black. Wondering how he could tell from looking at me that I was a Ducks fan, not a Beavers fan, I played along and asked him why. He winked and looked around conspiratorially. "It's so they can collect garbage along the highways during the day, then spend the evening relaxing in their prison cells."

That's got to be the lamest joke I ever heard.

We like it when contrasts between the good guys and bad guys are unmistakable. That's why we have a soft spot for stories like *Star Wars* that are Manichean in their plot line. Manicheism is an ancient moral doctrine that viewed the universe as an everlasting battleground between good and evil. Darth Vader gave into the dark side of the Force, while Obi-Wan Kenobi remained loyal to the Force's good side. What could be more black and white than that? We have a natural tendency to cast characters as either villains or heroes. It's a survival strategy. Instantaneous judgments enable us to identify likely competitors and enemies. There is no room for 50 shades of gray in the struggle for survival. That is also true in professional wrestling, which, ironically, occupies a gray space between "real" sports and the contrived theatrics of soap opera.

Professional wrestling matches are choreographed morality plays. I suspect that's why we love watching them so much. Villains, or heels, as they are called, square off against babyfaces. Babyfaces are a naïve version of the typical "good guy" character. They are convinced, as are their fans, that heels will fail because cheaters never win in the long run. If only life were that simple. Villains are adept at choking, stomping, biting, kneeing, kidney punching, and all manner of illegal maneuvers behind the back of the hapless referee who always seems to be looking the wrong way. By design, the crowd is all too aware of what is happening behind the referee's back. They howl their disapproval at every transgression. It's a vaudeville act (exaggerated drama) that agitates our sense of fair play and natural disdain for cheaters.

The popularity of professional wrestling correlates with its moral appeal. As fans and moral agents alike, we have a natural desire to protect the innocent from bullies. That's why we scream when the heel gets away with his dirty tricks. It's a tried and true formula of the ring. We empathize with babyfaces, although heels get the most fame and glory. Like the former, we bear the scars and humiliations from the sucker punches perpetrated against us by real-life bullies/villains. In our heart of hearts, we want to believe that every winner in the ring, as in life, must be as honest as the day is long. We are morally outraged at the thought that a cheater might win despite the evidence in life to the contrary. Our screams about the injustices that occur in the ring also serve as a proxy protest against injustices suffered in everyday life. Making that connection between what happens in the ring and what happens in our own lives is a cathartic (healing) experience. It's why we like to watch.

I haven't watched anything even remotely similar to a professional wrestling match since Muhammad Ali fought Japanese wrestler Antonio Inoki to a draw in 1976. (Ali is the only iconic athlete who I ever actually met in person: A friend and I visited his Catskills training camp in 1978.) Despite my own ambivalence toward the sport, I am familiar with the villainous personas of Rowdy Roddy Piper, Andre the Giant, and Randy Savage, to name a few famous wrestlers. Short of doing a Google search, I am unable to generate a comparable list of memorable babyfaces. Why is it easier for me to remember the heels of the ring? Why are they the bigger stars? I think it's because we have a natural tendency to pay more attention to someone who is a potential bully. We watch them like a hawk, just as any primate would track the movements of a predator passing nearby. To ignore such a danger would be foolish indeed. On the other hand, to pay the same level of attention to a nonthreatening person would probably be a waste of valuable mental resources. Memory becomes sharper as the potential for harm grows stronger. It's a survival mechanism that carries over into human culture. We like our heroes to have a little menace in them because it makes them that much more memorable—and irresistible. Wilt Chamberlain had that effect on people. So did Lawrence Taylor and Dick Butkus. Even imaginary superheroes have a foreboding element to their personas. Batman had his dark moods, the Incredible Hulk his unpredictable temper, and so on.

It isn't just contrived sports like professional wrestling that play on our fascination with good guy/bad guy moral scripts. It's an innate narrative template that we readily apply to all sports whenever the opportunity arises. The Oakland Raiders of the 1970s and 1980s were considered the "bad boys" of the NFL. They played aggressive, hard-nosed football that flirted with the edge of respectability. Their black and silver uniforms radiated potential menace. When you played them, you expected a street fight. The Detroit Pistons played a similarly physical (brutal) style of basketball in the 1990s. Many accused them of playing dirty. They embraced their controversial image, and it carried over into the stands. The rebels among us often loved them, while traditionalists loved to hate them.

Our inner sense of justice is naturally egalitarian. It's why we have always hated bullies and rooted for underdogs. We also have a natural tendency to admire athletes who are humble and gracious, like our hunter-gatherer forebears on the African savannah tended to be. There are exceptions, of course. Broadway Joe Namath was admired for his bravado. He guaranteed that the upstart New York Jets would win Super Bowl III, and they did just that. As baseball great Dizzy Dean said, "It ain't bragging if you can back it up." Muhammad Ali—the "Louisville Lip"—was flashy and outrageous as a young man. He didn't become humble and universally beloved until much later in life. A lot of football fans hate the New England Patriots. Some of it is probably rooted in jealousy since they have won six Super Bowls. That's not the only reason for the antipathy, however. The Spygate and Deflategate controversies add to the mix of suspicions about their willingness to cheat. Some believe they benefit from lucky plays more often than other teams do. Their win over the Seattle Seahawks in Super Bowl XLIX on a goal line interception at the end of the game was improbable at best. Interestingly, Tom Brady seems to get a pass from many Patriots haters. I think it's because he seems so humble.

I have been arguing that one of the reasons we love watching sports is because they mimic the survival conditions of our ancestral past. To be a fan is a homecoming of sorts, reminding us of what we once were. It's that connection to our past that invigorates our tribal tendencies and moral scripts as fans. We fall under the spell of that primordial nostalgia. There's one more additional perspective on why we care so much as fans that I want to explore now.

In *The Practice of Everyday Life*, Michel de Certeau claimed that reading is a subversive moral practice.[3] When we read a novel, for instance, we don't just accept the story as the author presents it. We read ourselves into the lives and situations of the characters. We make use of the story for our own purposes. We interpret the world in the same way, by reading it according to our own desires. Every act of reading is an editorial commentary of sorts, a form of rewriting that puts our interests first. This kind of moral appropriation extends to every aspect of our lives, including the consumption of manufactured products.

When we purchase clothes at the store, we don't just wear them as they were intended to be worn by the manufacturer. If it is a pair of jeans, we might distress their look by tearing holes in the knees. Manufacturers decide how something ought to be used, but consumers have their own ideas. They make use of things, repurposing them for other uses that are more to their own liking. Just as we rewrite what we read to suit ourselves, we remanufacture what we consume to create our own products that serve us better. Think of the disc jockeys who decided to create their own sound by intentionally skipping the turntable needle back and forth across a vinyl record. It's a creative act that was never intended by the original artists and producers. But it goes to the heart of how we feather our nests to make our lives reflect who we are. Everyday life is full of creative acts that subvert the intentions of the manufacturers and power brokers of the world.

Sports fans take creative liberties with what they consume (watch) as well. I like to watch multiple college football games at once by flipping channels. That's a little lame as a subversive activity, but I think it qualifies. At a recent Portland Trail Blazers game, I decided to conduct an amateur scientific experiment. Instead of watching the actual basketball game, I turned my ethnographer's gaze upon the fans to see what they were up to. Were they engrossed by Damian Lillard's ball-handling wizardry? Or were they mostly doing other things of their own design and choosing? That's what I wanted to know.

What I found most striking was the constant stream of people moving up and down the Moda Center stairs to the concourse exits, where bathrooms and food vendors could be found. It was like a pilgrimage, the faithful patiently lining up and waiting their turn to refresh themselves. One couple that I observed spent the entire two hours eating a giant bowl of nachos drenched with gooey cheese and topped with delicious meats. It was a feast, not a snack. The game ended before they were able to finish it. Another couple spent the entire game giggling and cuddling like newlyweds. Perhaps they were newlyweds. A lot of fans were preoccupied with their smart phones: texting, taking selfies, posting pictures, and so forth. Some fans preferred to watch the game on a flat screen monitor while sipping a brew at one of several arena bars. Based on what I saw, I suspect that most people weren't there to watch basketball per se. Instead, they were there to do other things of their own choosing, making their own uses of the game. That's my hypothesis anyway.

Sporting events are like clay in the hands of a sculptor. Rather than passively accepting games as prepackaged products, we make our own artful uses of them. We sculpt things to suit our purposes. We don't just watch, we take creative liberties to express ourselves. That's another reason why we love being sports fans. It provides us an opportunity to be subversive in entertaining fashion. We heckle referees, for instance, and scream at players to distract them so that they will make boneheaded mistakes. We make snide comments about the facilities, or the team mascot, or the ineptitude of the NFL commissioner, and so on, to entertain strangers sitting next to us in the stands. Humor and laughter are the most benign and universal methods we employ to personalize and redefine our experiences. Nothing is more infectious—and potentially deceptive—than a hearty laugh.

Fantasy sports represent the ultimate expression of subversive consumption. Every major sport has fantasy leagues, but nothing compares to the multibillion-dollar fantasy football scene. In fantasy football, you join a league and pick players from real football teams to be on your fantasy team. When those players accomplish something on the real football field, your fantasy team is awarded points in accordance with your league's scoring system. Generally speaking, offenses dominate fantasy football, not defenses. The most common type of fantasy football league is the head-to-head variety, where each week you compete against one other fantasy opponent. Fantasy football competitors are called GMs (general managers) because that's their basic function: to evaluate talent, pick players, monitor player injuries, trade players, and so on. For many competitors, fantasy football becomes an all-consuming obsession. As Mark St. Amant put it in his fantasy football memoir, "Fantasy football can seize you in its clutches and just *own* you, take over your life."[4]

St. Amant actually quit his job at the age of 30 so that he could devote his entire working life to fantasy football. He gave himself six months to see if he could master the game and somehow earn a living doing it. His gamble paid off when he was able to get a book contract about the experience.

Fantasy football competitors remake the game of football into something different than originally intended. They seem to care at least as much about their fantasy team results as they do real team results. It's possible to win prizes and money playing fantasy football, but most competitors play for bragging rights. They are highly motivated to humiliate (crush) their friends and competitors. I think that's a big part of the attraction in sports gambling, too, as I discuss in the next chapter.

In this chapter, I have tried to demonstrate that sports fandom is a complex experience with deeply held motivations that reach back to our origins as a species. We love to watch athletes perform because it excites the mirror neurons in our brains. It's how we evolved to understand one another. The fandom experience also rekindles our ancient tribal feelings of in-group solidarity and out-group mistrust. We have natural propensities to interpret contests using age-old scripts about good and evil. It pleases us to recognize events in such a manner. We also love to transform and rewrite what we observe on the field of play into something more suitable for our own purposes. For at least fifty thousand years, we have been the ethnographers and artists of our own experience.

There is light and darkness in the experience of being a sports fan. I think the good far outweighs the bad—fandom is not a Manichean tale, like *Star Wars*, with its eternal struggle between good and evil—although it would be foolish to overlook the dark side of fandom. Fighting and domestic violence are an ugly reality that is frequently associated with sports. Excessive gambling, drinking, and other self-destructive behaviors are common as well. As the story of *Friday Night Lights* revealed, entire towns can get turned sideways when they harbor unrealistic dreams and aspirations that are tied to the fate of their high school football teams. In its obsession to win a state championship, the town of Permian itself became dark and mean.

I believe the light side of fandom is considerably stronger than the dark side. More often than not, we make peaceful gestures toward our rivals in the stands. We share jokes and commiserate about losses endured. We overcome the natural xenophobia that separates us tribally, making new friends in the process. It helps us see the world from a different perspective, which enables our good manners to smother the distrust that can still bubble up from our competitive ancestral experience.

In sports as in life, hope is more resilient and uplifting than despair is debilitating. We are naturally inclined to be slightly more optimistic than not. We are able to call upon that resilience and optimism by entering into imaginary worlds of playfulness that refresh our spirits. The possibility of such recreation is the very beginning of sports and the play of intentionally organized games. When something so small in significance as an artificially contrived game can displace the seriousness of worldly cares, it borders on a spiritual experience. At their powwows, Native American dancers often imitate animal spirits. They try to leave themselves behind and enter into the animal spirit world. That is the epitome of what play and recreation mean: to be so engaged by an alternative world that when you return to your everyday world you feel refreshed. I think the closest thing to that kind of spiritual recreation that I ever experienced as a sports fan came from watching Michael Jordan play basketball.

It's hard to put into words just how significant Michael Jordan was when he and the Chicago Bulls dominated the world of basketball. Jordan's stature transcended sports in many ways. Larry Bird—a legend of the game in his own right—once described Jordan as a basketball god. It almost seemed to fit. That's how bright Jordan's star shone in the basketball heavens. Whenever he stepped onto the court, no matter what city the arena happened to be in, every watchful eye was glued to him. It was a magnetic attraction. Every fan hoped (expected) to see something impossible happen. Whether it was true or not, people believed that Jordan could hang suspended in midair a good beat or two longer than the laws of physics would allow. It was as if Jordan lived on a different planet. Watching him play enabled us to experience what life would be like in that other place for a little while.

8

COCKFIGHTING, GAMBLING, AND VILLAGES

American anthropologist Clifford Geertz and his wife, Hildred (also an anthropologist), spent a year studying the southeastern Bali village Tihingan in the 1950s. Geertz wrote about the experience in "Deep Play: Notes on the Balinese Cockfight," a now-famous essay about cockfighting.[1] While in Tihingan, he collected data on 57 different cockfights—a considerable number of cockfights given that it was illegal to hold such events at the time (with one or two exceptions). Obviously, the legal ban didn't deter the Balinese.

Geertz described the circumstances of his first cockfight in his essay. He and his wife were still newcomers, which meant that the Balinese hadn't yet accepted them into their village. In fact, they studiously ignored the American couple as if they didn't exist. It's a Balinese trait to avoid encounters with strangers. They are meticulously well-mannered, which is why Geertz became so fascinated by their love of cockfighting. The stark contrast between the quiet, almost shy, Balinese and the explosive violence of their favorite sport seemed to defy comprehension.

That first cockfight was raided by the police. Pandemonium broke out as the villagers scattered for cover. After a moment of uncertainty, Geertz and his wife ran from the police as well. That's what broke the ice and endeared them to the villagers. The next day, they took great pleasure in mimicking the awkward attempts of the scientists to find a place to hide from the police. It amused them to no end that these dignitaries with authorization papers from the government were afraid of the local police, who would never have dared to arrest them. "In Bali," Geertz explained, "to be teased is to be accepted."[2]

Cockfights are held in the late afternoon and usually include 10 different matches that last anywhere from 15 seconds to five minutes. An umpire helps select the combatant roosters between matches. They are fitted with razor-sharp spurs by an expert who attaches them to the cock's leg with string. If neither bird has perished by the end of a brief round, the birds are picked up and pampered until the next round begins. The ring is just large enough (about 50 square feet) to accommodate the birds and their handlers, plus the umpire. Only men of high standing in the village are allowed to stand next to the ring. The owner of the winning cock is awarded the bloodied carcass of the vanquished one, which becomes the main course of a prideful dinner.

Two different kinds of gambling take place at a Balinese cockfight. The most significant kind is "center" betting, the other being "peripheral." The peripheral variety is the easiest for Americans to understand: Odds would be shouted out (never greater than 2-to-1, and usually closer to even) and bets accepted from members of the crowd. Debts were always paid in full immediately after the contest. There was no such thing as an IOU.

Center bets involved the owners of the birds, in addition to their kin and alliance members. In the village of Tihingan, there were four major power alliances. Cockfighting etiquette required them to participate in the center bet if one of their members was a contestant. Relatives were also expected to support their kin in center bets. As a result, wagers sometimes became extremely large. Only high-status villagers had the connections and resources to mount such an event. The entire village often became part of the contest in one way or another. That is why Geertz claimed that cockfighting revealed the social structure of Balinese life. Observing a cockfight was like seeing the Balinese for who they really were.

Cockfighting was never about cocks, although they were cherished animals. Nor was it about the money that could be made from gambling. There were a few gambling addicts in the village, but they were despised for misunderstanding the nature of the contest. The real purpose of cockfighting was to provide villagers with an opportunity to display their status honorably. This blood sport illuminated the moral universe of the Balinese. Theirs was a strict society that forbade outward displays of emotion and aggression. Yet, in the explosive aggression that occurred in the ring, the Balinese were able to experience vicariously the aggressive feelings that they were duty bound to keep under wraps. The cock was a stand-in for male villagers, a symbol of their masculinity and unexpressed ferocity.

By underwriting a cockfight that enervated the entire village, a high-status male demonstrated what it meant to be Balinese. You flirt with violence and death but stop short of participating in the real thing; you relish the losses of your opponents but never gloat or brag outwardly; you live in harmony for the sake of the village but secretly desire to be admired and put on a pedestal. This razor's edge at the heart of Balinese life can only be expressed indirectly through the cockfight. Only the metaphorical cock gets to strut and preen, revealing what every Balinese secretly desired to do for himself.

Putting down the big-shot behavior of individuals to enhance the survival of the group is a moral universal among indigenous people. That's the basis for the discord between socially acceptable manners and secret desires that cockfighting exploits. The winner of a cockfight experiences a brief moment of personal glory that is safely constrained behind a public mask of seeming indifference to such vanities. Likewise, the loser of a cockfight experiences a brief moment of personal despair, also constrained behind a public mask of indifference. This secretive moral dance is reminiscent of the birth of conscience as an internal warning system that tells us when our bullying tendencies have gone too far. The Balinese are masters of such *oblique* experiences. They come right up to the threshold of lording it over their neighbors, then stop for the sake of decorum and peaceable relations. That glimpse—that oblique experience—is satisfying (and safe) enough.

To be able to land an oblique blow against one's opponents without disrupting village life was the entire purpose of cockfighting. The purpose of gambling on a cockfight was to enable more villagers to participate in the faux violence. Placing a bet on one of the cocks was like buying stock in the owner's alliance. By placing their bets, villagers became partial owners themselves, with a correspondingly strong rooting interest in the outcome. It enabled them to feel what it was like to be an owner. In that sense, Balinese gambling was a form of empathy. Like mirror neurons that enable us to comprehend what goes on in the minds of others, gambling enabled the Balinese to share the experience of cockfight sponsorship with their high-status neighbors. Like morality, it served an egalitarian purpose.

The original purpose of morality, remember, was to encourage the sharing of resources and responsibilities to enhance the survival of small bands of hunter-gatherers. That instinct to share, I suspect, is the moral basis for gambling, which appears to be universal across all cultures. Gambling is similar to the social contagion that occurs when a troop of monkeys spots a leopard lurking in the shadows. They point and scream until every last member of the troop has been put on full alert. Gambling is a form of hyperalertness in that sense, but the contagion pertains to the excitement of competition rather than the threat of predation. Gambling is to the sports fan what steroids are to the athletic competitor. In other words, gambling is a performance enhancer because it simulates the experience of being stalked by a metaphorical leopard. Nothing commands our attention quite like the threat of being devoured by a wild beast.

More than other primates, we have learned how to repurpose such biological survival mechanisms as the instinct to become hyperalert in the face of danger. We put our instinctual feelings to alternative uses in the imaginary worlds that populate our daily lives, including athletic contests, theatrical productions, and the like. All mammals engage their survival instincts in play situations. Lion cubs stalk one another and practice launching surprise attacks. Zebras run and kick up their heels as if being chased by imaginary lions. Yet, no species takes imaginary play as far as we do. When Gayle Sayers weaved his way through NFL defenses on hips that gyrated better than Elvis's, he wasn't just playing a game. He was running for his life, quite literally. At least that's what his instincts believed. We can trick ourselves into believing that our lives are at stake even when that isn't the case. To be able to cry on demand is a feat that any good actor can accomplish. We are all stage actors, to paraphrase Shakespeare's famous line.[3] As a species, we love to play fantasy roles/games as if they were as real as life itself. The distinction between make-believe and reality is easily blurred because of our powers of imagination. Sometimes that gets us into trouble. Performance anxiety, for instance, could be viewed as a problem of having too much imagination.

Imagination is a powerful tool in the human playbook. To win a bet is to win a contest of the imagination over the fates that would force us to curb our fantasies until they matched reality. We don't tilt at windmills, but at time itself, hoping to be spared the inability to foresee what might happen in a hard-fought competition between equals. That hope is what compels us to place a bet.

It is practically impossible for a primate to ignore a leopard. Survival depends upon becoming fully alert to the threat that it represents. It's an automatic response. (If you had to think about it first, you'd probably be dead already.) The artificial stimulation of our attention to the level of alertness that occurs in sporting contests is difficult to turn away from as well. That's one reason why gambling can become so addictive. The brain is tricked into thinking its survival is at stake; therefore, the addicted gambler cannot turn away from the prospect of one more bet. In moderation, gambling can serve an egalitarian purpose—enabling more Balinese to share the experience of owning a cock, for example. In excess, it can become a vice of bitter consequences, which is probably why modern morality has been critical of gambling. That appears to be changing, as more states aside from Nevada are coming on board with legal sports betting. I suspect that fantasy football's popularity has played a significant role in that attitude shift.

Fantasy football is unlike traditional gambling. You don't stand in line to place a bet like you would at a horse race. Instead, you create your own fantasy team of real players through a draft system. Your team's performance is based on the aggregate of each player's success during real-life games. It's a combination of fantasy and reality, as is a horse race or any other kind of betting situation. But the role that fantasy plays in fantasy sports is much larger. In a horse race, either your favorite horse wins or it doesn't. Nothing you can do will change that reality. In fantasy games, however, reality is already one step removed from the contest because the players have been selected to play for an imaginary team. There are two parts fantasy to one part reality in a fantasy contest, whereas in a traditional sports bet the reality-to-fantasy ratio is one-to-one: The horses run, and all you can do is fantasize about how they will finish. Fantasy football enables the gambler to be more actively engaged in the entire production of the game instead of passively awaiting the outcome of it.

Gambling is a way for a sports fan to become more invested in the contest. The bigger the role that fantasy plays in the contest, the more extensively fans will be able to invest themselves. Fantasy football fans are active contestants. There is no such thing as a fantasy football fan who isn't also a player/contestant. Contestants are called GMs (general managers), an indication of how important their role is to the entire enterprise. Without the fans, who are also the contestants, there is no fantasy football. That is a unique circumstance: The fan is both a consumer of the game and a contestant in the game.

In many ways, fantasy football is like the center bet of a Balinese cockfight. In a center bet, the entire village is drawn into alliances that become much more significant than the cockfighting. The "real" cockfight becomes a token or symbol for the "fantasy" competition that revolves around the status and honor of the villagers. The villagers themselves (the fans) are the real contestants, not the actual roosters. Fantasy football contestants dream about what it is like to be a GM, just as Balinese villagers dreamt about what it would be like to be a big shot (cock of the walk) for a day.

In circumstances where the fans are so actively invested that they take over the contest or its meaning, the outcome of betting becomes less about money and more about bragging rights. If you are focused on the money in a Balinese cockfight, you've missed the point. Judging from the numerous fantasy football memoirs I have read, the same can be said about fantasy football. No one plays for the money, or at least not for the money alone. As former NFL player Nate Jackson put it, what motivates his obsession with fantasy football is the desire to humiliate his friends.[4] Despite their preference for oblique forms of aggression, that is exactly what a Balinese would have said about a cockfighting wager.

Sports betting has recently become more customized to the preferences of fans. Fantasy sports stand at the extreme end of that trend, where the customization of the game by fans actually becomes a sport in itself. As a fan, I am no longer limited to betting on the outcome of a baseball game, for instance. Who wins and who loses isn't the only question of potential interest. Theoretically, I could place a bet on whether player X will hit better than .250 in his first three at-bats. Such fine-grained bets are possible because information about the game, including minutia about errors, at-bats, hits, and every newfangled analytic imaginable, is made available in real time by the booking agency's software system. Fan-centered betting up to and including fantasy football would not be possible without the real-time availability of game data that can be parsed and repackaged almost any way you like it. Sports betting in an automated, information-rich landscape is becoming an individualized experience, like the transformation that occurred in the beer industry when microbreweries began catering to the individual tastes of their customers.

In the Balinese cockfight, we get a glimpse of how sports and gambling coalesced into a complex moral drama that engaged the entire village. I suspect it takes a village, or a communal group of comparable complexity, to fully capture the tensions and subterfuges at play in the human effort to function as a moral hive. Here's a more forceful way to put it: The morally challenged village is the birthplace of sports and betting as we understand them today. That is the lesson I take from Geertz's interpretation of the Balinese cockfight. Other Stone Age village experiences seem to support that hypothesis.

Many Native American tribes played stickball, which is where the modern sport of lacrosse comes from. The game would often encompass entire villages and could last for days on end. As with the Balinese cockfight, the social stratifications and moral tensions of the village were revealed in the stickball contest. Disagreements between rival villages were sometimes resolved in a game of stickball, with hundreds of players competing on each side. It could get violent, even deadly. The rules of the game were amorphous and subject to change in varying circumstances. But the basic idea of using a sporting contest, along with betting as a means of cementing shared interests, to represent village society and resolve disputes was quite common in the Stone Age. The use of sports and betting in the village setting was, as Geertz observed, a creative way to dramatize the unresolved conflicts among villagers.

The group is more important than the individual, and yet every individual (males more egregiously than females) harbors a secret desire to bully or take advantage of others. That is a moral truism as old as human beings. Sports and betting emerged as a satisfactory expression of that ancient moral dilemma and a relatively safe means to resolve it peacefully. Only when the group got to the size and complexity of a village—several hundred people, roughly—could the full extent of the moral drama, along with its sporting resolution, become feasible.

Under the Mountain Wall chronicles Peter Mathiessen's experience with the Kurelu tribe in the Baliem Valley of New Guinea.[5] Mathiessen and colleagues on the Harvard–Peabody Expedition were the first Westerners to make contact with the Kurelu, who presumably were living in small villages much like humans had for tens of thousands of years. Interestingly, the male Kurelu spent most of their time engaged in ritualized war games with the tribe in the next valley. The groups would face one another from a distance and make menacing gestures with their Stone Age weaponry. It was rare for someone to be mortally injured. The social status of Kurelu warriors reflected their prowess on the front lines of the daily standoff. I think it is at least plausible that these Kurelu war games represent an earlier evolutionary form of such village sports as stickball and cockfighting, not to mention modern sports like lacrosse and American football. Football players, in particular, seem to line up and do "battle" in a similar fashion to the Kurelu. They have a warrior-like code as well, valuing strength, athletic prowess, bravery, loyalty, and aggression.

This kind of village morality, which encompassed conflicts of interest, power alliances, violent outbursts, masked hatred, glory and shame, status symbols, rituals, token fights, betting, and the like, is still visible in modern sports, although not always in the way that we might expect. I think the *Friday Night Lights* story discussed in a previous chapter is instructive as a cautionary example.[6] In the small towns of Texas, citizens invested their hopes and dreams in the fate of their high school football teams. The glorious fantasy of winning a state championship captivated the entire town. Each game became a referendum on the worthiness of their otherwise uneventful existence. One loss meant the postponement of happiness for yet another year in a life already inured to disappointment. Gridiron glory made small-town life tolerable, and the athletic prowess of local standout Boobie Miles represented an escape clause to a better life somewhere else. Then he got injured, and the better life went up in smoke.

A modern Texas town enraptured with its football team is only partially comparable to a Balinese village where life revolved around cockfighting. Both cockfighting and football represent means of escape from everyday constraints. To that extent, they are very similar. It is the purpose of their escapism that's so different, however. For the Balinese, cockfighting provided an escape from the rigid constraints of their manners. In the violent confrontation between the fighting cocks, the Balinese could symbolically let loose of their own pent-up aggressions. For the Texans, on the other hand, football provided an escape from their desperate belief that life had passed them by. In the achievements of the football team, their town found something to be proud of rather than one more thing to flee from. There are myriad ways to account for the differences and similarities between the Balinese and Texans. I offer one that makes sense to me.

According to Jared Diamond, the technological superiority that helped Europeans subjugate Native Americans and colonize the New World was an accident of geography.[7] It had nothing to do with their supposedly "superior" intelligence and values. Europe happened to lie on the edge of a continent with an axis that stretched from east to west, while the American colonies happened to lie on the edge of two continents that stretched from north to south. That's the only reason why Native Americans were a good thousand years behind the Europeans in their metallurgy and other critical capabilities.

Agriculture is the engine that made modern civilization possible. Twelve to fifteen thousand years ago, Stone Age hunter-gatherers gradually began domesticating plants and animals. That stable food source enabled them to settle down and build permanent villages, cities, and, eventually, vast empires. As empires grew and diversified their economies, more people were able to devote themselves to specialized professions for managing—and improving—practices pertinent to manufacturing, transportation, agricultural production, warfare, and other vital functions. Writing enabled them to preserve their knowledge and share it more easily with others. Libraries and schools became necessary, and the disciplined study of science and technology eventually accelerated the advances of civilization to a pace that we are familiar with today. The key to determining how far along the pathway toward modern civilization a given people had traveled was based almost exclusively on how long ago they had been exposed to domesticated plants and animals. The earlier in time they adopted an agricultural way of life, the further advanced their civilization would likely be. Europeans were exposed to agriculture much earlier than Native Americans because of the east-to-west axis of the Eurasian continent.

To lie on the same east-to-west axis as the Fertile Crescent, where agriculture first emerged, meant that Europe shared the same environmental conditions (soil, rainfall, growing season, etc.) that delimited the range within which newly domesticated grains could thrive. You can't grow wheat from the Middle East in the Arctic, for example. Plants need growing conditions that are similar to where they originated. They travel east to west successfully because geographies along the same latitude tend to be environmentally compatible. So Europeans benefited from lying to the west of the area where agriculture took root the earliest. Traveling merchants brought the new seeds and animals to European markets for barter.

The same benefits aren't available to continents that are aligned on a north-to-south axis because environmental conditions that are stable across latitudes change considerably as you move up and down longitudes. The further north you travel in North America, for instance, the shorter the growing season becomes. Domesticated plant species that migrate well from east to west don't migrate as well from south to north. That's the disadvantage Native Americans faced compared to Europeans. The potatoes, tomatoes, and llamas that were domesticated in South America never made it to North America because of the changing environmental conditions. Had they been domesticated on a continent more like Eurasia, the spread of agriculture could have been more uniform in the New World, as it was in the Old World.

Accidents of geography aside, one of the distinctive things about America is that we still have living memory of the frontier wilderness experiences that helped shape our national identity. To this day, our most precious mythologies are filled with a frontier spirit that is restless and optimistic about what might lie beyond the horizon. Instinctively, we identify with the free spirits of American folklore: cowboys on the open range; pioneers and settlers traversing half a continent in their prairie schooners; 49ers flocking to California in search of gold; mountain men living alongside Native Americans, who were all too often treated as subhuman. (Americans are more like the Native American tribes that were subjugated by white settlers than we care to admit, I suspect.)

As a modern civilization with unique connections to its wilderness past, the United States is a restless, roving (peripatetic) nation. We have a fear of being left behind, missing out on the next opportunity—the Big Rock Candy Mountain there for the pickings. Thomas Jefferson's Corp of Discovery Expedition, which sent Lewis and Clark from St.

Louis to the Oregon coast and back, still captivates us like no other adventure except perhaps the Apollo 11 mission to the moon. We overlook the moral shortcomings of Wild West gunfighters and outlaws, admiring their pluck and toughness. Football has become our most popular sport, eclipsing even baseball as the national pastime, because it is the epitome of a tough-guy sport. We believe that if you are tough enough—self-reliant, hardworking, uncomplaining—you can create your own destiny. That is the American dream.

America is a dreamer's paradise, a land of endless *new* opportunities and second chances. To be stuck without opportunity, tamed and saddle-broken, no longer free to pull up stakes and mosey along, is American-style despair. That's part of what makes a Texas town so different from a Balinese village. We dream of opportunities that are awaiting somewhere else, on the other side of the rainbow. Small-town football success is a ticket to that greater stage of imagination and possibility. I don't think it's a mindset that a Balinese villager would understand.

Many of the communal (village-like) qualities of our towns have been eroded by our individualistic inclinations. That's another thing that makes a Texas town different from a Balinese village. Alexis de Tocqueville, a Frenchman who studied American society in the 1830s with the same acuity that Geertz later studied the Balinese, was one of the first to recognize that Americans have a tendency to isolate themselves and pursue their own individualistic dreams of material success.[8] Over time, that indifference to the values and needs of a shared community life has led to even more isolation, loneliness, and, at times, incivility. It's a common debate in America today: Have we taken our concern for individual rights and freedoms too far? Has it led us to ignore the nurturing institutions and communitarian values that made individualism possible in the first place?[9] I think this helps explain why many small-town Texans (it happens in other states, too) are such fervent fans of their high school football teams.

Too much isolation in our towns is breaking the back of our natural moral preference for the welfare of the group over the individual. Instinctively, I think many of us sense that is the case, and it contributes to the small-town malaise that makes the football team that much more enticing. We rally behind the high school team because it reminds us of what it feels like to be part of something greater than ourselves. To be part of a moral community, a village, a team, is something that we naturally desire. We rely on sports to remind us of the communitarian nature of our moral experience. Happiness is a shared state of mind, not an individualistic one. Teams are happiest in their shared efforts. No one person is greater than the team, not even Boobie Miles. It is the absence, or paucity, of nonfootball-related community experiences that demonstrates the depth of similarity between a Texas town and a Balinese village. All people, no matter what level of civilization they may experience, have a need to be part of the hive. That is how we thrive as a species. Football and other sports remind us of that like few other experiences still can.

Finally, I want to close this chapter with a brief look at the concept of *Schadenfreude*. It's a German portmanteau that brings together two contradictory words: harm and joy. *Schadenfreude* refers to the pleasure or joy felt upon witnessing the misfortune or harm of others. It correlates well with the more familiar feeling of envy in a number of brain scan studies. In one study, 18 baseball fans (11 Red Sox fans, seven Yankee fans) were asked to rate their feelings when shown various game situations.[10] The results showed that fans experience slightly more pleasure at a rival team's failure than they do when their own team succeeds. It also found that negative feelings toward rival team fans correlates with a strong desire to heckle and harm them. That's not altogether surprising given the "us versus them" moral tribalism that undergirds our loyalties to sports teams, both as fans and players.

Schadenfreude isn't hard to comprehend when we are comparing different baseball fan bases, particularly ones with such ingrained odium for one another as the Yankees and Red Sox. Of course, a Red Sox fan would be delighted when a Yankee slugger strikes out. To expect a different reaction would be naïve at best. What about the Balinese villager who delights in delivering an oblique blow to a neighbor when he loses a cockfighting bet? That version of *Schadenfreude* seems a bit more complicated, and less comprehensible.

"Us versus them" animosity usually pertains to rival groups, not rival individuals within the same group. I think the desire to humiliate an in-group acquaintance is more akin to the egalitarian desire to put down big shots. In fact, *Schadenfreude* is often compared to the tall poppy syndrome, which is the resentment of high-status people. We like to see them get knocked down a peg or two. It's not "us versus them" so much as it is trying to prevent the potential for bullying. Recall that we developed a natural moral instinct to put down bullies so that our ancestors who lived in small egalitarian bands would stand a better chance of surviving.

We naturally care about our family and friends. There can be no doubt about that. Yet, we also enjoy besting them when we can in games and other "friendly" competitions. Not only that, sometimes we take a kind of moral pleasure when they suffer a setback if we believe the setback was warranted for some reason. Perhaps we thought our friend was too vain, or arrogant, or full of self-importance that needed to be corrected. Our moral feelings toward one another are complicated and varied. It would be naïve to think that we only have the best of intentions toward one another all of the time. Sometimes we have good moral reasons for not wishing the best for someone. Morality is a contact sport, and contradictory feelings like *Schadenfreude* are part of the picture.

Betting on a cockfight, or any other athletic contest, is born out of the secret desire to give someone else a metaphorical bloody nose. Betting is the antithesis of good manners. The lesson of this chapter is that you can't have one without the other. In sports, manners and betting go together. The tension between the two resides in our very nature, like yin and yang. Why else would it make sense to line up against one another and play fight in a rulebound, ritualized game that resembles warfare? Who would dream up such a pastime were it not within our nature to relish the endeavor?

Schadenfreude—taking pleasure in the misfortunes of others—is a complex moral feeling that gets to the heart of Balinese cockfighting. Balinese cockfighting, as I have tried to demonstrate, gets to the heart of what sports, betting, and morality are all about.

In the next chapter, I will explore the power of situations to manipulate and influence moral behavior in modern sports.

9

SITUATIONISM AND THE DYNAMICS OF MISBEHAVIOR

Most Americans believe that a person's behavior is a reflection of their settled character traits and integrity. For instance, we expect an honest person to tell the truth no matter what the consequences might be. That means we think of honesty as a habit or virtue that we feel obligated to uphold with few exceptions. If a thief were to ask where you hid your money, lying would be an acceptable (prudent) response. In most circumstances, however, the expectation is that a person of good character always tells the truth.

We assume that people of good character are reliable and trustworthy in their actions. When they don't measure up to that tacit reliability standard, we become suspicious of them. Lance Armstrong was banned from athletic competition for life because his egregious doping scheme rendered his character permanently suspect to authorities. We give people the benefit of the doubt—until they demonstrate that they can't be trusted. We might forgive mistakes, but we rarely forget them.

Does the natural instinct to judge people based on their character hold up under critical scrutiny? How sound is our everyday moral psychology? Surprisingly, there is an extensive body of scientific research that challenges the view that we behave consistently no matter what the circumstances. It turns out that even minor changes in situations can have a major impact on how we behave. This situationism research, as it is called, challenges the very idea that our lives are governed by something like a settled character or personality.[1] Instead, it seems to suggest that we are more fragmented and subject to the whims of slight changes in circumstances than we realize.

In this chapter, I will introduce several psychological studies of the situationism type and discuss their relevance to sports. I find that situationism provides an excellent lens through which to further refine my moral interpretation of sports.

In one study, 24 women and 17 men were observed using a pay phone in two different shopping malls.[2] The phones were rigged such that about half of the callers would find a free dime in the coin return slot, while the others would not find a dime. (Yes, in case you can't remember or weren't born yet, pay phones used to be ubiquitous prior to the advent of cell phones.) As subjects finished their calls and began walking away from the phone, an actress employed by the researchers "accidentally" dropped an envelope full of papers in their pathway. The purpose of the experiment was to see how many people would stop to help her pick up the papers. The results were startling. Fourteen out of the 16 subjects who found a dime stopped to help, whereas 24 of 25 subjects who didn't find a dime did not stop to help.

The study's conclusion that people are more likely to help when they are made to feel good isn't exactly earth-shaking news. Who hasn't experienced the benevolence that comes from being in a good mood? What is earth-shaking is that something as inconsequential as finding a dime could make such a big difference in how these people responded to the woman and her scattered papers. Common courtesy alone should have led a significant percentage of the subjects (if not all of them) to stop and help. That's what most of us would expect in such a situation. After all, we tend to believe that people of high character are courteous by nature, which requires that we render aid to those in need. Yet, that view isn't supported by the data. Almost every subject who didn't find a dime walked away without offering to help. Where's the courtesy and character in that? How on God's green Earth could a measly dime make such a Jekyll-and-Hyde-like difference?

This kind of counterintuitive result isn't just limited to situations where people find dimes. The smell of baking bread can put us into a helping mood just as effectively, as another study demonstrated.[3] Concern for others is an ethical universal in our society. Yet, in study after study, how people behave toward others is shown to depend upon minor changes in circumstances—a sniff of baked goods here, a dime found there, and so on. The threshold for inducing and/or inhibiting helping behavior is disturbingly low. These aren't heroic situations that subjects are facing. No one's life is being threatened. What gives?

Seinfeld is one of my all-time favorite television sitcoms. The clever premise of the show—to make a show about how two guys sold the concept of making a show about nothing to a major network—was fun and intriguing. I used to wonder, how long can they pull this thing off? A show about the frivolous details of their banal lives? It'll never last. It turns out I was dead wrong because the show lasted more than a decade. (Post-*Seinfeld* reality TV shows are even more frivolous, banal—and popular.) The two-part finale is what interests me here.

Jerry, George, Kramer, and Elaine are standing on the sidewalk watching a rotund man being robbed on the street in front of them. It never even occurs to them to try to intervene. Instead, they just stand there, making bemused jokes about fat people. After the robbery, as the insensitive foursome is about to leave, a policeman stops them for not trying to help the man. He explains the newly promulgated Good Samaritan law, requiring people to render aid in such situations. They reply that they've never heard of such a law. The officer arrests them anyway. In the second episode of the finale, the foursome stands trial, and every mean-spirited act from previous episodes of the show is used to malign them.

When I first saw the finale, I thought it was an ironic bit of self-criticism. Finally, these self-absorbed characters were getting what they deserved for being so damn shallow. That seemed to be the message. My interpretation is a little different now because of what I've learned about situationism research. We all have the capacity to behave as inconsiderately as the *Seinfeld* stars did. In fact, the greater the size of a group of bystanders who witness a crime, the less likely it is that any of them will render assistance to the victim. Bystander apathy, as it is called, is a social psychological effect that has been widely studied. In one such study, a group of subjects in an apartment was exposed to smoke from an apparent fire.[4] Instead of becoming concerned and calling for help, they ignored the problem. How could they disregard something so potentially dangerous?

It so happens that the presence of others sometimes inhibits us from taking action because we are unsure about whose responsibility it is to do something. Is it my job or yours? We also overestimate what other people seem to know, which allows their inaction to reinforce our own inaction. Everyone waits for someone else to do something, so nothing happens. As time passes, it gets easier to deny that anything is seriously wrong. (So there's a little smoke in the room, who cares?) It's like a vicious circle that inexorably leads to group paralysis.

Perhaps it is understandable that a sitcom like *Seinfeld* would depict the situational effects of bystander apathy with such trifling aplomb; however, the fact that the victim happened to be overweight is insufficient as an explanation of their failure to help. It doesn't require an insensitive prejudice to exhibit a lack of good character. Minor circumstances alone do the job all too well. That's true in sports also, as we will see shortly.

Situationism is not without its critics. The studies tend to be of the one-shot variety, which can't measure how we behave throughout time. Perhaps consistency of character fares better when people have the opportunity to face the same circumstances repeatedly. No one knows for sure. Nor can artificially constructed situations ever match the layered nuances of real-life experience. Psychological experiments oversimplify things practically by definition. It's a hazard of the scientific method that puts a premium on isolating single variables that can be tested against a control. Despite weaknesses, situationism still presents a formidable critique of traditional character-based perspectives in ethics and psychology. As one philosopher put it, "Experimental psychology is perhaps the worst available method for understanding human life. Except, I hasten to add, for all the other methods."[5] His point was that philosophers should give up their penchant for armchair speculation and start doing experimental research on morality and character for themselves.

Some of the most controversial psychological studies have been of the situationism variety. The Milgram Experiment is one of them. In the early 1960s, Yale psychologist Stanley Milgram explored the willingness of male subjects to follow instructions even when their own conscience told them to do otherwise.[6] What he discovered was quite surprising.

In one of his experiments, Milgram recruited 40 men who were told that they would be participating in a scientific study about the effects of punishment on memory and learning. That was a ruse, one of many Milgram employed. The subjects were cast in the role of "teacher," and an actor hired by Milgram played the role of "student." None of the subjects knew that the student was in on the experiment. They believed he was a volunteer just like them. The student was required to memorize word pairs, then recall one of them when prompted by the teacher. If he couldn't remember the words correctly, the teacher was instructed to administer an electrical shock as punishment. With each failure, the voltage of the shock was increased. The machine that administered the shocks was labeled to indicate that anything above 300 volts was dangerous, and that 450 volts—the highest setting—was lethal.

The shocks were faked, although the teachers didn't know that. The student did a good job of selling the fake punishment, moaning and screaming on cue when the shocks were administered. Most teachers found this situation very distressing. Some refused to administer another shock. When that occurred, the experimenter prodded them with increasingly stern instructions. The first one was totally benign: "Please continue." If that didn't work, the experimenter upped the ante, saying, "The experiment requires you to continue." "It is absolutely essential that you continue" was the next prod, and the final one was, "You have no other choice but to continue." If the teacher still refused to administer a shock, the experiment was ended. The teachers were not told any of this ahead of time.

Despite their visible discomfort at harming the student, each participant continued to administer the shocks up to the 300-volt level, and 65 percent of them continued to the "lethal" level of 450 volts. No teacher required a prod beyond "Please continue" to reach the 300-volt level of punishment. Here we have another illustration of a seemingly inconsequential circumstance—a mild directive to "Please continue"—that led subjects to do ostensibly harmful things to others. Why would they do such a thing, even beyond the point when they clearly felt uncomfortable?

According to Milgram, the subjects were willing to follow orders even when their own conscience told them not to continue because they respected the authority of the research scientist. They believed he was ultimately responsible for the consequences. That's the crucial point. We are willing to give up our autonomy—to do what others tell us even if we have doubts about it—if we feel that the person in charge is deserving of our trust. In that sense, we have a bias toward following the orders of authority figures. But it only extends so far, as another controversial study called the Stanford Prison Experiment makes clear.

In 1971, Philip Zimbardo created an artificial prison in the basement of the psychology building at Stanford University.[7] He recruited 24 male students to participate in his prison experiment. Half of the students were assigned the role of "prisoner" and the other half the role of "guard." The purpose of the experiment was to demonstrate how easy it is for normal people to be transformed into abusive tyrants and submissive victims by their circumstances. The disposition (character) of the person playing the role of guard or prisoner was supposedly irrelevant. That's what the experiment set out to prove.

As expected, some of the guards became aggressive and abusive, while some of the prisoners became overly submissive. Not everyone behaved according to plan, however. In one cell, the prisoners became rebellious and refused to cooperate. Nor did all of the guards follow their instructions to belittle (dehumanize) the prisoners. Five prisoners were removed from the study early for emotional trauma. The entire experiment was cut short after only six days due to the moral objections of an observer. It was supposed to last two weeks.

One common criticism of the experiment is that it was set up to encourage misbehavior, not just observe how circumstances might lead to misbehavior. If you are led to believe that your role is to be a bad ass prison guard, for example, that's probably what you will become. That doesn't necessarily mean that deep inside of us there exists a potential tyrant awaiting the right circumstances to emerge, which is what Zimbardo believed. He was overly enthusiastic in eliciting the kind of misbehavior he expected to see. I would call that confirmation bias.

Suffice it to say that no Institutional Review Board (IRB) would allow the Milgram or Stanford Prison experiments to take place today. Among other things, the potential psychological trauma to subjects would have doomed the studies. Ethical oversight of research involving human subjects wasn't standardized until the mid-1970s.

The authority bias that affected virtually every subject in the Milgram Experiment wasn't so pervasive in the Stanford Prison Experiment. Not everyone did what they were told by researchers in the latter case. Why the difference? I think it is due to the isolation of each subject in the Milgram Experiment. They weren't allowed to interact with one another. Nor did they interact directly with the student who received the shocks. That person was in a separate room, and teacher–student interactions were conducted via audio hookup. The experimenter was the only person the teachers (subjects) interacted with directly.

Contrast that with the experience of the prisoners and guards in the Stanford Prison Experiment. They interacted with one another, extensively so in some cases. That's why prisoners in one of the cells rebelled against guards rather than follow their orders. They became a cohesive group—a hive—and they took steps to subvert the authority of the guards. Like a hunter-gatherer band from our ancestral past, they resented "bullying" behavior. When an individual is isolated, he or she is more easily intimidated by an authority figure. Any hope of resisting is quashed. That's why solitary confinement is an effective method for controlling difficult prisoners. It's why bullies isolate their victims. When individuals band together, it empowers them to resist and fight back.

Not every group of prisoners at Stanford rebelled, but one of them did. That means subversive behavior—not just submissive behavior—is at least possible in circumstances where the exercise of authority is an important variable. That is especially true when people band together. For every case of *Seinfeld*-like bystander apathy, I suspect there is an alternative instance of bystander heroism. Remember what happened on Flight 93. The 9/11 hijackers intended to crash that United Airlines plane into the White House, or perhaps the capitol. They didn't reach their target because a number of passengers decided to fight back. We see this kind of dialectical switching between submissiveness and aggressiveness (and other variables as well) in sports. Behavior that is influenced by circumstances doesn't always unfold as predicted by a situationism study.

Consider, for example, the shifts in momentum that occur in athletic contests. One minute, a team appears to be listless and barely capable of hanging on. Then someone makes one good play—a basket, base hit, field goal, or whatever it might be—and suddenly they are off to the races. All it took was one little change in circumstances to flip the switch from submissiveness to aggressiveness. It's like finding a dime in a phone booth. The outcome of a game often does hinge on something that at first glance appears "inconsequential." A lucky break, like a fumble in a football game, can shift the momentum just as easily.

Yet, a change in momentum due to a lucky break or good play isn't quite the same thing as the refusal to help someone pick up her papers because you didn't find a dime. The latter situation has a moral weight—a misbehavior element—that isn't often part of a momentum swing. But the dynamics are similar. The boost in mood that predisposed subjects who found a dime to be helpful is comparable to a boost in confidence that predisposes athletes who make one good play to keep on fighting. Nothing is more vital to athletic performance than confidence. Mood and confidence may not be precisely the same thing, but clearly they are related phenomena that correlate well with one another. The more confidence you have, the brighter your mood and vice versa.

There's plenty of misbehavior in sports that we can point to in comparison to situationism studies. Losing your temper on the court is one obvious example. Athletes do it all the time. In the heat of competition, they push, kick, spit, swear, threaten, headbutt, scream, throw elbows, and commit every imaginable offense that a rage-filled meltdown is capable of producing. It's like being in a fugue state or under the influence of a mind-altering drug. I suppose that's why we describe a temper tantrum as a temporary loss of control. What we do in a fit of anger is inexcusable, of course, but it's also understandable. Every athlete knows how easy it is to overreact to some inconsequential thing and get mad. That's why they tend to overlook offenses of that kind so long as they don't become part of a pattern, lead to serious injury, or become overly personal. The perpetrator often apologizes, saying things like, "I don't know what came over me," "Normally, I don't behave like that," "I lost my temper," "I embarrassed myself," or "It'll never happen again." Most of the time, apologies are accepted and the incident is quickly forgotten.

Afterward, it is often impossible to remember exactly what triggered an outburst. Usually it is some insignificant thing that gets the better of us. Stress plays a role. It can distort our perspective, magnifying the significance of something that would normally be overlooked, for instance, a snide comment ("trash talk") or hard foul. Whatever the minor circumstance might be, it plays an outsized influence on the game if it causes us to go ballistic.

Temper tantrums are an accepted part of sports. Athletes, coaches, officials, and even fans brush them aside quickly. "It was just an emotional outburst," we say nonchalantly. Even Roger Federer—he of the ballet movements and unflappable demeanor—can be heard swearing on the court once in a while. It's to be expected. Surprisingly, showing excessive emotion can sometimes help settle down a player and bring out his or her best performance. John McEnroe was good at that. He would work himself into a screaming rage on the court, often regarding a questionable line call, then blithely go on to win the match. No big deal. Many fans appreciated his feistiness. I don't think that kind of behavior is tolerated today as much as it was 30 years ago.

In the 2018 U.S. Open final, Serena Williams had a McEnroe-like meltdown. It wasn't the first time she had a tantrum in the latter stages of the Open, either. She was playing Naomi Osaka, a young Japanese player. Osaka won the first set, 6–2, and was trailing in the second set when Carlos Ramos, the chair umpire, warned Williams for a coaching violation. A little later in the match, Williams was penalized a point for smashing her racquet. That's when she came unglued, calling Ramos a "liar" for accusing her of cheating and a "thief" for taking a point away from her. She pointed her finger at him, demanding an apology. Instead of apologizing, he penalized her a game for verbal abuse. That made the score in the second set 5–3 for Osaka, who went on to win the match, 6–2, 6–4.

Williams tried to make the conflict with Ramos about sexism. She said it was unfair to penalize her when men routinely get away with much worse behavior on court. Some in the tennis world supported Williams's claims, but not everyone saw it her way. What I find fascinating about this controversy is how the rhetoric of character was combined, or mixed, with the rhetoric of situationism. Both perspectives regarding the meaning of misbehavior were appealed to at the same time.

Look at how Williams reacted to Ramos. First, she demanded an apology from him for calling her a cheater. Ramos hadn't accused her of cheating, however. It was her coach, Patrick Mouratoglou, who was called for the coaching violation, not Williams. After the match, Mouratoglou admitted that he had been coaching her from the stands. He tried to justify it, saying, "Everybody does it." Yet, Williams took the violation as a personal attack on *her* character. That's what set her off. "I would rather lose than cheat," she said.

After she was assessed a penalty for verbal abuse, she switched tactics and began using a situationism argument to plea her case. It was no longer a question of her character (it would be hard to defend verbal abuse as virtuous behavior). Now she was claiming that the chair umpire wasn't allowing her to vent her feelings of anger and frustration the way a man would be allowed to do without incurring a penalty. In the stress of the moment, athletes lose their temper. That's not unusual. Instead of admitting that she overreacted and misbehaved, she was accusing Ramos of overreacting and misbehaving. The situation didn't get the better of her; it got the better of him.

Agree or disagree with Williams, I think this case illustrates how common it is in sports to find references to both a character ethic—"I'm not a cheater!"—and some minor situation or circumstance like a coaching violation that leads to an unexpected outcome. These two models for explaining why we misbehave (or don't misbehave) are not incompatible. It isn't an either-or where you must pick one model and reject another, as situationism studies seem to imply. Their purpose is to expose the ineffectiveness of character as an explanation of human behavior. I think they are mistaken about that, as I will explain in a minute. First, I want to look at another recent high-profile case in sports where there was an appeal to both character and extenuating circumstances (situationism) to fully grasp moral culpability.

Urban Meyer was the head football coach at Ohio State University (he resigned after the 2019 Rose Bowl). He is one of the most successful coaches in sports. His teams at the University of Florida and Ohio State University won three national championships. Despite his impeccable credentials, he got caught up in a situation that almost cost him his job in late summer of 2018.

The controversy surrounding Meyer has an eerie resemblance to Watergate in one sense. It wasn't the actual break-in at Democratic headquarters in the Watergate building that forced President Richard Nixon to resign from office. He wasn't involved in that malfeasance perpetrated by the committee to reelect him. Instead, what brought Nixon down was the fact that he lied to cover up what the committee had done without his knowledge.

Similarly, it wasn't his assistant coach's domestic violence issues that almost cost Meyer his job. Instead, what tripped him up—what made this case *the* story in sports for an entire month—was the question of whether he deliberately lied to a reporter during Big Ten Media Days on July 24. That's what set off the frenzied investigations surrounding what Meyer knew and didn't know regarding Zach Smith's troubled marriage to Courtney Smith, which ended in divorce in 2016.

Smith had been the wide receiver coach at Ohio State until Meyer fired him the day before Big Ten Media Days, after he learned that a domestic violence civil protection order had been issued against him on behalf of his former wife. Also relevant is the fact that Smith had been arrested for aggravated battery against Courtney Smith in 2009, while he was employed by Meyer as wide receiver coach for the University of Florida. She declined to press charges at that time, and the case was dropped. When Meyer hired Smith to work for him again at Ohio State University, the 2009 Florida arrest was not made known to college officials.

At Big Ten Media Days, Meyer was asked if he had known about an accusation of domestic violence made against Zach Smith by Courtney Smith in 2015. That's when Meyer said, "I don't know who creates a story like that." The implication was that the reporter was at fault for fabricating the allegation. Meyer was aware of the incident, as it turns out. Was he lying to the reporter? It certainly appeared that way. He claims that he was referencing the fact that there was no arrest made in 2015.

At an evening news conference following the Ohio State University Board of Trustees meeting, Meyer was given a three-game suspension without pay. He managed to save his job, although he dug himself a little deeper into the public perception hole he'd fallen into when he fumbled the opportunity to say how sorry he was for what Courtney Smith and her children had endured. It seemed as if he hadn't really gotten the message about how serious the problem of domestic violence is in the United States.

While serving his suspension, Meyer sat down with ESPN journalist Tom Rinaldi for a televised interview. Many of Rinaldi's questions were blunt and uncomfortable. When asked about his apparent lie at Big Ten Media Days, which precipitated the mess that led to his suspension, Meyer said, "I made a mistake, I did not lie." That's an interesting statement. To be caught in a lie would be a stain on his character. For Americans, in particular, honesty is perhaps the single most important attribute of their character. What makes a person good? Ask an

American that question and honesty is usually the first word that comes to mind. We still teach our children about George Washington's inability to tell a lie after he chopped down his father's favorite cherry tree. Honest Abe Lincoln's arduous journey to repay a client a few pennies that he was owed in change is part of our folklore. A mistake, on the other hand, does not carry the same moral weight.

In his own mind, Meyer's "mistake" was that he misremembered what he knew about 2015. It's not a lie if you don't remember something accurately. Lying implies the intent to deceive, whereas misremembering something doesn't involve such an intention. That's what Meyer believed. Leaving aside what we know about the mind's self-deception capabilities, I think what Meyer did was employ a situationism argument to preserve his own sense of being a person of good character. He mixed the two models for understanding misbehavior. Circumstances beyond his control—his faulty memory and the reprehensible actions of Zach Smith—led to an unnecessary crisis. That's his interpretation of events.

When asked to assess his own moral culpability, Meyer said, "I went too far in trying to help someone." Again, the implication is that his own virtuousness—in particular, his loyalty to Zach Smith, the grandson of Meyer's former mentor, Earle Bruce—blinded him from recognizing warning signs of trouble until it was too late. His intentions were good, yet the situation turned out to be horrific. Meyer readily admits that he should have been more diligent in monitoring and reporting Smith's misdeeds. Those are mistakes in judgment, unlike the faulty memory mistake that led to his misstatement at the Big Ten Media Days. Judgment carries considerable moral weight, and it does reflect upon a person's character.

There is a tactical interplay of taking responsibility while also denying responsibility in how we explain our own misdeeds. References to both character and circumstances are necessary to pull it off. We usually present ourselves to those around us as reliable and trustworthy in our character, while at the same time explaining any aberrations in our behavior pattern as mistakes triggered by unfortunate circumstances. That's the script Urban Meyer followed.

Situationism studies indicate that circumstances play a huge role in determining our behavior. Some advocates of the situationism perspective take the next step and suggest that there is no such thing as reliable character. They argue that we would be better off without references to character when we discuss human behavior.[8] I think that is a misinterpretation of what the results of their studies mean.

Could it be that character is a façade, or an illusion, that we employ to make ourselves look and feel good? Sure. But that doesn't mean it is something we can jettison like an old wives' tale. If it is a façade, it is a vital one that we couldn't easily live without. We use the language of character to understand and refer to ourselves. Character and selfhood have the same existential probity and utility. Is there such a thing as a real "self" that resides inside of me? It's probably an illusion—like the concept of character—that the mind constructed so that we could thrive as individual members of a hive. Could any of us live our lives without a sense of being a unique self with specific character traits, personalities, family backgrounds, friends, and so forth? Good luck with that project.

We live in a world that is filled with alternative worlds of our own making. Without the ability to create meaningful illusions, up to and including our own sense of selfhood and conscience, we would not be the creatures that we have become. Certainly there would be no sports. We enter into the make-believe world of football when we play the game and/or watch others play it as fans. Could we live without football? Sure. Could we live without the ability to construct make-believe worlds as a form of play? Not as human beings we couldn't. Just because something has an "illusory" quality doesn't mean it isn't vitally important to our identities and survival. Illusions are a necessary tool of evolution and human experience. That's why I think situationism advocates go too far in condemning character as an unimportant part of our moral universe. Make-believe is the basis for play, which is the basis for how we learn to get along with others and function as a moral hive.

Character is an ideal that we strive for, not a real thing that we possess. In many ways, it is an impossible ideal because egoism and nepotism are strong instincts that skew our behavior just like an incidental circumstance in a situationism study skews our behavior. To be fair-minded when our instinctive tendency is to look out for number one is an arduous task. Remember that morality evolved as a way to attenuate the self-serving desire to take advantage of others. It's never been an easy achievement because the self-serving tendencies in each of us are naturally very strong. It takes considerable effort to become a cooperative team player. Conscience alone has never been sufficient to the task because it too is susceptible to the cunning tactics of the miscreant. The watchful eyes of each member of the group are also necessary to insure moral decorum.

In the small bands of our ancestral past, we learned to cooperate just enough to thrive as a moral hive. That, in turn, enabled us to become the most imaginative and cunning species on Earth. We are opportunists who take advantage of others when we can get away with it. Ironically, that moral duplicity is what made us so flexible, another distinctive survival advantage of our species. Our moral evolution also involved the deceptive practice of convincing others that we are more generous than we actually are. That's what it took to build a reputation for generosity without having to pay the full price for it. Securing a good reputation was the Stone Age equivalent of buying health insurance. It paid big dividends down the road when you might need help because of an unforeseen setback.

From the beginning, morality has been a two-faced game, with plenty of fakery and deception but also just enough authenticity to make us a formidable species capable of transforming nature itself. We are the only species, so far as we know, that is no longer simply a pawn of evolution. We are on a moral trajectory that enables us to take charge of our own evolution. It started with our capacity to play roles and become characters of our own design. From the fictional experiences of our own play we have created a moral purpose that transcends our biological limits. We are the only creature that invents itself to be itself. Nothing in our modern experience teaches us that ancient lesson quite like sports. A skinny kid with an impoverished background can become a professional athlete if he or she dreams big enough and works hard enough to make the dream into reality. Making such dreams come true is a story as old as humanity. That's my moral theory of sports in a nutshell.

In the next chapter, which also happens to be the last chapter of this book, I will briefly ponder the future that might be awaiting us around the bend.

10

WHITHER THE FUTURE?

Throughout this book, I have been looking back to the ancestral environment to rediscover what our moral experience was like in its original form. Morality evolved to enhance the cooperative capabilities of small bands of hunter-gatherers. As Darwin pointed out, moral communities outcompete nonmoral ones because they work together more efficiently.[1] In that sense, morality is one of the crucial pillars of our incredible success as a species. Usually, it is the size of our brains that is credited with giving us the edge over other species. But how did our frontal lobes get to be so large in the first place? Many evolutionary biologists think it is because of the complex nature of our moral interactions. It takes a lot of brain power to coordinate the behavior of a small group of people beset with competing interests and desires.

Morality proved to be an effective yet conflicted system for promoting group harmony. Not only do we have competing interests and desires with other people. Paradoxically, our own psyches are riddled with them as well. Generous moral feelings must contend with strong self-serving instincts. Even conscience, the quintessential moral attribute, can be co-opted into the cunning schemes of the miscreant. Despite its quirks and limitations, morality served hunter-gatherer bands well enough. It helped that each member of the band kept a wary eye on the other members. Bullies, in particular, were punished by the group—often severely—which made them more cautious and calculating about when it might be safe to misbehave; however, nothing focused the group into a fine-tuned cooperative moral hive quite like the threat of competition from other bands. That gave rise to the xenophobic tribal feelings that continue to shape our behavior to this day.

Morality, as we understand it today, is not at all like what our ancestors experienced. We view it as a private and personal affair—an internal compass that steers us in the right direction—rather than a means to promote the welfare of the group. Of course we acknowledge the benefits of getting along well with others that stem from having good manners and other morally inspired characteristics. But group dynamics tend to be ancillary to our personalized moral sensibilities. For us, conscience is not a risk/reward calculator that tells us when it's safe to misbehave. It is, we believe, the voice of our authentic selves that is utterly incapable of duplicity. To heed one's conscience is to rise above petty acts of selfishness. It's a sign of moral purity for us, not moral cunning.

We abhor gossip, yet it was vital to the survival of the group in the ancestral environment. That is perhaps the most telling indicator of our moral differences.

Many of the original purposes of morality were upended due to the demands and stresses of living in increasingly large cities and empires following the agricultural revolution. Those momentous changes continue to challenge us even today. In the ancestral environment, morality helped us get along with people we knew almost as well as our own families. It wasn't such a huge leap forward to extend our natural feelings of nepotism to nonfamily members of the band or village who were already familiar to us as neighbors. On the other hand, how do you promote generous feelings toward absolute strangers? That has been the great moral struggle of every civilization since the invention of agriculture.

To help us live harmoniously among strangers in large cities, legal systems, religions, schools, and other civil institutions were created. These institutions have largely taken over the public responsibility side of our morality. That is one of the reasons why morality has become such a private affair today. The anonymity of our cities practically guarantees the flourishing of our most self-serving tendencies. There aren't enough civil authorities to keep a watchful eye on everyone. Isn't this what life has become for us? The police work endlessly to ferret out criminals who manage to stay one step ahead of them because defenders of the law are always reacting to what cunning offenders might dream up next. It's an arms race similar to what we find in basketball and other sports where the offense has a built-in advantage over the defense.

Why do hackers delight in creating viruses that destroy computer systems? Are they envious? Bored? What? I think the hacker mentality bewilders modern morality because we have polished it up so that only good behavior counts. But being good wasn't the original purpose of morality. The cunning side of it has been filtered out. That doesn't mean it isn't still operating inside of us as a moral force. I suspect that many subversive activities, like hacking, are somehow connected to the ancient moral desire to put down big shots. Powerful corporations are the modern version of hunter-gatherer big shots. I'm not trying to justify criminal behavior. But I do think we could benefit from reexamining the moral dynamics of many subversive activities. It isn't only do-gooders who are morally engaged in life. There is an egalitarian element to our moral feelings that is ancient and naturally suspicious of power and authority. Call it the Robin Hood effect.

There are remnants of our ancient morality that have survived into the modern world. In my view, there is no better example of such a remnant than modern sports. They bear a remarkable resemblance to hunter-gatherer moral life. Playing such modern games as football or basketball, or watching others play them, gets to the very heart of our aboriginal nature. The moral circumstances of our evolutionary beginnings are recapitulated in the contests of guile, athletic prowess, perseverance, tribal loyalty, and cooperative sacrifice that brighten our days. Freed from the drudgery of making a living, what do many of us do? We become weekend warriors who indulge an insatiable desire to play and compete, and watch others do likewise. We idolize virtuoso athletes like Michael Jordan and Secretariat. Far from being a trivial pursuit in our lives, sports represent something essential about us. To ignore their significance would be akin to misunderstanding what we are about as a species. That, briefly, is my moral theory of sports.

In this last chapter, I want to cast my gaze to the future rather than the past. For tens of thousands of years, our species has been on an evolutionary journey that, so far as we know, is unique upon this Earth. Where are we headed next as a species that is so passionately in love with sports? What new vistas might be lurking on the horizon or just beyond it? One potential disruptive change that is already making itself felt in the sports universe pertains to the issue of "transhumanism," defined as the effort to transform ourselves into something different than what nature made us. I briefly mention it in a previous chapter about advances in neuroscience. Before I explore the impact on sports of potential science fiction-like changes to our bodies and minds, I want to begin by discussing the sexism crisis that continues to haunt the credibility of testosterone-fueled modern sports like football. Transhumanism represents a potential problem of too much change for modern sports to absorb unscathed. But not enough change—too little of it rather than too much of it—can also be perilous. The ongoing disrespect toward women in many modern sports is of the latter variety.

Michelle Beadle is one of three cohosts on an ESPN morning talk show. The other cohosts are male. Since football is the most popular sport in the United States today, with not one but two television revenue juggernauts (college *and* professional), it isn't surprising that sports talk shows spend a great deal of time dissecting, analyzing, and Monday morning quarterbacking every nitpicking detail related to the gridiron. What is surprising—perhaps even shocking—is that Beadle recently announced that she is no longer going to watch football games of any kind. An ESPN analyst opting out on football? How is that even possible?

Beadle's opt-out regarding football was a protest against the sexism that is endemic to the sport. Players and coaches alike have repeatedly used their girlfriends and wives as punching bags, often without serious consequences. The Urban Meyer imbroglio at Ohio State regarding the issue of domestic violence is what pushed Beadle and many other women to the point of exasperation. Beadle felt that Meyer's three-game suspension was a mere slap on the wrist for repeatedly looking the other way while Zach Smith, his assistant coach, allegedly assaulted his former wife, Courtney Smith.

In modern sports, there is a tolerance for sexism and domestic violence that is out of step with the changing moral norms of American society. We are moving in a direction that is more inclusive and respectful toward women, yet many sports have lagged behind despite Title IX and other legal remedies meant to provide women with equal opportunities. What is behind this reluctance to change regarding the treatment of women that hangs like a dark cloud over football and many other sports?

Obviously, many sports are grounded in a male warrior-like culture that tolerates aggression and physical violence. Football is exhibit A for this kind of behavior. It would be naïve to think that doesn't spill over into family life on occasion. In a system that privileges stereotypical male tendencies to dominate and bully others, it is no wonder that women are sometimes reduced to crude caricatures of themselves as well. Female cheerleaders from many NFL teams have filed lawsuits in recent years for being underpaid and treated disrespectfully. In some egregious cases, they were sexually assaulted by fans, made to pose naked for photo shoots, and required to escort VIP males on dates.

Predatory sexual behavior toward women is a problem of ancient origin in our species and many other species as well. Using biology to make excuses for what occurs in sports is a fairly common "boys will be boys" tactic for preserving the status quo and tolerating misconduct. As a biological argument, it is utterly baseless. Our values are not biologically determined. Culture is a greater influence in that regard. We are creatures whose biology is attenuated and shaped by individual choices and cultural constructions. That has been our unique lot in life for a very long time. As I discuss in a previous chapter, we are just now learning how plastic our brains and genes truly are. We really do have the capacity to influence and change our own biology.

The #MeToo movement has called out powerful men in every industry who sexually assaulted women under the cloak of secrecy, shame, intimidation, and other predatory ploys. Yet, it seems that the power centers of professional and collegiate sports remain willfully tone-deaf to what is occurring in the broader culture around them. Perhaps that's why Michelle Beadle and many other women are turning their backs on football. As we saw in the last chapter, an incidental circumstance, for instance, finding a dime in a phone booth, can trigger a significant change in our moral outlook and willingness to help others. Rosa Parks refused to sit at the back of the bus one day, and afterward it became unthinkable to turn a blind eye to the injustices of racism. I wonder if we have reached a similar point of no return with regard to the exploitation of women in sports. A spell seems to have been broken.

The unofficial title of greatest male athlete in the world often goes to the Olympic gold medalist in the decathlon. There is some justification for that honorary designation since it requires excellence in 10 different track and field events, not just one. It's extremely difficult to become a world-class athlete in more than one sport. Just ask Michael Jordan. He was god-like in basketball but not even average as a professional baseball player.

Bruce Jenner won the decathlon gold medal in the 1976 Montreal Olympics. That world record–breaking feat catapulted him to international fame. After divorcing reality TV star Kris Kardashian in 2015—Jenner's third marriage—he shared the startling news that he had become a trans woman. Her name was now Caitlyn Jenner, and she completed sex reassignment surgery in 2017.

Jenner's gender transformation received a wide range of reactions from sports fans, from sympathy to indifference to hostile rejection. Some doubted the sincerity of her motives. After all, she was a member of the attention-grabbing Kardashian clan, the father of six children, and one of the most celebrated male athletes of recent memory. How could she now claim to have always been a woman in her true identity? Was this some sort of crazy publicity stunt? For many, it seemed unbelievable and surreal.

Can a man really become a woman? What is the difference between a trans woman (or man) and a naturally born one? Would it be fair for a trans woman to compete against a nontrans woman in a sporting event? That is a question that has been raised in Texas after a high school boy undergoing a change in gender identity won two consecutive state wrestling championships while competing against girls. Does a change in gender entail a predictable level of performance enhancement and/or decline? How do we measure differences of this kind and make judgments about what is fair?

I think the transgender issue that Americans are struggling to make sense of today represents a small foretaste of what is to come in the sports universe as we become more and more scientifically proficient about taking control of our own evolution.

The first test-tube baby was born in 1978. Today, more than 60,000 IVF (in vitro fertilization) babies are born each year in the United States.[2] Born in 2000, ANDi became the first transgenic primate. That means genetic material from another species (a jellyfish) was successfully inserted into his rhesus monkey DNA before birth. Geneticists are now capable of creating artificial chromosomes and inserting them into the DNA of germline cells (special reproductive cells). They have already done it with mice. It is only a matter of time before we add an extra chromosome pair to our own DNA. The scientific know-how is already available, and the implications are far-reaching. An artificial chromosome would allow parents to design their own children to some extent. It is doubtful that we will ever completely understand the complex interactions of our entire genome; however, there are enough genes that we do understand well enough to make "designer babies" a possibility in the near future.

Once we understand how something works, whether it's a mouse trap or a strand of DNA, we always want to tinker with it and make it work better. To be inventive in that way is part of our natural curiosity. According to geneticist Gregory Stock, the manipulation of our own genes could be the scientific equivalent of opening Pandora's Box. Once we open the box and begin tinkering with our own genes, it could lead to our own pseudo-extinction. "Progressive self-transformation," he said, "could change our descendants into something sufficiently different from our present selves to not be human in the sense we use the term now."[3] That our children could turn out to be different than we are as a species is a very strange prospect indeed.

Will we create a race of super-athletes? Stock is one scientist who doesn't think so. If it were possible to improve performance significantly through genetic manipulation, natural selection would probably already have done so. Not everyone agrees with that conservative assessment, however. Boosters for a genetically enhanced brave new world abound like stars in the night sky. Dreaming big is another irresistible aspect of our nature.

What if we did manage to create better athletes by tinkering with our genes. What then? Would the manipulation of one's own genes for competitive advantage be wrong in the same sense as taking steroids to get stronger and faster is perceived to be wrong today? Would basketball be the same game we know it to be today if every player was an eight-foot version of LeBron James? Would anyone care? Could the myth of a level playing field in sports survive a genetic free-for-all? (I think it barely survived the steroid era.)

Athletic performance has already been on a steady trajectory of improvement for more than a century. Training techniques have gotten better, as have sports equipment, nutrition, and medical care, coaching, and financial remuneration of professional athletes—the list goes on and on. Everything has been steadily improving, including results on the field. Imagine how an Olympian from the 1920s would fare in a foot race against Usain Bolt. It wouldn't be a fair contest. Does the genetic frontier that lies ahead represent just another evolutionary step in what has already been happening in modern sports for a long time? Or is it a harbinger of a revolution that will change the meaning of sports (and human existence) forever? We will have to wait and see.

Improving ourselves through genetic manipulation isn't the only transhumanism frontier. Perhaps even more hyped by enthusiasts is the prospect of a cyborg future for *Homo sapiens*. In a 2000 *Wired* magazine article, British engineer Kevin Warwick hailed his dream to become one with his computer.[4] His first step, "Cyborg 1.0," was to implant a RFID transmitter into his body. It enabled his computer to track basic information about his whereabouts and activities. Warwick confessed that he became emotionally attached to his implant. He was both surprised and encouraged by that. It led him to hope that more sophisticated computer implants would enable him to acquire additional senses, for example, the ability to perceive ultraviolet radiation.

What if we really are able to create hybrid humans that interface with computers and have machine-like parts? I imagine they would need to invent their own athletic contests if, like us, they wished to test their mettle against one another. Maybe it would be possible to play such games as mixed doubles in tennis where one team member is an enhanced cyborg and the other an ordinary human. In *Star Trek: The Next Generation*, Data, the cybernetic android officer, competes with humans in games like poker and chess but not in any kind of physical sport. His strength, endurance, agility, and so on, are far too superior for such contests to be fair or meaningful. Would ordinary humans be able to survive in a world where they are bettered in every way by robotic beings? At some point in the not too distant future, it is likely that the complexity of computers and artificial intelligence will exceed the complexity of our biological minds. What might happen after that is anyone's guess if computers are somehow able to achieve their own self-awareness or integrate themselves with our awareness and desires. Those are pretty big "ifs."

How likely is a cyborg future for us? Artificial chromosomes could represent a cyborg-like development, but it is highly unlikely that they would ever be able to control our entire genome. It is far too complex for that. Neuroscientists have created cochlear implants that interact directly with the brain to improve hearing. That's a far cry from fully integrating a computer with the human mind, however. The challenges are immense and the risks high. As we have learned with many psychotropic drugs, for instance, Prozac, each person has a slightly different reaction to them. Prozac doesn't work for everyone. Our brains and DNA have idiosyncrasies that are emergent and incapable of being accounted for ahead of time. Who is going to want to risk having a bad reaction to a procedure that could have permanent consequences?

According to Gregory Stock, our near-term future is much more likely to be enhanced via "fyborgization" rather than cyborgization.[5] Fyborgization allows us to fuse ourselves with machines, computers, tools, and so forth, in a functional way rather than a physically permanent one. We already employ many fyborg attachments—eye glasses, smart phones, and artificial limbs. Oscar Pistorius's carbon fiber blades are fyborg accessories, not cyborg leg implants that he can never remove or exchange for something more sensible when he needs to do something other than run a race. What's helpful as an enhancement for one purpose might be a burden if it can't be set aside when we want to do something else. The use of fyborg "wearable" technology makes more sense given the flexibility that it entails and the minimal risks.

In the near term, the convenience and interchangeability of fyborgization is likely to inhibit the quest to make permanent cyborgization changes to our bodies and minds. Football players wear pads and helmets. Those are fyborg technologies, and I can imagine a quarterback of the future wearing a computer that interfaces with his mind while he is on the field. Then, when the game is finished, he could take it off and hang it next to his shoulder pads and other gear. That kind of future would represent an evolutionary change in sports, not a revolutionary one as I suspect a cyborg future would almost certainly inaugurate. I can easily imagine an increasingly sophisticated fyborg future for athletes; a cyborg future, on the other hand, would be a different kind of reality that I have trouble imagining because it is so far beyond my everyday experience.

Will athletic contests as we understand them continue into the future? Yes, I think so. What if we become a different species through our own deliberate efforts and choices? Could that endanger sports as we understand them? I think the answer to that question is both yes and no. Yes, if cyborgs take over the world, they might lose interest in playing boring old human games. Who knows? However, I believe any sort of transhuman species would necessarily retain the moral impetus that has distinguished our species from the beginning. In that sense, no, I don't think it would be possible for any progeny of our species—even if they represent a different kind of being—to eclipse the joy of athletic performance. As I have tried to argue throughout this book, it is part of our moral nature to want to test our guile and strength in competition with one another.

Let me conclude this chapter by suggesting that transhumanism has a lot more in common with our ancestral morality than one might think. Neuroscientists and geneticists are leading us to where we have always been going—toward a future that exceeds the boundaries of the present moment. To reach beyond ourselves and expand the boundaries of our care and understanding is what we have been destined to do ever since we achieved self-awareness. It is our moral evolutionary heritage, and sports have been a significant expression of it. New technologies and scientific discoveries will accelerate the process of our own self-transformation. But we are on the same trail we have always been on. The path of self-transformation is as old as we are as a species. Transhumanists warn that we are now responsible for our own evolution. I think the reverse is true: We have always been responsible for our own evolution. That's what being self-aware means from a biological perspective. In human experience, life itself found a way to become aware of its own evolution.

Science will never eclipse our moral capacity to make sense of things because the project of science is itself an expression of our moral nature. So, too, is the project of sports.

APPENDIX

On Moral Psychology and Ethics

For those readers who wish to find out more about what morality was like in the ancestral environment and my views on how ethics, moral psychology, and sports fit into that picture, I offer this appendix.

Most of us use the terms morality and ethics interchangeably. When we do make a distinction, usually we think of morality as being more personal, ethics more theoretical. If I was a professional bicycle racer in the 1990s, for example, I probably considered the risks and rewards of taking EPO (erythropoietin), the hormonal drug developed to treat anemia that increases hemoglobin levels in the blood. That would have been a *moral* consideration because it pertained to my own personal life, and what I was willing or not willing to do to enhance my competitive advantages. On the other hand, the whole problem of PED (performance enhancing drug) use in sports is an *ethical* question. It's not about me personally; it's an abstract matter of defining principles that can help answer tough questions such as this one: Which medicinal products, if any, are appropriate for an otherwise healthy athlete to use in preparation for competition?

Morality is a human universal. Every archaic society studied by anthropologists has shown ample evidence of a moral life. No one doubts that it is part of human nature to be moral. We couldn't have become what we are today without it. The same can't be said about ethics. It's not necessary to be skilled at ethical reflection to be a moral person. On the other hand, isn't it reasonable to suppose that ethical literacy might help us to be a little more vigilant in our scruples—more honest, perhaps, or more generous, or happier and less cranky? Some moral psychologists don't seem to think so.

In recent decades, psychologists have studied morality extensively. The picture they have developed is quite surprising for someone like me with a background in ethics. Using a variety of experimental methods, they have discovered that moral experience pertains to feelings and intuitions, not thought processes. We make instantaneous moral judgments before we are even aware of having made them and without the benefit of any self-directed deliberations. It turns out that reasoning and thinking—hallmarks of *philosophical* ethics—have been vastly overrated. It's yet another reminder, reminiscent of Freud's elevation of the unconscious, that most of what goes on in our minds (and our moral lives) is out of our hands.

Jonathan Haidt, one of the moral psychologists I am referencing, uses the metaphor of an elephant with a human rider sitting on top to illustrate the significance of feelings and unconscious mental processes compared to reasoning and similar habits of the self-conscious mind.[1] The large elephant represents our feelings, while the tiny rider represents our intellect. Most of what we do in life—including the moral life—is handled by the elephant. It doesn't require our conscious attendance. The best we can do as self-aware moral agents is to steer the elephant in the right direction. It is beyond our abilities to overpower or supplant the elephant.

According to Haidt, philosophers have been misleading us for thousands of years about the primacy of the intellect over feelings.[2] The elephant metaphor is meant to correct Plato's allegory of the charioteer. In his *Phaedrus* dialogue, Plato depicted the path to enlightenment as a chariot ride. The charioteer, representing the intellect, must master the two winged horses that transport the soul to a more perfect world. One of the horses has a noble character, representing the moral sentiments. The other horse has a bad character, representing the base appetites. Plato's message is that reason must reign supreme over the feelings, whether noble or base. Research in moral psychology demonstrates just how wrong Plato was. If I might introduce one more animal metaphor, it's a case of the tail wagging the dog, which is exactly backward. It is feelings that matter most, not the intellect.

Moral judgments are based on instinctive feelings, not pro and con deliberations. There is something counterintuitive about that (at least for me). When asked about the choices we make, for example, most of us offer *reasons* for why we acted the way we did.

"Why did you steal that candy bar?"

"Well, I was hungry, and I didn't see anyone around, so I decided to take it. It was wrong of me, and I am sorry."

The way we talk about morality in everyday life privileges our conscious selves, which is partly why we are able to hold ourselves responsible for our actions. If I did something because an unconscious feeling compelled (tempted) me to do so, can (should) I be held responsible? Part of what it means to be held responsible for our behavior is the requirement that we provide a narrative explanation for it. "Why did you do that?" Translated, that means give me your *reasons* for why you did it.

Even though I agree with Haidt that our moral lives are governed more by the elephant than the rider, I am sympathetic to our customary ways of speaking about moral responsibility. Haidt calls the reasons that we give for our behavior *confabulations*: After-the-fact justifications for what we did.[3] First comes the affect driven decision, afterwards the fabricated rationalization for why we did it.

I readily concede that much of what matters most to us is attended to below the level of consciousness. That doesn't mean our subconscious decisions are an arbitrary stab in the dark, however. The feelings that instinctively tell us what to do before the conscious self has time to deliberate about it could actually be informed by calculations made automatically by the brain.

Evolutionary psychologists have argued that the brain is made up of dozens (perhaps even hundreds) of computational modules—mini computers, essentially—dedicated to managing specific aspects of our lives.[4] For example, there is a purported module for interpreting the data that streams to the brain from the eyes, enabling us to see. It entails the same sophisticated algorithms—instructions and formulas for calculating angles, distortions, color saturations, spatial orientations, and so on—that we would find in the most advanced camera systems. There is probably a module for language acquisition as well (a subconscious universal grammar, as one linguist put it)[5] and one for every other significant activity of the late Pleistocene epoch, when our species was evolving into its modern form.

Naturally, there is also a hypothetical moral module in the brain that instantaneously calculates risks, rewards, probabilities, consequences, and so forth, when we are faced with conundrums about how to behave. The prescribed course of action from those calculations reaches "us"— our conscious "moral" selves—through feelings triggered in other parts of the brain. It is those feelings (represented by the elephant) that motivate us to act in accordance with the "decision" calculated by the moral module. In a sense, the deliberations that we imagined occurring after the fact in our confabulations actually take place subconsciously in the split second before we instinctively know what to do without having to deliberate about it. So there is some number crunching and "reasoning" going on somewhere, just not where we thought it was. (Does that mean Plato was right?)

Not all neuroscientists are satisfied with computational theory, however. One alternative that has attracted the attention of moral evolution theorists pertains to a special kind of brain cell called *mirror neurons*. Discovered in Italy by scientists studying macaque monkeys, mirror neurons enable us to read one another's minds (literally).[6] When you smile at me, for example, the same brain neurons that triggered your smile also fire in my brain, motivating me to smile back at you. These specialized "mirror neurons"—I watch you do something, and my brain *simulates* what happened in your brain—could be the building blocks for empathy and imitation, key aspects of the moral life. With mirror neurons, there is no need to calculate how to behave in a hypothetical brain module. Instead, these special brain cells instantly connect us to one another, synchronizing our lives together in a brain-to-brain repartee (ballet).

Not all moral psychologists enjoy poking fun at philosophers as much as Jonathan Haidt seems to. Joshua Greene blends the new insights of science with traditional philosophy to tackle what he calls the tragedy of common sense morality.[7] We evolved to solve moral problems of the me versus us variety—how to temper our selfish tendencies for the good of the small groups we relied upon to survive in the Stone Age. Our moral feelings and gut instincts worked fine when faced with that kind of problem. But they don't work well when trying to solve the us versus them problems we face so often in the modern world. Our own interests and values often clash with those of other groups, or "tribes," as Greene calls them. The number of moral impasses of the pro life versus pro choice variety that we face is astounding and troubling. We weren't equipped to handle such an onslaught.

How to be less selfish toward those *within* my tribe is practically irrelevant when confronting animosity *between* different tribes. We need to transcend the limitations of our moral feelings and instincts, according to Greene. We need a common moral currency, like the greatest happiness principle, that all tribes throughout the world can appeal to as they attempt to adjudicate their conflicts. We need more thinking, more practical reasoning, not less, so that our moral instincts and gut reactions—our subconscious (automatic) behavioral tendencies—don't box us into rigid positions that we can't overcome. Just because the elephant rules doesn't mean the elephant knows how to help us in difficult circumstances.

Our knowledge about the ancestral environment from which anatomically modern humans first emerged approximately 200,000 years ago has grown by leaps and bounds since the 1980s. Anthropologist Christopher Boehm has taken advantage of that growing body of multidisciplinary research to offer a detailed analysis of our moral origins. He believes that we acquired a moral conscience sometime between 250,000 years ago (when archaeological evidence suggests that our immediate ancestor, *Homo erectus*, began systematically hunting large game) and 45,000 years ago (when archaeological evidence suggests that we reached modern cultural maturity).[8]

Boehm created an extensive database of the 339 hunter-gatherer societies that have been studied by modern ethnographers. From that database, he distilled a smaller subset of 150 groups that share similarities with early humans. He extrapolated what moral life in the ancestral environment must have been like by studying the moral systems of those 150 societies. Three things in particular stand out.

First, a late Pleistocene band of humans usually included six or seven male hunters who were treated as equals, with no dominant member. They hunted large game, and when someone was successful, the meat was distributed by a third party—not the hunter who killed the game—to each family in the band. The hunter didn't get to keep the large carcass for himself; it belonged to the group. It was this meat-sharing strategy, Boehm believes, that enabled humans to flourish in the often difficult climatic conditions of the late Pleistocene. This was the likely beginning of moral generosity as distinct from the much stronger instincts for self-preservation and nepotism.

Second, every member of the band actively participated in putting down what !Kung Bushmen call "big-shot" behavior. No one was allowed to lord it over anyone else. Humans are the only primate that has punished and suppressed the bullying behavior of alpha males. They used gossip to keep themselves informed about deviant behavior (bullying especially, but also cheating and stealing) that could jeopardize the group's harmony or, in extreme cases, survival. Morality evolved as a social control mechanism to keep male deviance in check. If necessary, the group banished or even took the life of an individual who couldn't learn to behave properly. Along with generosity, humility is a prized virtue in hunter-gatherer societies.

Third, archaic humans encouraged one another to cultivate generosity, humility, and other moral practices as a way to bolster social cohesion. They knew instinctively that selfishness is a much stronger motivator than other-regarding moral sentiments. So they preached about the importance of being generous. The golden rule was a human universal in the ancestral environment, as it is to this day. As a species, we need constant reminders and incentives to share because such sentiments are less significant (weaker) than the instincts to protect self and family. Moral feelings enabled hunter-gatherers to treat nonfamily members of their group as if they were family.

Early human bands were small (20 to 30 members typically), which made gossip and shared decisions regarding deviant behavior very effective. As the harsh and unpredictable Ice Age gave way to milder weather patterns that have persisted for the past 12,000 years, Paleolithic humans began to live in larger groups, and the initial stages of the agricultural revolution took root. Bands gave way to tribes, which eventually grew into civilizations. In every single instance where this transformation occurred, humans reverted back to the hierarchical model of self-governance that morality had helped to suppress for more than 100,000 years. Moral feelings had enabled early humans to manage their in-group conflicts in an egalitarian manner. Now—living among mostly *strangers* in burgeoning civilizations with censuses in the tens of thousands—they faced the greatest moral crisis of their existence.

It took tremendous ingenuity and effort to overcome the natural xenophobia that helped ancestral hunter-gatherers stick together as moral communities. They were forced to widen the circle of their cares and generosity, an ongoing task that we still struggle with today. The creation of kingdoms, laws, armies, gods, sacred texts, and schools of philosophy, along with the considerable retinues and artifacts necessary to support them, took up some of the burden from an archaic moral system floundering like a fish out of water. The results, as we know all too well from human history, have been mixed.

Morality is both irreplaceable and insufficient in its behavioral ministrations. The greatest preoccupation of every civilization has been how to buttress and support the cause of conscience, without which a life together in massive societies would be even more impossible than it often is. Ethics, like religion, has played an educational role in the moral life, a professionalized iteration of the old moral practice of encouraging members of the group to be more generous in their feelings. The story of the Good Samaritan, like the golden rule, is captivating because it both identifies the moral problem of civilization (how to live with people who aren't part of your tribe) and resolves it in a very familiar way (treat strangers like you would your own family).

Some of the earliest ethical manuals, like Confucius's *Analects* and Aristotle's *Nichomachean Ethics*, instructed students about how to improve their moral lives. In Aristotle's case, that meant acquiring virtues, which are dispositions to act and feel appropriately in given circumstances. We acquire virtues—courage, for example—by making it a habit to imitate what courageous people do (standing up to bullies, perhaps). The problem with the moral life, as Aristotle viewed it, was that we have too many bad habits.

The history of ethics, essentially, has been an effort to universalize our moral feelings. How can we learn to treat everyone—friend, foe, stranger, whomever—without prejudice? That is the ethical quest. Henry Sidgwick, one of the great ethicists of the 19th century, claimed that there are only three methods of ethics.[9] One is intuitionism, best represented by Kant's "moral law," which requires that we only act according to principles (intuitions) that can be universally applied to everyone. Take the intuition that stealing is wrong, for example. If I think it is okay for me to steal but not for others to do so, then I have not lived up to the moral law because my intuition isn't being applied universally.

The second method that Sidgwick identified is consequentialism, best represented by Mill's utilitarianism, which requires that we always act in accordance with the greatest happiness principle. According to that principle, we are obligated to increase the happiness of the greatest number of people possible, not just ourselves or our tribe. Taking the example of stealing again, it is wrong for anyone (including me) to steal because the *consequence* of stealing diminishes the happiness of those who are robbed, which is never acceptable.

The final method of ethics that Sidgwick identified is egoism, which he belittled as unworthy of us because it is essentially self-serving. It's not that concern for oneself first and foremost is inherently wrong; it's the prospect of living in a society made up entirely of such individuals that would be unbearable. Selfishness has always been a part of our moral lives, and it serves an important function when survival is at stake; however, it falls short as a means to expand our feelings of generosity.

As I mention earlier, Jonathan Haidt accused philosophers of subjecting feelings to reason. What do we mean when we appeal to reason? I think we are looking for impartiality or objectivity: the absence of prejudice and favoritism. Being reasonable and applying our principles universally probably amount to the same thing. Yes, philosophers have attempted to subject feelings to reason (Aristotle would call it *educating our feelings*).[10] They did so (and still do) in the ongoing effort to solve the moral problem of civilization, which is to expand the circle of our generous feelings beyond the confines of our own tribe. What philosophers keep forgetting (subverting), however, is that the elephant is really in charge.

I have spent some time discussing the difference between morality and ethics because it is important for understanding what I mean by a moral theory of sports. Morality is more basic than ethics; it pertains to the altruistic feelings and instincts that evolved in the long gestation of our hunter-gatherer past. Ethics, on the other hand, is of more recent vintage. Grounded in the ideas and practices of civilization, it has systematically attempted to remake our moral lives. While I think both morality and ethics are vitally important to modern sports, this book focuses on the moral aspects of sports rather than the ethical conundrums that often bedevil it, for example, the cat-and-mouse game of catching cheaters who take PEDs.

The moral life was propped up by legal systems, religions, and ethical theories once we started living together in large civilizations. We could add sports to that list as well. The ancient Olympics illustrates just how interconnected these efforts to buttress morality were in the early centuries of post–Stone Age civilizations.[11] The games were religiously and politically significant, in addition to being athletic contests. The temple of Zeus was the largest structure at Olympia, which is saying something since the hippodrome for chariot racing could seat 80,000 bellicose fans. The statue of Zeus was considered one of the Seven Wonders of the Ancient World. There was only one foot race at the first Olympics, believed to be held in 776 BC. Other contests were added in later years. It is unknown why athletes competed naked, but we know that their trainers had to undress because of an incident involving a married woman named Pherenike. She had disguised herself as a trainer so she could watch her son compete. Married women were not allowed to attend. It is probably a myth that warfare ceased during the games, but safe passage was granted to those making the journey by the battle-prone Greeks.

One of the oldest platitudes about modern sports is that they are a training ground for the improvement of character. Children are encouraged—and often required—to participate in sports as a way of ensuring their moral development. Important as that might be, it's not what I mean by suggesting that morality and sports are intimately related. Sports are not just a "training ground" for morality, nor are they simply *like* morality in promoting this or that social benefit. Instead, they constitute a moral system in their own right that is the nearest thing to a remnant or vestige of the original moral system of our remote ancestors.

Sports offers a unique window into what it means to be moral in the fullest sense, and morality—particularly as it was practiced by our hunter-gatherer ancestors—returns the favor. Their interconnectedness is unique in modern times. I believe that the common sense morality we take for granted today has been sanitized and diminished in its scope when compared to what it was long ago. No doubt such diminishment is an inevitable consequence of the encroachments on the moral life from legal systems, religious traditions, political movements, and myriad other efforts to help us get along with one another on a shrinking planet with at least two nations now exceeding one billion citizens each. The complexities of life today are astonishing indeed and the inadequacies of morality as our sole guiding light all too obvious.

There is a rich texture to the moral life—a *thickness*, as anthropologist Clifford Geertz might say[12]—that has been weeded out throughout the years. Currently, we have what I would call a thin "goody two-shoes" sense of morality shorn of its full-bodied portfolio. My hope is that by viewing morality from the rough-and-tumble perspective of sports, we will come to appreciate all of the tactics and strategies that figure into the social calculus of being (and sometimes merely appearing to be) generous and good. The moral life is an extremely sophisticated and plastic social system. The secret of our success as a species is linked to our moral adaptability.

I'm also convinced that the reverse is equally enlightening: Viewing sports from the full-bodied moral perspective of our remote ancestors will help us understand the irresistible attraction so many of us have for sports. Why are we so serious about the games we watch and play? Why is it so mesmerizing to follow a tennis ball hit back and forth over a net? It's as if we were designed for such experiences—and, of course, we were. Understanding sports as an agonistic moral drama, we also begin to understand how our being here in this life is a peculiar kind of game playing. That was the message of Bernard Suits's quirky fable about the wise grasshopper, which has become a paradigm of sports philosophy.[13] Play is one of the few things we do for its own sake, as is the practice of moral virtue. The two belong to one another. That is my hunch, and it's why I wrote this book.

NOTES

INTRODUCTION

1. Malcolm Gladwell, *Outliers: The Story of Success* (Boston: Little, Brown and Company, 2008).
2. Johannes Fuss et al., "A Runner's High Depends on Cannabinoid Receptors in Mice," *PNAS* 112, no. 42 (October 20, 2015), 13105-08. Accessed October 23, 2017, https://www.researchgate.net/publication/282604724_A_Runner's_high_depends_on_cannabinoid_receptors_in_mice.
3. Peter Kramer, *Listening to Prozac* (New York: Penguin, 1993).
4. Jane Goodall, *The Chimpanzees of Gombe: Patterns of Behavior* (Cambridge, MA: Belknap, 1986), 61.
5. Frans de Waal, *Chimpanzee Politics: Power and Sex among Apes* (Baltimore, MD: Johns Hopkins University Press, 2007).
6. Christopher Boehm, *Moral Origins: The Evolution of Virtue, Altruism, and Shame* (New York: Basic Books, 2012).
7. Daniel Lieberman, *The Story of the Human Body: Evolution, Health, and Disease* (New York: Pantheon, 2013).
8. Charles Darwin, *The Descent of Man* (London: John Murray, 1882).
9. David Wilson, *Darwin's Cathedral: Evolution, Religion, and the Nature of Society* (Chicago: University of Chicago Press, 2002), 17.
10. Frans de Waal, *Primates and Philosophers: How Mortality Evolved* (Princeton, NJ: Princeton University Press, 2006), 7.

1. BULLYING, TEASING, AND THE BIRTH OF CONSCIENCE

1. Richard Alexander, *The Biology of Moral Systems* (Hawthorne, NY: De Gruyter, 1987).
2. Alexander, *The Biology of Moral Systems*, 113.
3. Benjamin Franklin, *The Autobiography of Benjamin Franklin* (New Haven, CT: Yale University Press, 1964), 125.
4. Alexander, *The Biology of Moral Systems*.
5. Alexander, *The Biology of Moral Systems*.
6. Mark Fainaru-Wada and Steve Fainaru, *League of Denial: The NFL, Concussions, and the Battle for Truth* (New York: Crown, 2013).
7. A. Bart Giamatti, "Baseball and the American Character," *Harper's* 273, no. 1,637 (October 1986): 27.
8. Giamatti, "Baseball and the American Character," 27.
9. Bonaventura Majolo and Laetitia Marechal, "Between-Group Competition Elicits Within-Group Cooperation in Children," *Scientific Reports* 7, article no. 43277 (2017). Accessed February 7, 2018, https://www.nature.com/articles/srep43277.
10. Christopher Boehm, *Moral Origins: The Evolution of Virtue, Altruism, and Shame* (New York: Basic Books, 2012), 158.
11. Boehm, *Moral Origins*.
12. Gina Perry, "Real-Life Lord of the Flies," *New Scientist*, vol. 237, no. 3,165 (February 17, 2018): 41–43.
13. Rayvon Fouche, *Game Changer: The Technoscientific Revolution in Sports* (Baltimore, MD: Johns Hopkins University Press, 2017).
14. Fouche, *Game Changer*, 162.
15. Fouche, *Game Changer*.
16. Boehm, *Moral Origins*.
17. Don Banks, "Back in Buffalo: Richie Incognito's Long Road from Pariah to Relevancy," *Sports Illustrated*, June 2, 2016. Accessed January 13, 2018, https://www.si.com/nfl/2016/06/02/richie-incognito-buffalo-bills-dolphins-bullying-scandal.
18. Ted Wells, *Report to the National Football League Concerning Issues of Workplace Conduct at the Miami Dolphins*. Accessed February 1, 2018, http://www.nfl.com/news/story/0ap2000000325899/article/summary-of-ted-wells-report-on-miami-dolphins.
19. *Jacobellis v. Ohio*, 378 U.S. 184 (1964).
20. Andrew George, trans. *The Epic of Gilgamesh: The Babylonian Epic Poem and Other Texts in Akkadian and Sumerian*, introduction by Andrew George (New York: Penguin, 2003).

21. Jean Briggs, *Inuit Morality Play: The Emotional Education of a Three-Year-Old* (New Haven, CT: Yale University Press, 1999), 8.
22. Kristen Fleming, "Why Everyone in Tennis Hates Maria Sharapova," *New York Post*, March 29, 2016. Accessed March 24, 2018, https://nypost.com/2016/03/29/why-everyone-in-tennis-hates-maria-sharapova/.

2. THE LAND OF PRETEND

1. Richard Alexander, *The Biology of Moral Systems* (Hawthorne, NY: De Gruyter, 1987).
2. Alexander, *The Biology of Moral Systems*.
3. Frans de Waal, *Primates and Philosophers: How Morality Evolved* (Princeton, NJ: Princeton University Press, 2006), 7–12.
4. Alexander, *The Biology of Moral Systems*.
5. Christopher Boehm, *Moral Origins: The Evolution of Virtue, Altruism, and Shame* (New York: Basic Books, 2012).
6. Adam Smith, *The Wealth of Nations* (New York: Prometheus Books, 1991).
7. L. Jon Wertheim, *Strokes of Genius: Federer, Nadal, and the Greatest Match Ever Played* (Boston: Houghton Mifflin Harcourt, 2009).
8. Jared Diamond, *The Third Chimpanzee: The Evolution and Future of the Human Animal* (New York: HarperCollins, 1992), 48.
9. Julian Jaynes, *The Origin of Consciousness in the Breakdown of the Bicameral Mind* (Boston: Houghton Mifflin, 2000).
10. Jaynes, *The Origin of Consciousness in the Breakdown of the Bicameral Mind*.
11. John Geiger, *The Third Man Factor: Surviving the Impossible* (Edinburgh: Canongate, 2009).
12. Jon Krakauer, *Into Thin Air: A Personal Account of the Mt. Everest Disaster* (New York: Villard, 1998).
13. Sarah Brosnan and Frans de Waal, "Monkeys Reject Unequal Pay," *Nature* 425 (September 18, 2003).
14. Michael McCann, "Deflategate, One Year Later: The Anatomy of a Failed Controversy," *Sports Illustrated*, January 17, 2016. Accessed April 4, 2018, https://www.si.com/nfl/2016/01/18/deflategate-one-year-later-tom-brady-bill-belichick.
15. John Leonard, "Tom Brady Has Done His Time for Deflategate, but the Science Says He's Not Guilty," *Sports Illustrated*, October 4, 2016. Accessed April 4, 2018, https://www.si.com/nfl/2016/10/04/tom-brady-deflategate-ideal-gas-law.

16. Samuel Horovitz, "If You Ain't Cheating You Ain't Trying: 'Spygate' and the Legal Implications of Trying Too Hard," *Texas Intellectual Property Law Journal* 17, no. 305 (2009).

17. Ted Wells, *Investigative Report Concerning Footballs Used during the AFC Championship Game on January 18, 2015*. Accessed April 4, 2018, https://nfllabor.files.wordpress.com/2015/05/investigative-and-expert-reports-re-footballs-used-during-afc-championsh.pdf.

3. COACHES AND REFEREES

1. Seth Davis, "The Hell of Fame," *Sports Illustrated* 118, no. 13 (March 25, 2013).

2. Anders Ericsson and Robert Pool, *Peak: Secrets from the New Science of Expertise* (Boston: Houghton Mifflin Harcourt, 2016).

3. Neil Amdur, "The Three Seconds That Never Seem to Run Out," *New York Times*, July 28, 2012. Accessed May 4, 2018, https://www.nytimes.com/2012/07/29/sports/olympics/three-seconds-of-the-munich-olympics-that-never-seem-to-run-out.html.

4. Joseph Price, Marc Remer, and Daniel Stone, "Sub-Perfect Game: Profitable Biases of NBA Referees," *Journal of Economics and Management Strategy* 21, no. 1 (2012).

5. Lawrence Pedowitz, *Report to the Board of Governors of the National Basketball Association*. Accessed May 5, 2018, https://www.nba.com/media/PedowitzReport.pdf.

6. Michel de Certeau, *The Practice of Everyday Life*, trans. Steven Rendall (Berkeley: University of California Press, 1984).

7. Jean Bottero, *Mesopotamia: Writing, Reasoning, and the Gods* (Chicago: University of Chicago Press, 1992), 210.

8. Associated Press, "Parents Go to Court to Boot 30-Year-Old Son from Their N.Y. Home," *Minneapolis Star-Tribune*, May 23, 2018. Accessed May 25, 2018, http://www.startribune.com/judge-sides-with-parents-boots-adult-son-from-new-york-home/483373871/.

9. Garrett Broshuis, "Restoring Integrity to America's Pastime," *Texas Review of Entertainment and Sports Law* 14, no. 2 (2013).

10. *New Oxford Annotated Bible* (Oxford, UK: Oxford University Press, 1977), *I Samuel* 17.

11. Lindsay Schnell, "Blowing up the BCS," *Sports Illustrated* 125, no. 19 (December 12, 2016).

4. IMITATION, RITUAL, AND TRANSCENDENCE

1. Elizabeth Anscombe, "Modern Moral Philosophy," *Philosophy* 33, no. 124 (January 1958).
2. Alasdair MacIntyre, *After Virtue: A Study in Moral Theory* (Notre Dame, IN: University of Notre Dame, 1981).
3. Stephen Covey, *The 7 Habits of Highly Effective People* (New York: Simon and Schuster, 1989).
4. Benjamin Franklin, *The Autobiography of Benjamin Franklin*, ed. Leonard Labaree et al. (New Haven, CT: Yale University Press, 1964), 148. Franklin's 13 virtues are as follows: temperance, silence, order, resolution, frugality, industry, sincerity, justice, moderation, cleanliness, tranquility, chastity, and humility.
5. Aristotle, *Nichomachean Ethics*, trans. Martin Ostwald (New York: Liberal Arts Press, 1962).
6. Christopher Peterson and Martin Seligman, *Character Strengths and Virtues: A Handbook and Classification* (New York: Oxford University Press, 2004).
7. A. Porteous, "Platonist or Aristotelian?" *Classical Review* 48, no. 3 (July 1934).
8. St. Augustine, "On the Morals of the Catholic Church," in *Augustin: The Writings against the Manichaeans and against the Donatists*, ed. Phillip Schaff (Peabody, MA: Hendrickson, 1994).
9. Aristotle, *Nichomachean Ethics*, 50.
10. Anders Ericsson and Robert Pool, *Peak: Secrets from the New Science of Expertise* (Boston: Houghton Mifflin Harcourt, 2016).
11. Ericsson and Pool, *Peak*.
12. Malcolm Gladwell, *Outliers: The Story of Success* (Boston: Little, Brown and Company, 2008).
13. Matthew Syed, *Bounce: Mozart, Federer, Picasso, Beckham, and the Science of Success* (New York: Harper, 2010).
14. John Rawls, *A Theory of Justice* (Cambridge, MA: Belknap, 1971).
15. Robert Bellah, *Religion in Human Evolution* (Cambridge, MA: Harvard University Press, 2011).
16. *Bull Durham*, directed by Ron Shelton (Orion Pictures, 1988).
17. Oscar Fernandez and Roberto Cachan-Cruz, "An Assessment of the Dynamic of Religious Ritualism in Sporting Environments," *Journal of Religious Health* 53, no. 6 (2014).
18. *Field of Dreams*, directed by Phil Robinson (Universal Pictures, 1989). The movie is based on the novel *Shoeless Joe* (Boston: Houghton Mifflin, 1982), by W. P. Kinsella.

19. David Foster Wallace, "Roger Federer as Religious Experience," *New York Times*, August 20, 2006. Accessed May 10, 2017, https://www.nytimes.com/2006/08/20/sports/playmagazine/20federer.html.

5. EXCELLENCE WITHOUT END

1. Bowen McCoy, "The Parable of the Sadhu," *Harvard Business Review*, May–June 1997. Accessed February 20, 2017, http://dhensley.com/wp-content/uploads/2017/06/parable-of-sadhu.pdf.
2. Jim Collins, *Good to Great* (New York: HarperAudio, 2001). See also Tom Peters and Robert Waterman, *In Search of Excellence: Lessons from America's Best-Run Companies* (New York: Harper and Row, 1982).
3. Lutz Bornmann and Ruediger Mutz, "Growth Rates of Modern Science," *Journal of the Association for Information Science and Technology* 66, no, 11 (2015).
4. Mark Fainaru-Wada and Steve Fainaru, *League of Denial: The NFL, Concussions, and the Battle for Truth* (New York: Crown, 2013), 79.
5. Mick Power, *Understanding Happiness: A Critical Review of Positive Psychology* (New York: Routledge, 2016).
6. Jonathan Raban, *Bad Land: An American Romance* (New York: Pantheon, 1996).
7. H. G. Bissinger, *Friday Night Lights: A Town, a Team, a Dream* (Reading, MA: Addison-Wesley, 1990). The film adaptation was directed by Peter Berg (Imagine Entertainment, 2004).
8. Angela Duckworth, *Grit: The Power of Passion and Perseverance* (New York: Scribner, 2016).
9. Jared Diamond, *Collapse: How Societies Choose to Fail or Succeed* (New York: Viking, 2005).
10. Michael Lewis, *Moneyball: The Art of Winning an Unfair Game* (New York: W. W. Norton, 2003).
11. David Wilson, *Darwin's Cathedral: Evolution, Religion, and the Nature of Society* (Chicago: University of Chicago Press, 2002).
12. Jay Busbee, "Why Rooting for Lindsey Vonn to Fail Is Un-American," *Yahoo Sports Online*, February 27, 2018. Accessed February 18, 2018, https://sports.yahoo.com/rooting-lindsey-vonn-fail-un-american-035939602.html.
13. Neil Young, "Heart of Gold," *Harvest* [album], Reprise Records, 1972.

6. NEUROSCIENCE, MIRRORING, AND COMPLEMENTARITY

1. Jocelyn Faubert, "Professional Athletes Have Extraordinary Skills for Rapidly Learning Complex and Neutral Dynamic Visual Scenes," *Scientific Reports* Vol. 3 (January 31, 2013). Accessed June 24, 2018, https://www.nature.com/articles/srep01154.
2. Brandon Sneed, *Head in the Game: The Mental Engineering of the World's Greatest Athletes* (New York: HarperCollins, 2017).
3. Sneed, *Head in the Game*.
4. Sneed, *Head in the Game*.
5. Marco Iacoboni, *Mirroring People: The New Science of How We Connect with Others* (New York: Farrar, Straus and Giroux, 2008), 18.

7. FANDOM: WHY WE WATCH AND CARE SO MUCH

1. Marco Iacoboni, *Mirroring People: The New Science of How We Connect with Others* (New York: Farrar, Straus and Giroux, 2008), 5.
2. Jack London, *The Call of the Wild* (New York: Macmillan, 1903).
3. Michel de Certeau, *The Practice of Everyday Life*, trans. Steven Rendall (Berkeley: University of California Press, 1984).
4. Mark St. Amant, *Committed: Confessions of a Fantasy Football Junkie* (Scribner, 2004), 6.

8. COCKFIGHTING, GAMBLING, AND VILLAGES

1. Clifford Geertz, *The Interpretation of Cultures* (New York: Basic Books, 1973).
2. Geertz, *The Interpretation of Cultures*, 421.
3. William Shakespeare, *As You Like It* (New York: Oxford University Press, 1993), Act II, Scene VII, "All the world's a stage, And all the men and women merely players . . ."
4. Nate Jackson, *Fantasy Man: A Former NFL Player's Descent into the Brutality of Fantasy Football* (New York: Harper, 2016).
5. Peter Matthiessen, *Under the Mountain Wall* (New York: Viking, 1962).
6. H. G. Bissinger, *Friday Night Lights: A Town, a Team, a Dream* (Reading, MA: Addison-Wesley, 1990). See chapter 5 for my earlier discussion of the story.

7. Jared Diamond, *Guns, Germs, and Steel: The Fates of Human Societies* (New York: W. W. Norton, 1999).

8. Alexis de Tocqueville, *Democracy in America* (Indianapolis, IN: Liberty Fund, 2012).

9. Michael Sandel, *Democracy's Discontent* (Harvard, 1996). Sandel articulates the communitarian case against radical individualism and the liberal political philosophy of the Enlightenment that is the basis for American politics.

10. Mina Cikara, M. Botvinick, and S. Fiske, "Us versus Them: Social Identity Shapes Neural Responses to Intergroup Competition and Harm," *Psychological Science* 22, no. 3 (2011).

9. SITUATIONISM AND THE DYNAMICS OF MISBEHAVIOR

1. John Doris, *Lack of Character: Personality and Moral Behavior* (New York: Cambridge University Press, 2002).

2. Alice Isen and Paula Levin, "Effect of Feeling Good on Helping: Cookies and Kindness," *Journal of Personality and Social Psychology* 21, no. 3 (1972).

3. Robert Baron and Jill Thomley, "A Whiff of Reality: Positive Affect as a Potential Mediator of the Effects of Pleasant Fragrances on Task Performance and Helping," *Environment and Behavior* 26 (1994).

4. Bibb Latane and John Darley, "Group Inhibition of Bystander Intervention in Emergencies," *Journal of Personality and Social Psychology* 10 (1968).

5. Doris, *Lack of Character*, 8.

6. Stanley Milgram, "Behavioral Study of Obedience," *Journal of Abnormal and Social Psychology* 67 (1963).

7. Craig Haney, Curtis Banks, and Philip Zimbardo, "A Study of Prisoners and Guards in a Simulated Prison," *Naval Research Review* 30 (1973).

8. Doris, *Lack of Character*.

10. WHITHER THE FUTURE?

1. Charles Darwin, *The Descent of Man* (London: John Murray, 1882).

2. Society for Assisted Reproductive Technology, "National Summary Report." Accessed September 23, 2018, https://www.sartcorsonline.com/rptCSR_PublicMultYear.aspx?reportingYear=2015.

NOTES

3. Gregory Stock, *Redesigning Humans: Choosing Our Children's Genes* (Boston: Houghton Mifflin Harcourt, 2002), 4.

4. Kevin Warwick, "Cyborg 1.0," *Wired* (February 2000).

5. Stock, *Redesigning Humans*, 29.

APPENDIX

1. Jonathan Haidt, *The Happiness Hypothesis: Finding Modern Truth in Ancient Wisdom* (New York: Basic Books, 2006).

2. Haidt, *The Happiness Hypothesis*.

3. Haidt, *The Happiness Hypothesis*.

4. Steven Pinker, *How the Mind Works* (New York: W. W. Norton, 1997).

5. Noam Chomsky, "The Universal Man," *New Scientist* 213, no. 2,856 (March 17, 2012).

6. Marco Iacoboni, *Mirroring People: The New Science of How We Connect with Others* (New York: Farrar, Straus and Giroux, 2008).

7. Joshua Greene, *Moral Tribes: Emotion, Reason, and the Gap between Us and Them* (New York: Penguin, 2013).

8. Christopher Boehm, *Moral Origins: The Evolution of Virtue, Altruism, and Shame* (New York: Basic Books, 2012).

9. Henry Sidgwick, *The Methods of Ethics* (Chicago: University of Chicago Press, 1962).

10. Aristotle, *Nichomachean Ethics*. Trans. Martin Ostwald. (New York: Liberal Arts Press, 1962).

11. Allen Guttmann, *Sports: The First Five Millenia* (Amherst: University of Massachusetts, 2004).

12. Clifford Geertz, *The Interpretation of Cultures* (New York: Basic Books, 1973), 430.

13. Bernard Suits, *The Grasshopper: Games, Life, and Utopia* (Toronto: University of Toronto Press, 1978).

BIBLIOGRAPHY

Alexander, Richard. *The Biology of Moral Systems*. Hawthorne, NY: De Gruyter, 1987.
Amdur, Neil. "The Three Seconds That Never Seem to Run Out." *New York Times*, July 28, 2012. Accessed May 4, 2018. https://www.nytimes.com/2012/07/29/sports/olympics/three-seconds-of-the-munich-olympics-that-never-seem-to-run-out.html.
Anscombe, Elizabeth. "Modern Moral Philosophy." *Philosophy* 33, no. 124 (January 1958): 1–19.
Aristotle [384–322 BC]. *Nichomachean Ethics*. Trans. Martin Ostwald. New York: Liberal Arts Press, 1962.
Associated Press. "Parents Go to Court to Boot 30-Year-Old Son from Their N.Y. Home." *Minneapolis Star-Tribune*, May 23, 2018. Accessed May 25, 2018, http://www.startribune.com/judge-sides-with-parents-boots-adult-son-from-new-york-home/483373871/.
Augustine, St. [354–430]. "On the Morals of the Catholic Church." In *Augustin: The Writings against the Manichaeans and against the Donatists*, ed. Phillip Schaff, pp. 231–39. Peabody, MA: Hendrickson, 1994.
Banks, Don. "Back in Buffalo: Richie Incognito's Long Road from Pariah to Relevancy." *Sports Illustrated*, June 2, 2016. Accessed January 13, 2018, https://www.si.com/nfl/2016/06/02/richie-incognito-buffalo-bills-dolphins-bullying-scandal.
Barkow, Jerome, Leda Cosmides, and John Tooby. *The Adapted Mind: Evolutionary Psychology and the Generation of Culture*. New York: Oxford University Press, 1992.
Baron, Robert, and Jill Thomley. "A Whiff of Reality: Positive Affect as a Potential Mediator of the Effects of Pleasant Fragrances on Task Performance and Helping." *Environment and Behavior* 26 (1994): 766–84.
Barrett, Deidre. *Supernormal Stimuli: How Primal Urges Overran Their Evolutionary Purposes*. New York: W. W. Norton, 2010.
Bateson, Gregory. "A Theory of Play and Fantasy." In *Ritual, Play, and Performance: Readings in the Social Sciences/Theatre*, ed. Richard Schechner, pp. 67–73. New York: Seabury Press, 1976.
Bellah, Robert. *Religion in Human Evolution*. Harvard University Press, 2011.
Bissinger, H. G. *Friday Night Lights: A Town, a Team, a Dream*. Reading, MA: Addison-Wesley, 1990.
Boehm, Christopher. *Moral Origins: The Evolution of Virtue, Altruism, and Shame*. New York: Basic Books, 2012.
Bornmann, Lutz, and Ruediger Mutz. "Growth Rates of Modern Science." *Journal of the Association for Information Science and Technology* 66, no. 11 (2015): 2,215–22.
Boterro, Jean. *Mesopotamia: Writing, Reasoning, and the Gods*. Chicago: University of Chicago Press, 1992.

Bowerman, William, and W. E. Harris. *Jogging, Etc.* London: Transworld Publishers, 1968.
Boxill, Jan, ed. *Sports Ethics: An Anthology.* Malden, MA: Blackwell, 2003.
Briggs, Jean. *Inuit Morality Play: The Emotional Education of a Three-Year-Old.* New Haven, CT: Yale University Press, 1999.
Brooks, David. *The Road to Character.* New York: Random House, 2015.
Broshius, Garrett. "Restoring Integrity to America's Pastime." *Texas Review of Entertainment and Sports Law* 14, no. 2 (2013): 119–44.
Brosnan, Sarah, and Frans de Waal. "Monkeys Reject Unequal Pay." *Nature* 425 (September 18, 2003): 297–99.
Buller, David. *Adapting Minds: Evolutionary Psychology and the Persistent Quest for Human Nature.* Cambridge, MA: MIT Press, 2005.
Busbee, Jay. "Why Rooting for Lindsey Vonn to Fail Is Un-American." *Yahoo Sports Online*, February 27, 2018. Accessed February 18, 2018, https://sports.yahoo.com/rooting-lindsey-vonn-fail-un-american-035939602.html.
Chomsky, Noam. *Syntactic Structures.* The Hague, NL: Mouton, 1964.
———. "The Universal Man." *New Scientist* 213, no. 2,856 (March 17, 2012): 28–29.
Christian, David. *Maps of Time: An Introduction to Big History.* Berkeley: University of California Press, 2004.
Cikara, M., M. Botvinick, and S. Fiske. "Us versus Them: Social Identity Shapes Neural Responses to Intergroup Competition and Harm." *Psychological Science* 22, no. 3 (2011): 306–13.
Collins, Jim. *Good to Great.* New York: HarperAudio, 2001.
Confucius [551–479 BC]. *The Analects.* Trans. Raymond Dawson. New York: Oxford University Press, 2000.
Covey, Stephen. *The 7 Habits of Highly Effective People.* New York: Simon and Schuster, 1989.
Darwin, Charles [1809–1882]. *The Descent of Man.* London: John Murray, 1882.
———. *On the Origin of Species.* New York: Cambridge University Press, 2009.
Davis, Seth. "The Hell of Fame." *Sports Illustrated* 118, no. 13 (March 25, 2013): 64 ff.
De Block, Andreas, and Siegfried Dewitte. "Darwinism and the Cultural Evolution of Sports." *Perspectives in Biology and Medicine* 52, no. 1 (Winter 2009): 1–16.
de Certeau, Michel. *The Practice of Everyday Life.* Trans. Steven Rendall. Berkeley: University of California Press, 1984.
de Tocqueville, Alexis [1805–1859]. *Democracy in America.* Indianapolis, IN: Liberty Fund, 2012.
de Waal, Frans. *The Bonobo and the Atheist.* New York: W. W. Norton, 2013.
———. *Chimpanzee Politics: Power and Sex among Apes.* Baltimore, MD: Johns Hopkins University Press, 2007.
———. *Primates and Philosophers: How Morality Evolved.* Princeton, NJ: Princeton University Press, 2006.
Diamond, Jared. *Collapse: How Societies Choose to Fail or Succeed.* New York: Viking, 2005.
———. *Guns, Germs, and Steel: The Fates of Human Societies.* New York: W. W. Norton, 1999.
———. *The Third Chimpanzee: The Evolution and Future of the Human Animal.* New York: HarperCollins, 1992.
Doris, John. *Lack of Character: Personality and Moral Behavior.* New York: Cambridge University Press, 2002.
Duckworth, Angela. *Grit: The Power of Passion and Perseverance.* New York: Scribner, 2016.
Elliott, Carl. *Better Than Well: American Medicine Meets the American Dream.* New York: W. W. Norton, 2003.
Epstein, David. *The Sports Gene: Inside the Science of Extraordinary Athletic Performance.* New York: Current, 2013.
Ericsson, Anders, and Robert Pool. *Peak: Secrets from the New Science of Expertise.* Boston: Houghton Mifflin Harcourt, 2016.

Fainaru-Wada, Mark, and Steve Fainaru. *League of Denial: The NFL, Concussions, and the Battle for Truth.* New York: Crown, 2013.
Faubert, Jocelyn. "Professional Athletes Have Extraordinary Skills for Rapidly Learning Complex and Neutral Dynamic Visual Scenes." *Scientific Reports* 3 (January 31, 2013). Accessed June 24, 2018, https://www.nature.com/articles/srep01154.
Fernandez, Oscar, and Roberto Cachan-Cruz. "An Assessment of the Dynamic of Religious Ritualism in Sporting Environments." *Journal of Religious Health* 53, no. 6 (2014): 1,653–61.
Fleming, Kristen. "Why Everyone in Tennis Hates Maria Sharapova." *New York Post*, March 29, 2016. Accessed March 24, 2018, https://nypost.com/2016/03/29/why-everyone-in-tennis-hates-maria-sharapova/.
Fouche, Rayvon. *Game Changer: The Technoscientific Revolution in Sports.* Baltimore, MD: Johns Hopkins University Press, 2017.
Franklin, Benjamin. *The Autobiography of Benjamin Franklin.* Ed. Leonard Labaree et al. New Haven, CT: Yale University Press, 1964.
Fuss, Johannes, Jörg Steinle, Laura Bindila, Matthias K. Aver, Hartmut Kirchherr, Beat Lutz, and Peter Gass. "A Runner's High Depends on Cannabinoid Receptors in Mice." *PNAS* 112, no. 42 (October 20, 2015), 13105-08. Accessed October 23, 2017. https://www.researchgate.net/publication/282604724_A_Runner's_high_depends_on_cannabinoid_receptors_in_mice.
Geertz, Clifford. *The Interpretation of Cultures.* New York: Basic Books, 1973.
Geiger, John. *The Third-Man Factor: Surviving the Impossible.* Edinburgh: Canongate, 2009.
George, Andrew, trans. *The Epic of Gilgamesh: The Babylonian Epic Poem and Other Texts in Akkadian and Sumerian.* Introduction by Andrew George. New York: Penguin, 2003.
Giamatti, A. Bart. "Baseball and the American Character." *Harper's* 273, no. 1,637 (October 1986): 27–30.
Gladwell, Malcolm. *Outliers: The Story of Success.* Boston: Little, Brown and Company, 2008.
Goodall, Jane. *The Chimpanzees of Gombe: Patterns of Behavior.* Cambridge, MA: Belknap, 1986.
Greene, Joshua. *Moral Tribes: Emotion, Reason, and the Gap between Us and Them.* New York: Penguin, 2013.
Guttmann, Allen. *Sports: The First Five Millenia.* Amherst: University of Massachusetts Press, 2004.
Hacking, Ian. *Historical Ontology.* Cambridge, MA: Harvard University Press, 2002.
Haerens, Margaret, ed. *Doping.* Opposing Viewpoints Series. Farmington Hills, MI: Greenhaven, 2014.
Haidt, Jonathan. *The Happiness Hypothesis: Finding Modern Truth in Ancient Wisdom.* New York: Basic Books, 2006.
_____. *The Righteous Mind: Why Good People Are Divided by Politics and Religion.* New York: Pantheon, 2012.
Haney, Craig, Curtis Banks, and Philip Zimbardo. "A Study of Prisoners and Guards in a Simulated Prison." *Naval Research Review* 30 (1973): 4–17.
Hauser, Marc. *Moral Minds.* New York: HarperCollins, 2006.
Homer [8th century BC]. *The Iliad.* Trans. Richmond Lattimore. Chicago: University of Chicago Press, 1951.
_____. *The Odyssey.* Trans. Albert Cook. New York: W. W. Norton, 1967.
Horovitz, Samuel. "If You Ain't Cheating You Ain't Trying: 'Spygate' and the Legal Implications of Trying Too Hard." *Texas Intellectual Property Law Journal* 17, no. 305 (2009): 305–31.
Iacoboni, Marco. *Mirroring People: The New Science of How We Connect with Others.* New York: Farrar, Straus and Giroux, 2008.
Isen, Alice, and Paula Levin. "Effect of Feeling Good on Helping: Cookies and Kindness." *Journal of Personality and Social Psychology* 21, no. 3 (1972): 384–88.

Jackson, Nate. *Fantasy Man: A Former NFL Player's Descent into the Brutality of Fantasy Football*. New York: Harper, 2016.
James, Scott. *An Introduction to Evolutionary Ethics*. Malden, MA: Blackwell, 2011.
Jaynes, Julian. *The Origin of Consciousness in the Breakdown of the Bicameral Mind*. Boston: Houghton Mifflin, 2000.
Johnson, Steven. *Mind Wide Open*. New York: Scribner, 2004.
Joyce, Richard. *The Evolutmion of Morality*. Cambridge, MA: MIT Press, 2007.
Kant, Immanuel [1724–1804]. *Critique of Practical Reason*. Indianapolis, IN: Bobbs-Merrill, 1956.
———. *Grounding for the Metaphysics of Morals*, 3rd ed. London: Hackett, 1993.
Krakauer, Jon. *Into Thin Air: A Personal Account of the Mt. Everest Disaster*. New York: Villard, 1998.
Kramer, Peter. *Listening to Prozac*. New York: Penguin, 1993.
Latane, Bibb, and John Darley. "Group Inhibition of Bystander Intervention in Emergencies." *Journal of Personality and Social Psychology* 10 (1968): 308–24.
Leonard, John. "Tom Brady Has Done His Time for Deflategate, but the Science Says He's Not Guilty." *Sports Illustrated*, October 4, 2016. Accessed April 4, 2018, https://www.si.com/nfl/2016/10/04/tom-brady-deflategate-ideal-gas-law.
Lewis, Michael. *Moneyball: The Art of Winning an Unfair Game*. New York: W. W. Norton, 2003.
Lieberman, Daniel. *The Story of the Human Body: Evolution, Health, and Disease*. New York: Pantheon, 2013.
London, Jack. *The Call of the Wild*. London: Macmillan, 1903.
Machiavelli, Niccolo [1469–1527]. *The Prince*. Chicago: University of Chicago Press, 1998.
MacIntyre, Alasdair. *After Virtue: A Study in Moral Theory*. Notre Dame, IN: University of Notre Dame Press, 1981.
Majolo, Bonaventura, and Laetitia Marechal. "Between-Group Competition Elicits Within-Group Cooperation in Children." *Scientific Reports* 7, article no. 43277 (2017). Accessed February 7, 2018, https://www.nature.com/articles/srep43277.
Matthiessen, Peter. *Under the Mountain Wall*. New York: Viking, 1962.
McCann, Michael. "Deflategate, One Year Later: The Anatomy of a Failed Controversy." *Sports Illustrated*, January 17, 2016. Accessed April 4, 2018, https://www.si.com/nfl/2016/01/18/deflategate-one-year-later-tom-brady-bill-belichick.
McCoy, Bowen. "The Parable of the Sadhu." *Harvard Business Review*, May–June 1997. Accessed February 20, 2017, http://dhensley.com/wp-content/uploads/2017/06/parable-of-sadhu.pdf.
McDonald, Melissa, Carlos Navarrete, and Mark Van Vugt. "Evolution and the Psychology of Intergroup Conflict: The Male Warrior Hypothesis." *Philosophical Transactions of the Royal Society B* 367 (2012): 670–79.
Milgram, Stanley. "Behavioral Study of Obedience." *Journal of Abnormal and Social Psychology* 67 (1963): 371–78.
Mill, John Stuart [1806–1873]. *Utilitarianism*. Indianapolis, IN: Bobbs-Merrill, 1957.
Nack, William. "Pure Heart: The Life and Death of the Racehorse Secretariat." *Sports Illustrated*, June 1990. Accessed April 4, 2018, https://www.si.com/longform/belmont/index.html.
New Oxford Annotated Bible, rev. standard version. Oxford, UK: Oxford University Press, 1977.
Papineau, David. *Knowing the Score: What Sports Can Teach Us about Philosophy (and What Philosophy Can Teach Us about Sports)*. New York: Basic Books, 2017.
Pedowitz, Lawrence. *Report to the Board of Governors of the National Basketball Association*. Accessed May 5, 2018, https://www.nba.com/media/PedowitzReport.pdf.
Perry, Gina. "Real-Life Lord of the Flies." *New Scientist*, vol. 237, no. 3,165 (February 17, 2018): 41–43.
Peters, Tom, and Robert Waterman. *In Search of Excellence: Lessons from America's Best-Run Companies*. New York: Harper and Row, 1982.

Peterson, Christopher, and Martin Seligman. *Character Strengths and Virtues: A Handbook and Classification*. New York: Oxford University Press, 2004.
Pigliucci, Massimo. *Answers for Aristotle*. New York: Basic Books, 2012.
Pinker, Steven. *How the Mind Works*. New York: W. W. Norton, 1997.
Plato [427–347 BC]. *The Dialogues of Plato*. New York: Oxford University Press, 1924.
Porteous, A. "Platonist or Aristotelian?" *Classical Review* 48, no. 3 (July 1934): 97–105.
Power, Mick. *Understanding Happiness: A Critical Review of Positive Psychology*. New York: Routledge, 2016.
Price, Joseph, Marc Remer, and Daniel Stone. "Sub-Perfect Game: Profitable Biases of NBA Referees." *Journal of Economics and Management Strategy* 21, no. 1 (2012): 271–300.
Raban, Jonathan. *Bad Land: An American Romance*. New York: Pantheon, 1996.
Rawls, John. *A Theory of Justice*. Cambridge, MA: Belknap, 1971.
Rieff, Philip. *Freud: The Mind of the Moralist*. New York: Viking, 1959.
———. *The Triumph of the Therapeutic: Uses of Faith after Freud*. Chicago: University of Chicago Press, 1966.
Rose, Nikolas. *Governing the Soul: The Shaping of the Private Self*, 2nd ed. London: Free Association of Books, 1999.
Rose, Nikolas, and Joelle Abi-Rached. *Neuro: The New Brain Sciences and the Management of the Mind*. Princeton, NJ: Princeton University Press, 2013.
Sandel, Michael. *The Case against Perfection: Ethics in the Age of Genetic Engineering*. Cambridge, MA: Harvard University Press, 2007.
———. *Democracy's Discontent: America in Search of a Public Philosophy*. Cambridge, MA: Harvard University Press, 1996.
Schnell, Lindsay. "Blowing up the BCS." *Sports Illustrated* 125, no. 19 (December 12, 2016): 52–59.
Seinfeld, Jerry, and Larry David. *Seinfeld*. NBC television series. Columbia Tristar Television Distribution, 1989–1998.
Shackleton, Ernest [1874–1922]. *South: A Memoir of the Endurance Voyage*. New York: Carroll and Graf, 1998.
Shakespeare, William [1564–1616]. *As You Like It*. Ed. Alan Brissenden. New York: Oxford University Press, 1993.
Shelton, Ron. *Bull Durham*. Motion picture. Orion Pictures, 1988.
Sidgwick, Henry [1838–1900]. *The Methods of Ethics*. Chicago: University of Chicago Press, 1962.
Singer, Peter. *The Expanding Circle: Ethics, Evolution, and Moral Progress*. New York: Farrar, Straus and Giroux, 1981.
Smith, Adam [1723–1790]. *The Theory of Moral Sentiments*. Cambridge, UK: Cambridge University Press, 2002.
———. *The Wealth of Nations*. New York: Prometheus Books, 1991.
Sneed, Brandon. *Head in the Game: The Mental Engineering of the World's Greatest Athletes*. New York: HarperCollins, 2017.
St. Amant, Mark. *Committed: Confessions of a Fantasy Football Junkie*. New York: Scribner, 2004.
Stock, Gregory. *Redesigning Humans: Choosing Our Children's Genes*. Boston: Houghton Mifflin Harcourt, 2002.
Suits, Bernard. *The Grasshopper: Games, Life, and Utopia*. Toronto: University of Toronto Press, 1978.
Syed, Matthew. *Bounce: Mozart, Federer, Picasso, Beckham, and the Science of Success*. New York: Harper, 2010.
Virgil [70–19 BC]. *The Aeneid*. Trans. Robert Fitzgerald. New York: Random House, 1983.
Wallace, David Foster. "Federer as Religious Experience." *New York Times*, August 20, 2006. Accessed May 10, 2017, https://www.nytimes.com/2006/08/20/sports/playmagazine/20federer.html.
Warwick, Kevin. "Cyborg 1.0." *Wired* (February 2000): 145–51.

Wells, Ted. *Investigative Report Concerning Footballs Used during the AFC Championship Game on January 18, 2015.* Accessed April 4, 2018. https://nfllabor.files.wordpress.com/2015/05/investigative-and-expert-reports-re-footballs-used-during-afc-championsh.pdf.

———. *Report to the National Football League Concerning Issues of Workplace Conduct at the Miami Dolphins.* Accessed February 1, 2018, http://www.nfl.com/news/story/0ap2000000325899/article/summary-of-ted-wells-report-on-miami-dolphins.

Wertheim, L. Jon. *Strokes of Genius: Federer, Nadal, and the Greatest Match Ever Played.* Boston: Houghton Mifflin Harcourt, 2009.

Wertheim, L. Jon, and Sam Sommers. *This Is Your Brain on Sports: The Science of Underdogs, the Value of Rivalry, and What We Can Learn from the T-Shirt Cannon.* New York: Crown Archetype, 2016.

Wilson, David. *Darwin's Cathedral: Evolution, Religion, and the Nature of Society.* Chicago: University of Chicago Press, 2002.

Wilson, Edward. *The Social Conquest of Earth.* New York: Liveright, 2012.

Young, Neil. "Heart of Gold." *Harvest.* Album. Reprise Records, 1972.

INDEX

The 7 Habits of Highly Effective People, 53–54
1972 Munich Olympics, 39, 45–46
1976 Montreal Olympics, 73, 152
1980 Lake Placid Olympics, 68
2018 Pyeongchang Olympics, 84

Abdul-Jabbar, Kareem, 98
addiction, 82–83
agricultural revolution, xv, xvi, 5, 22, 61, 68, 78, 80, 127–128, 148, 162
Aikman, Troy, 97
Alexander, Richard, biological evolution of psyche, 1–3, 20
Ali, Muhammad, 29–30, 65, 112, 113
American dream, 129
anabolic steroids, xiii, 122, 153
analytics, use of in making baseball player decisions. *See* moneyball
ancestral environment. *See* hunter-gatherer way of life
ancient Olympics, 165
Andre the Giant, 112
Anscombe, Elizabeth, revival of virtue ethics, 53
Apollo 11 mission to the moon, 129
appetites, insatiability of. *See* scarcity, role of in moral evolution
Aristotle, acquisition of virtues, 54, 55–57, 61, 96, 163, 164

Armstrong, Lance, role of bullying in doping scandal, 8–10
artificial chromosomes, 152, 154
athletic skills, acquisition of, 57–60
authenticity, scarcity of, 85
aversion to being cheated, 29, 31–32
awakening of ancient instincts. *See* call of the wild

babyfaces in professional wrestling. *See* professional wrestling
Balinese cockfighting: origins of gambling, 120, 121–122, 125; village life compared to Texas town, 126–129
banishment as hunter-gatherer moral punishment, 5, 162
baseball. *See Bull Durham*; *Field of Dreams*; gambling as social contagion; Giamatti, A. Bart; moneyball; natural law tradition in sports; neuroscience uses in athletic training; *schadenfreude*; seventh-inning stretch; small ball baseball strategy; stolen base baseball tactic
basketball. *See* 1972 Munich Olympics; Curry, Stephen; hack-a-Shaq strategy; intrastate rivalries; James, Lebron; Jordan, Michael; March madness; NBA; neuroscience uses in athletic training; pick-and-role play in basketball

INDEX

Beadle, Michelle, ESPN cohost, 150–151
bees, social insects, 22, 106
Belichick, Bill, 24–25, 86
betting, meaning of. *See* gambling as social contagion
bias confirmation, 34, 138
bicameral theory of consciousness, 27–28
biofeedback, 92
Boise State University Fiesta Bowl, 51
Bolt, Usain, 154
boosterism, exaggerated expectations, 74, 75, 89, 90, 153, 154
Boston Red Sox, use of neuroscouting, 91
Bowerman, Bill. *See* Nike
boxing. *See* Ali, Muhammad; Foreman, George; Frazier, Joe
Brady, Tom, 25, 32, 34, 113. *See also* Deflategate
brain plasticity, 90, 94, 151
brain synchronicity. *See* mirror neurons
bronc riding, 38
bucket list solipsism, 72
Bull Durham, 66–67
bullying, role of in morality. *See* conscience, evolution of
Butkus, Dick, 112
bystander apathy, 135–136

Cain and Abel, Bible story, 81
call of the wild, awakening ancient instincts and memories, xii, 65, 108, 110
de Certeau, Michel. *See* subversive behavior, moral significance of
Chamberlain, Wilt, 112
character as basis for behavior, 133, 134, 136, 141, 142, 143–145
cheating. *See* moral deception
chess, 42, 43, 154
Chicago Bulls. *See* Jordan, Michael
Chicago Cubs, 75
chimpanzees and bonobos. *See* primatology research
choking, cause of, 60
chunking, seeing what is about to happen, 43, 58–59, 60, 90
climate change influence on evolution, 78, 162

coaching. *See* strategy in coaching; tactics in coaching
Code of Hammurabi, 49
Collins, Doug, 45
Comaneci, Nadia, 73
complementarity thesis for neuroscience, 100–102
computer hacking as morally subversive, 149
concussions in football. *See* CTE
conscience, evolution of, xv, 2, 5, 6, 15, 19–20, 22, 50, 80, 83, 94, 99, 100, 101, 121, 145, 147, 163
consequentialism (ethical method), 164
Costner, Kevin, baseball movies. *See Bull Durham*; *Field of Dreams*
CTE (chronic traumatic encephalopathy), 3, 73
cunning, importance of in moral life. *See* moral deception; tricksters and trickery
Curry, Stephen, 73, 90–91
cyborgization, 154, 155, 156

Darwin, Charles, xvi, 147
Data, *Star Trek: The Next Generation*, 42, 154
David and Goliath, Bible story, 50, 51
deception. *See* moral deception
Deflategate, 32–34, 113
deliberate practice, 58, 60, 83, 90, 94
Detroit Pistons, 113
dime in payphone psychology experiment, 134, 139–140, 151
domestic violence. *See* #MeToo movement
Donaghy, Tim, NBA referee, 47
doping. *See* PEDs
dreaming and sports analogy, 26
Duckworth, Angela. *See* grit

Easter Island, collapse of civilization, 76–77
EEG (electroencephalogram) use in training, 91–92
egalitarian preference in morality, xvii, 10, 15, 48, 113, 122, 130–131, 149, 162
egoism, natural instinct for, 5, 23, 93, 145, 164

INDEX

Epic of Gilgamesh, 12
epigenetics, 89–90
EPO (erythropoietin), 9, 17, 157
ethical idealism as distinct from morality, 1, 2, 19, 53, 57, 63, 134, 157, 158, 163
ethology. *See* Goodall, Jane
evolution of *Homo sapiens*, xiv–xv, xvi, 1–3, 15, 20, 97, 108, 154, 161
excellence, potential harm of, 72, 73, 74, 75, 76–77. *See also* addiction; moneyball; scarcity, role of in evolution
expertise, acquisition of, 43, 58, 59, 62. *See also* chunking

failure as learning experience, x, 81, 86
fairness, sense of, xiv, 31–32, 44. *See also* Deflategate; justice as epitome of virtue; moral deception
false hope. *See* boosterism, exaggerated expectations
fantasy football, 103, 104, 115–116, 123–124
Favre, Brett, gunslinger mentality, 81, 82
Federer, Roger, 31, 42, 69–70, 84, 140
Field of Dreams, 69
flexibility, importance of, 23, 74, 80, 155
flow of the game, being in the, 44, 45, 64
football. *See* Boise State University Fiesta Bowl; CTE; Deflategate; fantasy football; *Friday Night Lights*; Hail Mary pass; Incognito, Richie; #MeToo movement; Meyer, Urban; NFL; spread offense in football; Spygate; strategy in coaching; tactics in coaching; zone read, football tactic
Foreman, George, 29
Franklin, Benjamin, 2, 57, 171n4
Frazier, Joe, 29, 65
Friday Night Lights, 75, 116, 126. *See also* Balinese cockfighting
friendship, importance of, ix, xi, 1, 12, 16, 17, 24, 28, 31, 56, 57, 67, 106, 116, 124, 131, 145, 163
frontier mythologies, importance of, 14, 81, 128, 129, 154
fyborgization, 155

Gable, Dan, 39

gambling as social contagion, 122, 123. *See also* Balinese cockfighting; fantasy football
gamesmanship, 34–35
Garden of Eden, Bible story, 109
Gay-Lussac's gas law, 33, 34
Geertz, Clifford. *See* Balinese cockfighting
generosity, importance of for hunter-gatherers, 4, 16, 21, 23, 82, 85, 93, 94, 95, 102, 146, 162, 163
genetics, future implications of, 89–90, 152–154
Giamatti, A. Bart, paradoxical nature of baseball, 4–5
Gladwell, Malcolm, ix; 10,000 hour rule, 59
Goodall, Jane, xiii–xiv, xv
Good Samaritan law, 135
Grant, Bud, 39
The Grasshopper, parable about games, 166
Greenland, settlement of, 77–80
Gretzky, Wayne, 97
grit, 55, 76, 77
gunslinger mentality, 81

hack-a-Shaq strategy, 29
Hail Mary pass, 68
hallucinatory voices, 27–28
Himalayas, 28, 71–72
hive behavior, moral significance of, 22–23, 24, 25, 97, 106, 125, 130, 145, 146, 147
honesty, importance of, 3, 85, 133, 143
human genome, 6, 89
humility, importance of for hunter-gatherers, 21, 82, 85, 162
hunter-gatherer way of life, xvii, 4, 5, 6, 7, 15–16, 19, 23, 30, 48, 49, 61, 62, 63, 66, 77–78, 80, 82, 84, 85, 86, 94, 113, 122, 127, 139, 147, 149, 163, 165

Ice Age, importance of for human evolution. *See* climate change
Iceland, settlement of, 77
The Iliad (Homer), 26, 27–28
illusion, use of. *See* make-believe, importance of

imaginary worlds. *See* make-believe, importance of
imitation, importance of, 54, 60, 64, 96, 160. *See also* play, importance of; rituals, importance of
immune system, flexibility of, 80
Incognito, Richie, 11–12, 14, 15
instinct. *See* moral instinct
intentional fouling, 29
Into Thin Air, Everest disaster. *See* Himalayas
intrastate rivalries, 110
intuitionism (ethical method), 163
Inuit, 16, 77–78, 80, 86
IRB (Institutional Review Board), 138
Irvin, Michael, 97
IVF (in vitro fertilization), 152

jackrabbits. *See* South Dakota State University
Jackson, Nate, fantasy football player, 124
Jackson, Reggie, 65
James, LaMichael, Oregon football, 41
James, Lebron, 6, 73, 85, 98, 153
Jenner, Bruce/Caitlyn, transgender issue, 152
Jennings, Kerri Walsh, 92
jogging, 1970s fitness craze, xi–xii
Jordan, Michael, 86, 105, 106, 107, 117, 149, 152
justice as epitome of virtue, 56; Rawlsian original position, 61

Kaepernick, Colin, 84
Kalahari bushmen bigshot avoidance behavior, 30
Kansas City Royals, 43
Kardashians. *See* Jenner, Bruce/Caitlyn, transgender issue
Kelly, Chip, Oregon football. *See* tactics in coaching
Knight, Bobby, 39
Knight, Phil. *See* Nike
!Kung Bushmen, 162
Kurelu tribe, New Guinea, 126

Lewis and Clark expedition, 128–129
loneliness, 110, 129
lost fountain of youth, xvii

Lucy, archaic hominid skeleton, xiv
lying. *See* moral deception

MacIntyre, Alasdair, revival of virtue ethics, 53, 54
make-believe, importance of, 110, 145
Malone, Karl. *See* pick-and-roll play in basketball
Manicheism, battle between good and evil, 111
manners, importance of, 4, 30–31, 34, 116, 121, 131, 148
March madness, 24, 103–104
Mariota, Marcus, Oregon football, 41
The Matrix, 92
McEnroe, John, 141
meat sharing, importance of in hunter-gatherer society, 5, 20, 30, 161
medicalization of life, 54
meditation, 65, 92
metis. *See* Odysseus
#MeToo movement, 10, 151
Meyer, Urban, 142–144, 150
Miami Dolphins. *See* Incognito, Richie
Milgram experiment, 136–138
mimesis. *See* imitation, importance of
miracle on ice. *See* 1980 Lake Placid Olympics
mirror neurons, 87, 93, 95–99, 100–101, 105, 106–107, 116, 121, 160
mismatch diseases, 83
MMA (mixed martial arts), 30
moneyball, new analytics in baseball, 78–80, 91
Montana, Joe, 97
Montana land boosterism, 74
moral deception, 2–4, 6, 20, 23, 29, 30, 35, 144. *See also* tricksters and trickery
moral evolution. *See* evolution of *Homo sapiens*
moral-free zone. *See* Himalayas
moral imperfection, saving grace of, 23
moral law. *See* intuitionism
moral psychology criticism of ethics, 19, 53, 133, 158, 160
moral tribes. *See* tribalism as moral feeling
mountain climbing. *See* Himalayas

Nadal, Rafael, 25, 31, 63, 70, 73
Namath, Joe, 113
Native Americans: ritual dancing and spiritual transcendence, 64, 68; stickball, 125, 126; subjugation of, 127–128
natural law tradition in sports, 50
NBA (National Basketball Association), 29, 47, 86, 90, 98
nepotism instinct, 5, 22, 23, 93, 145, 148
neuroscience uses in athletic training, 59, 90–92, 94, 153
New England Patriots, 21, 24, 32–34, 86, 113
NFL (National Football League), 3, 11, 33, 34, 76, 81, 84, 92, 97, 112, 115, 122, 124, 151
Nicklaus, Jack, 64
Nike, xii, 9, 105, 110
Norman, Josh, 92
nostalgia in sports, 65, 109, 113

Oakland Athletics. *See* moneyball, new analytics in baseball
Oakland Raiders, 112
Odysseus, 26–27. *See also* The Iliad; moral deception; tricksters and trickery
Ohio State University. *See* Meyer, Urban
Olympics. *See* 1972 Munich Olympics; 1976 Montreal Olympics; 1980 Lake Placid Olympics; 2018 Pyeongchang Olympics; ancient Olympics
Oregon State University, 110
overabundance. *See* scarcity, role of in moral evolution

parable of the Sadhu, 71–72
Payne, Brandon, neurocognitive efficiency trainer. *See* Curry, Stephen
Pedowitz report on NBA referee malfeasance, 47
PEDs (performance enhancing drugs), xiii, 8, 9, 16–17, 133, 157
performance anxiety, x, 122
Petersen, Chris, football coach, 51
Philadelphia Eagles, 21
pick-and-roll play in basketball, 98–99
Piper, Rowdy Roddy, 112

Pittsburg Steelers. *See* Webster, Mike
placebo effect, 29, 66
Plato, 55, 158
play, importance of in evolution, 54, 62–63, 66
Popovich, Greg, 86
Portland Trail Blazers, 114–115
positive psychology, 54–55, 74, 76
practice. *See* deliberate practice
predatory sexual behavior. *See* #MeToo movement
Presley, Elvis, 41, 122
pretending, importance of, 3, 4, 20, 25, 26, 31, 34, 48. *See also* make-believe, importance of
primatology research, xiii–xiv, xvii, 10, 31–32, 95, 152, 160
professional wrestling, moral appeal of, 111–112
prudence, importance of, 56, 60, 76, 80
psychotropic drug research, xiii

Rapa Nui people. *See* Easter Island
Rawls, John, *A Theory of Justice*, 61, 62
referees, role of, 35, 39, 40, 41, 43–45, 46, 47, 48, 49, 111. *See also* 1972 Munich Olympics
religion in sports: moral versus spiritual transcendence, 67–69; watching Roger Federer play tennis, 69
Rice, Jerry, 97
risk-taking calculations. *See* conscience, evolution of
rituals, importance of, 63–67, 69, 109, 131
Robber's Cave psychological experiments, 7–8
Robin Hood as moral exemplar, 34, 49, 149
Rodman, Dennis, 14
rope-a-dope strategy. *See* Ali, Muhammad
Rose, Pete, 15, 31
rudeness. *See* Sharapova, Maria
rule mongers, 47, 81
rules, creative use of. *See* subversive behavior, moral significance of
runner's high, xiii, xv
running as evolutionary adaptation. *See* jogging, 1970s fitness craze

Saban, Nick, 40
sabermetrics, 78
SABR (Sneak Attack by Roger), 42
Savage, Randy, 112
Sayers, Gayle, 122
SBNR (spiritual but not religious), 63
scarcity, role of in moral evolution, 82–85
schadenfreude, 130–131
schizophrenia. *See* hallucinatory voices
Seattle Seahawks, 92, 113
Seau, Junior, 76
Secretariat, 149
Seinfeld, bystander apathy episodes, 135–136
self-esteem among children, 86
selfish gene theory of evolution, xvi, 21
seventh-inning stretch, 7, 67
Severson, Red, basketball coach. *See* St. Cloud State basketball team
sexism in sports, 141, 150–151
Shakespeare, William, 122
Sharapova, Maria, 16–17
sheriff and referee analogy, 49
Sidgwick, Henry, three methods of ethics, 163–164
Simpson, O. J., 20
situationism psychology studies of morality, 133–134. *See also* Milgram experiment; *Seinfeld*, bystander apathy episodes; Stanford prison experiment
small ball baseball strategy, 42–43
small town isolation, 129
Smith, Adam, invisible hand concept, 23
social insects as super-organisms. *See* hive behavior, moral significance of
somatic ethic, 93
South Dakota, growing up in, ix–xii, 13–14, 37–38
South Dakota State University: Jackrabbit Stampede rodeo, 37–38. *See also* intrastate rivalry
space, strategic significance of, 40
spirituality in sports, 67–70
spread offense in football, 40–41
Spygate, 33, 113. *See also* Deflategate
St. Amant, Mark, fantasy football player, 115
St. Cloud State basketball team, 38
Stanford prison experiment, 138–139

Star Wars, 109, 111, 116
steroids. *See* anabolic steroids
Stockton, John. *See* pick-and-roll play in basketball
stolen base baseball tactic, 42–43
Stone Age. *See* hunter-gatherer way of life
strangers, crisis of getting along with, 68, 148, 162
strategy in coaching, 29, 40, 41, 42–43
STS (superior temporal sulcus), 90
subversive behavior, moral significance of, 2, 26, 47–48, 113–115, 139, 149
success (self-help) literature, 53, 57, 61, 72, 93
superheroes, 64, 86, 112
superstition in sports, 31, 63

table tennis: Chinese training techniques, 59–60, 91; Rafael Nadal's tennis racquet grip, 25
tactics in coaching, 40–41, 42–43
tailgating, 109
Taylor, Lawrence, 112
teasing, moral purpose of, xviii, 12–16
Temple of Zeus. *See* ancient Olympics
tennis. *See* Federer, Roger; McEnroe, John; Nadal, Rafael; Sharapova, Maria; Williams, Serena
third-man factor, coping with extreme stress, 28, 29, 96. *See also* illusion, importance of
time, tactical significance of, 41
TMS (transcranial magnetic stimulation), 95
too much abundance, moral problem of. *See* scarcity, role of in moral evolution
de Tocqueville, Alexis, *Democracy in America*, 129
transgender issue in sports, 152
transhumanism, 93, 149, 154, 156
tribalism as moral feeling, 7, 108, 109, 113, 116, 130, 148, 163
tricksters and trickery, xvii, 3–4, 20, 21, 26, 35, 40, 41, 43, 46, 48, 50, 51, 59, 111, 123. *See also* moral deception
Trojan War, role of cunning, 26
Trump, Donald, president of the United States, 84–85

INDEX

unconscious, role of in morality, 2, 3, 6, 20, 21, 32, 93–94, 100, 158, 159
underdogs, moral preference for, 48, 113
University of Iowa, xvi, 39, 69, 104
University of Notre Dame, 104
University of Oklahoma Fiesta Bowl, 51
University of Oregon blur offense, 41. *See also* Bowerman, Bill; Kelly, Chip; Knight, Phil; James, LaMichael; Mariota, Marcus; Nike
University of South Dakota, 110
Utah Jazz. *See* pick-and-roll play in basketball
utilitarianism, 164

veneer theory of morality. *See* de Waal, Frans, primatologist
Vietnam, xi
village life and sports. *See* Balinese cockfighting
villains in professional wrestling. *See* professional wrestling
virtual reality as athletic training tool, 92
virtue ethics. *See* Aristotle
virtues and vices, their complementary roles, 56, 74, 76, 87

virtuoso performance, 60
Vonn, Lindsey, 84–86
de Waal, Frans, primatologist, xiv, xvi, 21, 31
WADA (World Anti-Doping Association), 9
Warwick, Kevin. *See* cyborgization
Webster, Mike, 3, 73
Wells, Ted. *See* Deflategate; Incognito, Richie
Western grebe synchronized mating dance, 97
Williams, Serena, chair umpire incident, 141–142
Wilson, Russell, 92
winning, meaning of, x, 24–25
Woods, Tiger, 63, 64
wrestling, x, 3–4, 35. *See also* professional wrestling; Gable, Dan

xenophobia. *See* tribalism as moral feeling

zone, being in the, 64–65
zone read, football tactic, 40, 98

ABOUT THE AUTHOR

Richard J. Severson grew up playing tennis, golf, football, basketball, hockey, and innumerable other neighborhood games on the windswept plains of South Dakota. He studied biology in college and later earned his PhD in religion and ethics from the University of Iowa. Severson worked for 29 years in higher education and is the author of *The Principles of Information Ethics* (1997). He and his wife live in Lake Oswego, Oregon.

www.ingramcontent.com/pod-product-compliance
Lightning Source LLC
Chambersburg PA
CBHW021849300426
44115CB00005B/78